SIGNPOSTS

ERIC KAMPMANN

BEAUFORT
BOOKS

First edition was published by WND Books.

For inquiries about volume orders, please contact:
Beaufort Books27 West 20th Street, Suite 1103
New York, NY 10011sales@beaufortbooks.com

Published in the United States by Beaufort Books www.beaufortbooks.com

Distributed by Midpoint Trade Books,
a division of Independent Book Publishers

www.midpointtrade.com
www.ipgbook.com

Interior design by Neuwirth & Associates, Inc.
Cover design by Mark Karis
Cover photo by Eric Kampmann

Library of Congress Data on file

ISBN: 9780825309366 (paperback)
ISBN: 9780825308185 (ebook)

"The safest road to hell is the gradual one—the gentle slope, soft underfoot, without sudden turnings, without milestones, without signposts."

—C. S. LEWIS

FOREWORD

Anyone who has spent much time in the Scriptures knows that the writers of the Bible loved to use metaphors, or word pictures, to illustrate eternal truths. Some of those word pictures can be earthy—like Solomon referring to dead flies that ruin the perfume in Ecclesiastes 10:1, or Peter talking about a washed pig that immediately returns to wallowing in the mud in 2 Peter 2:22. Other pictures are more poetic . . . like Paul comparing our new resurrection bodies to the way star differs from star in heavenly splendor, or David describing the rising sun as a "bridegroom coming forth from his pavilion" and "a champion rejoicing to run his course" (Psalm 19:5).

God paints the most poignant pictures of His love that you and I can imagine . . . a father grieving over a wandering child . . . a husband longing after his unfaithful wife . . . a shepherd cradling a lamb in his arms.

Some of the word pictures I like best, however, are those that refer to life as a journey through uncharted territory. Scripture is chock-full of references to paths and roads, trails and highways—and all the dangers, snares, and incredible vistas along the way. You get the sense that the Bible was intended as a guidebook, an almanac, or a GPS to help a traveler keep on the best route through his years of life on earth.

> *You broaden the path beneath me,*
> *so that my ankles do not turn.*
> —2 SAMUEL 22:37

> *You have made known to me the path of life;*
> —PSALM 16:11

Teach me your way, O Lord;
lead me in a straight path because of my oppressors.
—PSALM 27:11

Teach me to do your will, for you are my God;
may your good Spirit lead me on level ground.
—PSALM 143:10

Whether you turn to the right or to the left, your ears will hear
a voice behind you, saying, "This is the way; walk in it."
—ISAIAH 30:21

There is a way that seems right to a man,
but in the end it leads to death.
—PROVERBS 14:12

Set up road signs; put up guideposts.
Take note of the highway, the road that you take.
—JEREMIAH 31:21

I am the way and the truth and the life.
No one comes to the Father except through me.
—JOHN 14:6

And so it goes, through the Old Testament and the New, over and over again. Life is like a road with a million twists and turns, climbing over mountains, and dipping down into deep valleys. And God's Word is like a map or a well-thumbed guidebook to help a person avoid the hidden dangers and enjoy the viewpoints along the way.

Eric Kampmann not only writes from the perspective of someone who knows and loves the Word, he also writes as one who loves being out on the trail. One of his driving desires in recent years has been to hike the entire length of the Appalachian Trail—all 2,178 miles of it. I'm impressed with myself when I walk a couple of miles!

Along the way, he has recorded his observations and photographed its wonders—and related it all to our daily walk of faith.

This book truly is a *daily* companion. Unlike the Appalachian Trail, you can hike straight through it, day by day, in one year. If you first pick up this book in March, pick up the trail right there. If you get it in December, start your hike immediately. Carefully consider the author's quoted Scripture excerpts and—if you have time—go back and read the whole chapter from the Bible in its original context. Ask the Lord to expand your heart to embrace new truths and open your eyes to every divine signpost along the path.

Some of those signposts will be warnings: *Caution! Beware! Danger! Thin Ice! Stay on the Trail!* Others will be words of encouragement: *Persevere, Take Courage, Press On, Follow Your Guide, Be of Good Cheer.* The simple fact is, God has not left us without guidance, help, and His own companionship on this trek through life.

I think you're in for a real adventure.

—GREG LAURIE

PREFACE

The heart of a man plans his way,
but the LORD establishes his steps.

—PROVERBS 16:9

John Eldredge in his short book *Epic* uses this as his subtitle: "The Story God is Telling and the Role that is Yours to Play." In the first chapter Eldredge quotes Sam, the Hobbit, in *The Lord of the Rings* asking, "I wonder what sort of tale we've fallen into?" Eldredge goes on to say, "Sam assumes that there is a story; there is something larger going on. He also assumes that they have tumbled into it, been swept up into it." Before 1987, I would not have believed that I was in any story but my own. But in the spring of that year my whole concept of story would be turned on its head

As a young boy, I thought Manhattan was the center of everything that was romantic and mysterious. I would occasionally travel to the city with my father by train and would come away with the conviction that New York was my city and that I would someday move there.

My attraction to the great city would later take on a literary cast. As I grew older, New York became for me the city of Melville, Whitman and Fitzgerald, a never ceasing engine of dreams and money, drawing people from around the world to live and work in the steel and glass canyons that tower above the churning streets. F. Scott Fitzgerald particularly influenced my thinking as when in *The*

Great Gatsby he describes the experience of approaching the city from afar:

"Over the great bridge, with the sunlight through the girders making a constant flicker upon the moving cars, with the city rising up across the river in white heaps and sugar lumps all built with a wish out of non-olfactory money. The city seen from the Queensboro Bridge is always the city seen for the first time, in its first wild promise of all the mystery and beauty in the world."

In September 1969 I was married in New York City and soon secured a job as a sales rep for a book publisher. Ten years later, I was vice president, director of sales at a major publishing house. In 1981, I left that job to launch my own start up, but by 1987 I realized my company was in trouble and was skidding off the side of the road and then....

And then, one spring day I took an unscheduled detour by entering a church on Park Avenue. I was alone and the church was empty. Silence hung over the vast space and instead of turning back to rejoin the flood of people going somewhere in a hurry, I sat down. I had entered the church on an impulse and then I said a prayer on impulse. I did not expect anything to happen one way or the other and soon enough I reemerged into the light and the flowing stream of seemingly determined people passing by.

Two weeks later, an angel must have entered my office because I received a very explicit message to get up, leave the building, find a bookstore and buy a Bible. Amazingly, I did just that: I found a bookstore a few blocks away and bought a beautifully made leather-bound Bible. And with that one act, everything in my life would begin to change.

In 1989, my company did declare Chapter 11. It should have disappeared forever at that point, but it emerged in 1991 from bankruptcy. Real miracles happened during this period. It was also in 1991 that I discovered a lectionary that gave me an excellent roadmap in my new quest to know the Old and New Testaments. Using the lectionary, I immersed myself in daily reading year after year. I also began to attend church, participate in Bible studies, listen to tapes and read as much as I could to supplement my daily biblical readings.

By 2001, I began compiling passages from the wisdom books in the Old Testament for my children mostly, but for other purposes as well. Those passages became a book I would call Tree of Life. Once the book was finished, I began to write short commentaries for each of the 365 wisdom passages chosen for the book.

By the end of the first full year of writing, I realized I wasn't ready for prime time, to put it mildly. I returned to the keyboard and for the next two years I rewrote and rewrote until I became confident in what was being said and how it was being said.

The first version of this book was published in 2008 and was called *Trail Thoughts*. In 2011, the book was reissued as *Signposts* and became the basis for a series of 365 daily podcasts with Senior Pastor Chuck Davis of Stanwich Church.

While in Israel in 2012, Chuck Davis and I committed to embarking on a new series of daily podcasts on Jesus as He is revealed to us in the four Gospels. After those were completed, I decided to write a new book based on the content of the podcasts. That book, *Getting to Know Jesus*, was published in 2016.

Finally, in November 2017, I started posting a psalm and a short commentary on Twitter and Facebook. In addition to the psalm, I included a photograph as a way of adding a new dimension to the experience of being in the Word of God daily.

What began as a short prayer in an empty church in Manhattan in 1987 had, unexpectedly, grown into a trilogy of devotionals that has put me in the middle of a story that I never expected to be in. At that time, I would have been incapable of thinking I was in any story but my own. But as I came to know the Bible, I began to see the larger narrative Eldredge writes about; I began to see that when I prayed to God for help that day in 1987, I opened a way through a door that revealed to me that I was being invited into a story that has been unfolding since the beginning.

—Eric Kampmann, January 2020

Restore to me the joy of your salvation and grant me
a willing spirit, to sustain me.

—PSALM 51:12

A NEW YOU

THE CALENDAR HAS turned a new page, and we find ourselves confronted by a new year. The revels have ended, and we awake to the prospects of new goals, new challenges, even "a new you"! Of course, most of us know that nothing much has changed since yesterday. The past has not been wiped clean; our little foibles are still tapping us on the shoulder. Our regrets and sorrows did not disappear when the clock struck twelve.

So here we are on the edge of a new year, and we are not sure what we should do about it. Where do we start? Perhaps the introductory deal at the health club is just the ticket. Or maybe a trip to the self-help section of a nearby bookstore will be the needed answer. Of course, the deeper question remains to be answered: How can we escape the habits and hidden desires that continue to weigh us down?

Could it be that the urge is the ancient inclination of the heart for reconcilliation to the holiness of God? While we may think of ourselves as mere wandering shadows of the earth, alienated from God and not worthy of His love and attention, we still seem to feel the need to fill that emptiness in the heart with the fullness that can only come from Him.

The biblical narrative shows us why we often feel so forlorn. The good news is that the lost can be found. While the idea of a "New You" has taken on a strong commercial coloration, the deeper truth is that each one of us yearns for transformation. Let this be the moment when we decide to embrace genuine change that will finally bring peace, love, and joy into our lives every day of the year.

The highest heavens belong to the LORD, but the earth he has
given to man. It is not the dead who praise the LORD, those who
go down to silence; it is we who extol the LORD, both now and
forevermore. Praise the LORD.

—PSALM 115:16–18

RETURNING TO THE ORIGINAL STORY LINE

THE BIBLICAL ACCOUNT of the first man begins in a garden: "Now the LORD God had planted a garden in the east, in Eden, and there he put the man he had formed" (Genesis 2:8). The garden was designed to be a good place for man, a place he could enjoy and cultivate: "The LORD God took the man and put him in the Garden of Eden to work it and take care of it (Genesis 2:15)."

God planted all kinds of trees and brought beasts of the field for the man to name. And God created a companion for the man so that together the man and the woman would fulfill God's purposes for them. From the very beginning, God created the earth for man's dominion. It was only when the man and the woman defied God's one prohibition that a very different story began to unfold.

At the center of the new story is betrayal, for where there was harmony, now we find rebellion; where there was a home, now we find exile; and where there was abundance, now we find hard labor and travail.

The original story line was radically changed by one act of thoughtless defiance. The new story is the tale that culminates as a sacrificial act of love on a cross on a mound outside the gates of Jerusalem. At that moment, all men and women once again could enter the original story line that had its origin in Eden.

For you created my inmost being;
you knit me together in my mother's womb.
I praise you because I am fearfully and wonderfully made;
your works are wonderful, I know that full well.

—PSALM 139:13–14

A MATTER OF FAITH

DAVID SAYS, "I am fearfully and wonderfully made" because he is ever marveling at the mystery and miracle of God's creation and the creature He created in His own image (Genesis 1:27). But while David expresses awe at the depth of the mystery and complexity of man and this world, he also tells us that man without God is little more than a handful of dust: "For you created my inmost being; you knit me together in my mother's womb."

David is a biblical colossus; he is a giant killer, a great leader and warrior, a poet, and a king. But he is also an adulterer and murderer and in the case of his son, Absalom, a failed father. David, like every other man and woman, is composed of divinity and dust, but in the end, it is the divinity part we love about David.

Throughout his long life, David maintained an intimate relationship to his creator. David wandered away, but he would always return to the one who created him, who chose to lift him out of the sheep pens and who had him anointed to be the king of Israel. David lived in closest relationship with God even when the times and circumstances would have tried the faith of other men. David's faith is indivisible and is a model for each one of us: "My frame was not hidden from you when I was made in the secret place. When I was woven together in the depths of the earth, your eyes saw my unformed body. All the days ordained for me were written in your book before one of them came to be" (Psalm 139:15–16).

Blessed is the man who does not walk in the counsel of the
wicked or stand in the way of sinners or sit in the seat of
mockers. But his delight is in the law of the LORD,
and on his law he meditates day and night.

—PSALM 1:1–2

WALKING THE STRAIGHT PATH

LIFE HAS OFTEN been compared to a journey with many paths, and some tell us that all those paths lead to God. This, though, is comforting because it is so inclusive, but unfortunately for those pushing this line, they have wandered away from biblical truth. David tells us that it is just as easy to "walk in the counsel of the wicked" as it is to walk in the way of the Lord. We set off on a journey armed with map, compass, and book, only to become utterly lost by taking a wrong turn here or by not paying attention there. If we want to stay on the straight path, then we should pay attention to "the law of the Lord, and on his law meditate day and night."

The right way is not always an easy way; we are called to exercise wakefulness and exert effort. The wisdom of the Lord suggests that we seek the Lord in everything we do: "Seek the Lord while he may be found; call upon him while he is near" (Isaiah 55:6). Otherwise, we may find ourselves on a trackless path with little hope of ever finding our way back to where the Lord always intended us to be. A journey may have many roads, but only one leads to the Lord, for "narrow is the road that leads to life . . ." (Matthew 7:14).

It was not by their sword that they won the land,
nor did their arm bring them victory; it was your right hand,
your arm, and the light of your face, for you loved them.

—PSALM 44:3

HISTORY

IN MOST CONTEMPORARY accounts of historical events, man plays the central role of hero or villain. In Winston Churchill's four-volume *History of the English Speaking Peoples*, for example, the real hero is the genius of the peoples of the British nation. It is essentially a progressive view of history and, therefore, modern because it tells a tale of greater and greater national triumphs. It is a wonderful story of kings and queens and leaders of all sorts carrying the growing empire forward to its ordained destiny of a saving civilization. Yet in a sense, Churchill's account is a surprisingly unsatisfying account because the hand of God is nowhere to be found.

The Bible is also a work of history with its own kings and queens, battles won and lost, civilizations rising and falling, warriors and cowards, saints and villains. But while earthly events are important to the unfolding story, the supernatural hand of God is everywhere from the first page through the last.

If we subscribe to the biblical account of history, then the importance of particular civilizations diminishes substantially, while the salvation of the individual soul becomes paramount. From the fall in the Garden of Eden to the resurrection of Jesus Christ and the bestowing of the Holy Spirit, it is a story that continues to unfold to this very moment through people just like you and me. This history becomes the revelation of God's compelling purpose, with each one of us as participants in His great narrative: "It was not by their sword that they won the land . . . it was your right hand, your arm, and the light of your face, for you loved them."

You, O LORD, keep my lamp burning;
my God turns my darkness into light.

—PSALM 18:28

ILLUMINATION

A RENOWNED LANDSCAPE photographer once told me, "I am just an average photographer with a very great God." I am an average photographer, but I know the truth of his observation through an experience of my own.

It began on an early spring climb to the summit of Mt. Whitney in the High Sierras. This climb was not the usual hike up to the summit, but a four-day adventure that required heavy backpacking up to snow-filled Boy Scout Lake, a flat bowl surrounded on three sides by sharp, jutting peaks. This natural platform was our base camp; from there, we ascended Whitney by heading up a long, steep, icy shoot to the right of the imposing headwall. About five hundred feet below the summit, we clamped onto fixed ropes for the final push.

After descending, we spent that night once again at Boy Scout Lake. The next morning, we awoke before sunrise to begin the job of packing up to head down to the Portal and the road out to Lone Pine. At higher elevations, the world before sunrise can be cold and miserable, but when the rising sun appeared and its ascending light hit the dormant gray rocks, the rocks seemed to awaken and catch fire and dance with the new dawn.

Just south of our tent site stand the Needles, four sculpted spires that rise up out of the mountain massif. They appear to the eye to be four steeples of a natural cathedral standing guard against the brutal wind that is constantly besieging this massive wall.

For the most part, I was busy packing up for our departure, but when I chanced to look up, I could see that the light had transformed the stone spires of the Needles into a luminous, serrated gold bulwark set against the deep blue of a desert morning sky. Luckily, my camera was resting on my sleeping bag; I picked it up and without hesitation, shot four or five frames with black and white film. I wanted to catch the gold rocks, but I had run out of color film, so I had no choice but to go with what was in the camera.

When I later developed the film, I could see that the gold that had caught my eye became, in the picture, vibrantly beautiful rock formations. I had caught the light as it reflected off the Needles in just the right way at just the right moment. If I had hesitated, the light would have changed, and my exceptional black and white picture would have lost all its life. Instead, I became a very average photographer recording the work of a very great God.

The Lord brought me forth as the first of his works,
before his deeds of old; I was appointed from eternity, from the
beginning, before the world began. When there were no oceans, I
was given birth, when there were no springs abounding with
water; before the mountains were settled in place, before the
hills, I was given birth, before he made the earth or its fields
or any of the dust of the world.

—PROVERBS 8:22–26

BEFORE THE CREATION OF THE WORLD

TODAY MANY ARE taught that life begins at birth and ends with the finality of death; they are taught that there is no reality to either God or to eternal life. The Bible, however, tells another story. According to Scripture, you and I were created by God before we were born. And from the beginning, He had a purpose for us.

Solomon tells us that God's wisdom was "appointed from eternity, from the beginning before the world began." This spiritual truth is echoed throughout the Bible. From David: "When I was woven together in the depths of the earth, your eyes saw my unformed body" (Psalm 139:15–16). From Jeremiah: "Before I formed you in the womb, I knew you; before you were born I set you apart" (Jeremiah 1:5). From Isaiah: "Before I was born the LORD called me, from my birth he has made mention of my name" (Isaiah 49:1). From Paul: "For he chose us in him before the creation of the world" (Ephesians 1:4). And Jesus says this at the end of His prayer for all believers: "Father, I want those you have given me to be with me where I am, and to see my glory, the glory you have given me because you loved me before the creation of the world" (John 17:24).

In our thoughtlessness, we can choose to disregard the reality of the existence of God. We are free to choose to live without Him, but like everything else, that choice has profound implications.

Even from birth the wicked go astray;
from the womb they are wayward and speak lies.

—PSALM 58:3

A GOOD AND RIGHTEOUS RULER

ANYONE WHO HAS lived through the twentieth century with its wars and cataclysmic violence knows that an unjust and violent ruler will bring misery to the people and to the land. But at the end of his life, King David spoke of the blessings that come from a righteous ruler: "When one rules over men in righteousness, when he rules in the fear of God, he is like the light of morning at sunrise on a cloudless morning, like the brightness after rain that brings the grass from the earth" (2 Samuel 23:3–4).

The tyrant scorches the land and decimates the prosperity of the people. The righteous ruler is a servant of the people and acknowledges that all genuine blessings come not from his political or military power, but from God alone.

Why do the nations say, "Where is their God?" Our God is in heaven; he does whatever pleases him.

—PSALM 115:2–3

IN THE IMAGE OF GOD OR IN THE IMAGE OF MAN

EVEN WHEN PEOPLE deny the existence of God, they seem to show a need to substitute something godlike for the God they have denied. There is plenty of evidence that man has a hard time explaining existence without some reference to a creator or creative force. And many nonbelievers speak enthusiastically about spirits and spiritual reality. They just don't accept the God of the Bible.

It might be reasonable to suggest that their denial of the God of Holy Scripture is little more than an unconscious reenactment of the original sin of Adam and Eve in the Garden. Remember, their act of rebellion was based on the false promise of becoming like God by coming to know what God knows.

The promise, of course, was a lie. Adam and Eve chose to overreach God's design for them, and so they paid a dear penalty for their choice. Today, by denying the reality of God, men and women have fallen into a pattern of trying to reverse the design of creation. Creating idols or substitute gods is the natural result of denying God. It is merely an attempt at reversing the biblical account by creating a creator in the image of man.

*The words of the wise are like goads, their collected sayings like
firmly embedded nails—given by one Shepherd. Be warned, my
son, of anything in addition to them. Of making many books
there is no end, and much study wearies the body.*

—ECCLESIASTES 12:11–12

THE LANGUAGE OF GOD

How DO WE become literate in the language of the spirit of God?
What are the "right words" given by "one Shepherd"?

Jesus is that "one Shepherd," but when He spoke, He was often
misunderstood because He spoke in the figurative language of the
Holy Spirit. Nicodemus came to Jesus with a literal spirit and so was
bewildered when Jesus told him, "I tell you the truth, no one can see
the kingdom of God unless he is born again" (John 3:3). Likewise,
the Samaritan woman is blinded at first by her ethnic literalism: "You
are a Jew and I am a Samaritan woman. How can you ask me for a
drink?" (John 4:9). But Jesus speaks of another kind of water that
never fails and that wells "up to eternal life" (John 4:14).

Then Jesus speaks of a time when all barriers will be broken
down and one language will be spoken: "Yet a time is coming and
has now come when the true worshipers will worship the Father in
spirit and truth, for they are the kind of worshipers the Father
seeks. God is spirit, and His worshipers must worship in spirit and
in truth" (John 4:23–24).

If we are trapped in a spiritual literalism, then we should pray that
our Emmaus moment will come: "And beginning with Moses and all
the Prophets, he explained to them what was said in all the Scriptures
concerning himself.... Then their eyes were opened and they
recognized him, and he disappeared from their sight. They asked each
other, 'Were not our hearts burning within us while he talked with us
on the road and opened the Scriptures to us?'" (Luke 24:27, 31–32).

Then the LORD said to Satan, "Have you considered my servant
Job? There is no one on earth like him; he is blameless and
upright, a man who fears God and shuns evil. And he still
maintains his integrity, though you incited me against him to
ruin him without any reason."

—JOB 2:3

ARMED FOR BATTLE

THE CONFLICT IN heaven over the integrity of Job may seem to be a battle over the soul of one man, but as we will see later, this represents the struggle faced by all men and women. For the struggle of Job foreshadows the epic battle that will become engaged with the birth of Jesus Christ. At the very beginning of his ministry, Satan tempts Jesus in the wilderness, by attacking His integrity. Satan offers Jesus an easy way out with promises of kingdoms, sustenance, and earthly salvation.

Every man engages in a struggle within his heart over what his heart will believe and how he will act upon it. "For our struggle is not against flesh and blood, but against the rulers, against the authorities, against the powers of this dark world and against the spiritual forces of evil in the heavenly realms" (Ephesians 6:12). When Job says, "Till I die, I will not deny my integrity. I will maintain my righteousness and never let go of it" (Job 27:5–6), he is laying down the marker for each one of us. For the external battle has an internal antecedent within the heart of each man and woman.

We live on a battlefield. Do we know the terrain? Are we properly armed? Do we even know the maneuvers of the enemy?

*O L*ORD*, do not rebuke me in your anger or discipline me in
your wrath. For your arrows have pierced me, and your hand has
come down upon me. Because of your wrath there is no health in my
body; my bones have no soundness because of my sin. My guilt
has overwhelmed me like a burden too heavy to bear.*

—PSALM 38:1–4

A PAINFUL BURDEN

ON ONE LEVEL, King David's situation seems comparable to Job's. Both are suffering. But where the cause of Job's suffering is mysterious to him, the cause of David's heavy burden is clear to both him and to God. He also says in the same psalm, "I confess my iniquity; I am troubled by my sin" (Psalm 38:18). Although David has become the most powerful of men and was anointed by God, David, as a mere mortal, is capable of falling away from God through sin: "My guilt has overwhelmed me like a burden too heavy to bear."

If a man as great and blessed as David was felled by sin, why do we believe we can withstand the power of its attraction? We can't, but God has provided a way out of the trap that torments us. In the New Testament we are promised that when we are tempted, God will provide a way of escape. Often the liberating road away from the misery of our hidden guilt comes through earnest prayer. We must ask for the freedom we long for and the promise will be fulfilled in our lives, but we must ask before we can receive.

Man born of woman is of few days and full of trouble.
He springs up like a flower and withers away; like a fleeting
shadow, he does not endure. Do you fix your eye on such a
one? Will you bring him before you for judgment?

—JOB 14:1–3

WILL HE LIVE AGAIN?

JOB HAS LOST everything; he is suffering from unimaginable afflictions, and in his misery he seems to despair even life itself. But we should understand that while it is generally true that "man born of woman is of few days and full of trouble," this is not the full story, nor does Job imply that it is. Job never says that God has caused this or any misery. In fact, the suffering is inflicted by the hand of Satan and not by God.

In order to understand Job better, we need to attend to everything he says, including this: "If a man dies, will he live again? All the days of my hard service I will wait for my renewal to come. You will call and I will answer you; you will long for the creature you have made" (Job 14:14–15).

The hardships of the present are real, but for Job and for us, they are mitigated by the knowledge of the mercy and love of God for each one of His children.

Every word of God is flawless; he is a shield to those
who take refuge in him. Do not add to his words,
or he will rebuke you and prove you a liar.

—PROVERBS 30:5–6

DO NOT ADD . . . OR SUBTRACT

FOR THOSE WHO consider God optional, the words of the Bible mean very little. There are others, however, who seem to take the Word of God seriously but want to add to it or subtract from it for their own purposes. For example, Thomas Jefferson excised the miracles because his eighteenth-century sensibility was offended by the improbability of the supernatural.

At the other end of the spectrum are the high-octane embellishers who believe that the Bible needs to be added to in order to be relevant to modern readers.

Either way, the authority of the biblical witness of God's Word is placed in doubt. If the enemies of God can find a small thread to unravel, then they can proceed to cast doubt on the whole fabric of God's revelation. In speaking about God's law, Moses warned against altering any of it: "Do not add to what I command you and do not subtract from it, but keep the commands of the LORD your God that I give you" (Deuteronomy 4:2).

The truth is that we should approach the Word of God with humility; we should have the attitude of a thirsty sojourner who wishes to drink in every word that God has blessed us with through His Holy Scripture.

Do not say, "Why were the old days better than these?"

For it is not wise to ask such questions.

—ECCLESIASTES 7:10

THE PRESENT MOMENT

MEMORIES CAN BE sweet as well as bitter. "I thought about the former days, the years of long ago; I remembered my songs in the night" (Psalm 77:5–6). It is hard to pass through a day without a smell or an image or a conversation summoning memories of a far away time that we might wish to recapture or obliterate.

At the same time, it is wrong to magnify the importance of the past because then we diminish the importance of the present. The past was never better or worse—only different—with different possibilities that cannot now longer be grasped.

We need to be aware that the present is the most important moment of our life. Jesus never tired of calling His followers to the present moment. His first words reported in the Gospel of Mark are, "The time has come. . . . The kingdom of God is near. Repent and believe the good news!" (Mark 1:15).

Jesus is calling us to engage the present moment *now*. Through what He accomplished on the cross for us, we have been truly freed to follow Him.

The heavens praise your wonders, O LORD,
your faithfulness too, in the assembly of the holy ones.
For who in the skies above can compare with the LORD?
Who is like the LORD among the heavenly beings?

—PSALM 89:5–6

CHOOSE WISELY

THE HAND OF God in creation should be obvious to all, but since the nineteenth century many leaders, under the influence of the philosophy of scientific progress, have proclaimed that God is dead and, therefore, is not the cause of the creation of the world.

Matthew Arnold, the poet, captures the desolate spirit of this "enlightened" period in his poem "Dover Beach":

The Sea of Faith was once, too, at the full,
and round earth's shore lay like the folds of a bright girdle furled.
But now I only hear its melancholy, long, withdrawing roar,
retreating, to the breath of the night-wind,
down the vast edges drear and naked shingles of the world.

As we now know, the god of that age became the shipwreck of the next century with its sinister technologies resulting in world wars, mass murders, and atomic bombs. When we no longer see God's hand in the stars and the seas and splendors of the earth itself, we consign ourselves to the desolate and dark places of this world without any possibility of rescue.

As Moses approached the end of his long journey, he told the people of Israel that they have a choice and they should choose wisely: "See, I set before you today life and prosperity, death and destruction. . . . Now choose life, so that you and your children may live and that you may love the LORD your God, listen to his voice and hold fast to him" (Deuteronomy 30:15, 19–20).

Naked a man comes from his mother's womb,
and as he comes, so he departs. He takes nothing
from his labor that he can carry in his hand.

—ECCLESIASTES 5:15

———⊸⊷⊶⊷⊸———

MEANINGLESS

WHEN WE SPEND the best days of our lives chasing after fame or wealth, then, according to the Teacher, we are to be pitied, for in the end nothing of lasting value will be ours. "Meaningless! Meaningless! . . . Everything is meaningless" (Ecclesiastes 1:2).

But unlike many of the popular writers of the "lost generation" who reflected a world stripped of God, Solomon is not writing as a stoic or nihilist. He is simply describing a truth that seems to have been lost in our time: "All things are wearisome, more than one can say. The eye never has enough of seeing, nor the ear its fill of hearing. What has been will be again, what has been done will be done again; there is nothing new under the sun" (Ecclesiastes 1:8–9).

Why are you downcast, O my soul? Why so disturbed within me?
Put your hope in God, for I will yet praise him, my Savior and my
God . . . Deep calls to deep in the roar of your waterfalls;
all your waves and breakers have swept over me.

—PSALM 42:5–7

SEEK THE LORD

SOMETIMES A DARK mood comes upon us unexpectedly. Maybe it was hovering at the edge of our consciousness like a fog bank at the edge of a placid sea. The wind shifts, and what was bright sunlight becomes a wall of gray. And so it happens that the sunshine disposition is enshrouded by feelings of longing, loneliness, and anxiety.

We suffer through these moments, saying with the Psalmist, "Why are you downcast, O my soul? Why so disturbed within me?" We long for the sunlit moments again, but no amount of distracting activity seems to help. Out of desperation we may seek relief through an addictive diversion, or we may anesthetize our suffering through medication. But none of it works for long because we are seeking physical relief with merely physical implements.

David seems to be saying that the cause of his despair is rooted in a broken relationship with God. Healing begins when David says, "Put your hope in God." When we depart from the company of God to pursue our own purposes, we allow ourselves to become vulnerable to all life's afflictions, and we experience what it is like to be unarmed in the midst of battle. "The LORD is with you when you are with him. If you seek him, he will be found by you." (2 Chronicles 15:2). Life presents many calamities, but comfort and safety come when we walk with the Lord: "Seek the LORD, all you humble of the land, you who do what he commands" (Zephaniah 2:3).

Praise the Lord from the earth . . .
Let them praise the name of the LORD,
for his name alone is exalted;
his splendor is above the earth and the heavens.

—PSALM 148:7, 13

TEACH US TO PRAY

THE LORD, WHOSE "splendor is above the earth and the heavens," stooped to take us by the hand to teach us how to speak to Him in prayer. Jesus gave us the Lord's Prayer in His Sermon on the Mount, but He did not ask us to slavishly memorize it and repeat it by rote. He wanted it to come from a heart filled with love, devotion, and gratitude. He gave us the form of prayer to pray and asked each of His followers to fill it in with the words that come from the heart.

Paraphrasing Jesus, we might pray: *Father, holy is your name. I pray that you will bring revival to the land. I pray that you will provide your children with bread for this day. I pray that you will forgive us for our sins, conscious and unconscious. I pray that you will teach us compassion so that we will learn to forgive as you have forgiven us. I pray that your hand will guide us on good paths and away from temptations and you will strengthen us so that we will resist all deceptions. I pray this because you are God. To you be all glory and power forever. Amen.*

Eat honey, my son, for it is good;
honey from the comb is sweet to your taste.
Know also that wisdom is sweet to your soul;
if you find it, there is a future hope for you,
and your hope will not be cut off.

—PROVERBS 24:13–14

PRINCES AND PRESIDENTS

EVERY FOUR YEARS on this day in the United States a president is sworn in. This civic celebration represents a national moment of hope and renewal; America entrusts the future of the nation to a new leader who will need to call upon all his or her wisdom to fulfill the promise of the moment. Unhappily, when it comes to princes and presidents, wisdom and good judgment have often been in short supply, and the people and their nations suffer as a result. One Old Testament story illustrates the inevitable consequences when a leader lacks wisdom in fulfilling his trust.

When King Solomon died, his son, Rehoboam, ascended to the throne. Shortly after assuming power, representatives of the people of Israel petitioned the new king to lift the crushing burden of taxes that had been imposed in earlier years. The people could no longer bear the excessively heavy load and sought relief from the new king.

Rehoboam sent the people away while he conferred with his advisors. First, he consulted with the elders who said, "If today you will be a servant to these people and serve them and give them a favorable answer, they will always be your servants" (1 Kings 12:7). Then Rehoboam turned to his youthful companions who told him to assert his power over the people by saying, "My father laid on you a heavy yoke; I will make it even heavier. My father scourged you with whips; I will scourge you with scorpions" (1 Kings 12:11). The king rejected wise counsel and followed the misguided advice of the foolish and inexperienced companions, and so peace in the land was fractured. The people rose up, and civil war broke out.

The wise ruler should always think of himself as the servant of the people. The foolish leader will always think that the people are only there to serve him.

The fruit of the righteous is a tree of life, and he who wins souls
is wise. If the righteous receive their due on earth, how much
more the ungodly and the sinner!

—PROVERBS 11:30–31

RESTORATION

THE TREE OF life appears in several places in the book of Proverbs, but it did not originate there. It can be found at the very beginning of the Bible in Genesis and at the very end in Revelation.

In Genesis, almost everyone remembers the tree of knowledge of good and evil. God commanded Adam not to eat of its fruit, "for when you eat of it you will surely die" (Genesis 2:17). And we remember what happens. Adam and Eve are deceived into tasting the forbidden fruit of that tree, which leads to the consequences that are felt even to this day. But what of that other tree, the tree of life? If Adam and Eve must suffer death, then they cannot have access to the tree of life: "'The man has now become like one of us, knowing good and evil. He must not be allowed to reach out his hand and take also from the tree of life and eat, and live forever.' So the Lord God banished them from the Garden of Eden." (Genesis 3:22–23).

The sin is rebellion against God and his purpose and sin can lead to separation from eternal life. One could summarize the rest of the story of mankind by saying it is a story of finding our way back to the tree of life through Jesus' work on the cross for our sake.

> *But to the wicked, God says: "What right have you to*
> *recite my laws or take my covenant on your lips? You hate my*
> *instruction and cast my words behind you. When you see a thief,*
> *you join with him; you throw in your lot with adulterers. You use*
> *your mouth for evil and harness your tongue to deceit. You speak*
> *continually against your brother and slander your own mother's*
> *son. These things you have done and I kept silent; you thought*
> *I was altogether like you. But I will rebuke you and*
> *accuse you to your face."*

—PSALM 50:16–21

BY THEIR FRUIT

IT IS OFTEN difficult for us to distinguish the reality behind the appearance of things. But what we are incapable of doing, God can.

The reality here is one of wickedness, but the appearance is one of righteousness. While God can never be fooled, men can easily be blinded by the smooth words of charlatans and false purveyors of the Word. One of the most reprehensible examples of this is the deceitful and self-serving holy man who steals from God's vineyard and spreads corruption amongst the people.

Before the fall of Jerusalem, Jeremiah proclaimed that false priests would bring devastation to the land: "From the least to the greatest, all are greedy for gain; prophets and priests alike, all practice deceit. They dress the wound of my people as though it were not serious. 'Peace, peace,' they say, when there is no peace" (Jeremiah 6:13–14). Any society that substitutes licentiousness and greed for virtue and goodness has intentionally or unintentionally chosen a path that will lead to corruption, decline and, if not reversed, a fall as severe as the destruction of ancient Jerusalem.

Why do the nations conspire and the peoples plot in vain? ...
The One enthroned in heaven laughs; the Lord scoffs at them.

—PSALM 2:1,4

THE WAR WITHIN

WHEN WE SPEAK of war, we usually think of epic conflicts like the World Wars of the last century. But according to the second psalm, our earthly battles began as an act of war against God Himself. Our defiance began in the Garden of Eden when both the man and the woman allowed themselves to be deceived by listening to the subtle lies of Satan while disregarding the warning of God Himself.

The choice of Adam and Eve had universal consequences. Every generation that followed seemed to inherit the same rebellious characteristics. Tragically, each one of us is born with the contradictory impulse to worship and rebel, to serve God and to serve ourselves. Only through painful experience and God's grace do we come to understand what Jesus meant when He said, "Just as the Son of Man did not come to be served, but to serve, and to give his life as a ransom for many" (Matthew 20:28).

Thus, the peace spoken of in the Bible must begin within the heart of every man and woman. Until that happens, we will know only conflict, division, and discord and not the peace that flows out of a restored relationship with God.

Then the LORD said to Satan, "Have you considered my servant
Job? There is no one on earth like him; he is blameless and
upright, a man who fears God and shuns evil."

—JOB 1:8

———— ⌾ ————

WILL WE TURN AWAY

WHO, AT SOME point in life, has not experienced contrarian impulses? And who, if they probe deeply enough, does not think of himself as a genuinely good person? So why should it be surprising when an afflicted person cries out against the injustice of God?

At first glance, Job would seem to fit this description perfectly, but throughout the time of his suffering, he never claims to be a man without sin. In fact, it is God who claims that Job is "blameless and upright, a man who fears God and shuns evil." While terrible things come to afflict Job, including the deaths of his children, the loss of his wealth, and the pain of disease, the key question is whether or not Job will lose patience with God, blame Him, and turn on Him.

Loss of faith and betrayal are central realities in the Old and New Testaments, and understanding the example of Job's crisis is important if we are to understand our own response to crisis. Will we remain faithful no matter what? Will we humble ourselves before God no matter what the circumstance? Or will we turn our backs on God, rejecting Him in anger because we have come to believe that He has not been faithful to us?

There are six things the LORD hates, seven that are detestable to
him: haughty eyes, a lying tongue, hands that shed innocent
blood, a heart that devises wicked schemes, feet that are quick to
rush into evil, a false witness who pours out lies and a man who
stirs up dissension among brothers.

—PROVERBS 6:16–19

DETESTABLE IN THE EYES OF GOD

How can God hate when everyone says that God is love? If God is love, then it would be illogical to assume that God can hate.

If you take the biblical perspective, however, then it becomes clear that while God loves us, He hates anything that separates us from Him. The verse says that He hates haughty eyes, which I take to mean pride. And it was pride that brought Eve low when she was deceived into believing that by eating the forbidden fruit from the tree, she would "be like God, knowing good and evil" (Genesis 3:5).

But rather than bringing Adam and Eve closer to God, their act violated their relationship to Him. Oswald Chambers in his book *Biblical Psychology* puts it this way: "God loves the world so much that he hates with a perfect hatred the thing that is twisting people away from him." Here we have seven things that twist us away and are truly detestable in the eyes of God.

You turn men back to dust, saying, "Return to dust,
O sons of men." For a thousand years in your sight are like
a day that has just gone by, or like a watch in the night.

—PSALM 90:3–4

REALITY CHECK

AS WE GROW older, time begins to play unexpected tricks on us. What once took forever now passes by with lightning speed. Often, when we sense time accelerating, we may default to crisis mode because we feel suddenly trapped by the constrictions of limited time. We are frustrated that we have accomplished so little with so little time left to do the things we always planned to do. We may begin to feel a sense of panic, and an air of regret can form within us that may lead us to depression and a sense of purposelessness.

It is at this moment, when we are experiencing one of life's reality checks, that either we hide or we embrace the moment, taking what we have left and building from it. For while "death is the destiny of every man" (Ecclesiastes 7:2), God is calling us to his purpose now; the minute or the hour is not important, for the laborer will receive his wage, and the wage, for the good servant is the abundance that comes through joy.

No king is saved by the size of his army; no warrior escapes
by his great strength. A horse is a vain hope for deliverance;
despite all its great strength it cannot save.

—PSALM 33:16–17

A MERE MORTAL

IN THE MID-1990s, I decided to learn about winter mountaineering. I enrolled in a class sponsored by a credible climbing school and, at the appointed time, travelled to northern New Hampshire and the White Mountains to join other like-minded neophytes for a four-day adventure of survival in the rough, rocky, and frozen terrain of the Franconia Range.

My assembled group of ten was pretty diverse; it was made up of young and old people of varying levels of experience. There was one guy, though, who stood out from the rest of us. Bill was about thirty-five years old, tall, good looking with a mop of flowing blond hair. He exuded the confidence of an athletic natural, a born star who instantly intimidated the rest of us by his very demeanor.

Furthermore, Bill was adorned with every piece of up-to-the-minute name brand equipment you could buy. He was loaded with stuff from Marmot, Mountain Hardwear, Asolo, and much more. It was as if Bill had climbed out of the pages of *Backpacker Magazine*. He appeared to be everything a first class mountaineer should be.

As we went through the usual gear check the night before setting out, Bill recounted tales of mountain adventures from times past, and we listened as he talked the talk. I would have felt completely intimidated if I had not remembered that sometimes giants were pigmies in disguise and that the only place to truly assess talent is out on the cold mountain.

On day one, we set out on a practice climb to a location just above tree line. We used our crampons and ice axes, but the climb was easy because we were not loaded down with overnight packs. Everyone kept pace for about an hour, but then Bill began to fall behind. He would pause to rest every so often, complaining about a previous leg injury. By the time we returned to our base camp, Bill announced he was finished, and he packed up all that gear to leave the rest of us to think about the often strange disconnect between appearance and reality. Bill seemed like a genuine Master of the Universe; he seemed to have it all, but in the end he proved to be a mere mortal just like the rest of us.

The first to present his case seems right,
till another comes forward and questions him.

—PROVERBS 18:17

STANDING FIRM ON THE FIELD OF BATTLE

MANY WANT TO believe what they are told, but this passage suggests that the buyer should always beware because it is easy to be fooled, just as it is easy for some to fool. We hear a persuasive argument, and we automatically say, "That's right!" when we should have said, "No, that can't be what he means."

Eventually, though, experience, knowledge and a certain level of natural skepticism should alert us to the danger of listening to only one voice when we know that another side of the story might exist. In order to question a false argument, we must be armed with knowledge; in the case of Scripture, we are called to know the entire story, the "full counsel of God."

Otherwise, when the worldly man makes his case, there will be no one to answer, leaving the field open to those who represent, consciously or unconsciously, the interests of the rulers, the authorities, against the cosmic powers and "against the spiritual forces of evil in the heavenly realms." (Ephesians 6:12).

Show me your ways, O LORD, teach me your paths;
guide me in your truth and teach me, for you are God my Savior,
and my hope is in you all day long.

—PSALM 25:4–5

A GREAT TEACHER

HOW WE LONG for a great teacher! All these years later, I still remember the teachers of my youth who had the skill, character, and heart to reach me in all my reluctant and rebellious ignorance. What patience and forbearance they had!

Still vivid in my memory are Mr. Charles and Mr. Briggs, my English teachers; Mr. Wales, my math teacher; and, most of all, Mr. Keller, a man with great musical talent and great compassion. Yet none of these men, or any teacher for that matter, can compare to the profound wisdom God can convey, if only we will approach Him with an attitude of humility and prayer.

James says, "If any of you lacks wisdom, he should ask God, who gives generously to all without finding fault, and it will be given to him" (James 1:5). Remember to acknowledge all men and women who have helped lead you toward wisdom and knowledge, but understand that behind each one of them stands God who wants you to draw ever closer to the source of all wisdom and truth.

I will praise God's name in song and glorify him with thanksgiving.

—PSALM 69:30

———&

THE SWEET POWER OF MUSIC

THE PSALMIST SAYS man is "made . . . a little lower than the heavenly beings and crowned . . . with glory and honor" (Psalm 8:5). If in the whole hierarchy of creation we hold this unique closeness to the heavenly sphere, then it is no wonder that man feels drawn to "the sweet sounds of music." How sterile and desolate life would be without music. In the book of Job, we are told that music was present at the beginning when God created the universe "while the morning stars sang together and all the angels shouted for joy" (Job 38:7).

When music is absent, the door opens to a world of discord and conflict, and man's mortal nature asserts itself or, as Shakespeare says, "The man that hath no music in himself, nor is not mov'd with concord of sweet sounds, is fit for treasons, stratagems, and spoils; the motions of his spirit are dull as night, and his affections dark as Erebus. Let no such man be trusted" (*Merchant of Venice*).

Elsewhere in the play, Shakespeare says that music mirrors the harmonious hand of God behind everything in the natural world: "For do but note a wild and wanton herd, or race of youthful and unhandled colts, fetching mad bounds, bellowing and neighing loud, which is the hot condition of their blood; if they but hear perchance a trumpet sound, or any air of music touch their ears, you shall perceive them make a mutual stand, their savage eyes turn'd to modest gaze by the sweet power of music."

Music opens the heart to the harmony that existed between God and man, the creature He created in His own image (Genesis 1:27-28). It is as if music lifts the heart up into the company of angels choiring in heaven. In its holist expression, music speaks to us about the presence of God in all dimensions of creation, both at the beginning and even now at this very moment.

Generations come and generations go, but the earth remains
forever. . . . All things are wearisome, more than one can say.
The eye never has enough of seeing, nor the ear its fill of
hearing. What has been will be again, what has been done will be
done again; there is nothing new under the sun.

—ECCLESIASTES 1:4, 8–9

A HANDFUL OF DUST

IT IS A truism that "generations come and generations go." And all can see that "the sun rises and the sun sets, and hurries back to where it rises."

Solomon provides a vision devoid of hope and passion. He seems to be saying that life is purposeless and futile and, in the end, everything we strive to create will disintegrate into a handful of dust. But is Solomon expressing a universal truth, or is he merely voicing the sad reality of his own excesses when he says, "the eye never has enough of seeing, nor the ear its fill of hearing"?

In old age, Solomon's life had declined into pitiful self-indulgence; the futility he expresses reveals that it is nearly impossible ever to quench the lusts of the sinful nature once it has gained a foothold. When men live under the burden of sin, nothing good seems possible. When that heavy load is lifted (and it can be lifted), then what once seemed impossible becomes probable; and what was once heavy, now is light.

There are three things that are too amazing for me,
four that I do not understand: the way of an eagle in the sky,
the way of a snake on a rock, the way of a ship on the high seas,
and the way of a man with a maiden.

—PROVERBS 30:18–19

WINTER LIGHT

IN EARLY FEBRUARY the light begins to change. Without much warning, the steel gray of deep winter gives way to intimations of a softer season ahead. Daylight lingers longer into the afternoon, and the warmth of the light reflecting off distant skyscrapers seems to battle the forbidding coldness of the moment. And in the late afternoon, when the sky is clear, the setting sun paints the western horizon in orange and reds, intimating that the cloistered winter months will soon be past.

This is the time when I begin to feel the draw of the hills and mountains of the country beyond the shores of this water-bound city. Though snow and ice still cover much of the surrounding land, I instinctively begin to plan to head out to the territory of the Appalachian Mountains and the trail that connects the twelve states between Georgia and Maine.

I am often asked why I leave the comforts of home to walk the many miles of the Appalachian Trail, and I suppose I have many reasons, but what I always come back to is the way the trail connects me to the mysteries of this life we have all fallen into. I may inhabit a world constructed by the hands of man, and I may marvel at all its complexity and brilliance, but the city of man with its activities and diversions is never enough.

Solomon attributes this longing to the way God made men and women, for while we live in the temporal, we yearn for things eternal (Ecclesiastes 3:11). When the Psalmist says, "The meadows are covered with flocks and the valleys are mantled with grain; they shout for joy and sing" (Psalm 65:13), he sees the loving handprint of God in everything. So even though my feet are planted firmly on the hard ground of this world, my heart tells me that eternal inclinations buried deep within my soul urge me on to walk where "the hills are clothed with gladness" (Psalm 65:12).

My days are swifter than a runner; they fly away without
a glimpse of joy. They skim past like boats of papyrus,
like eagles swooping down on their prey.

—JOB 9:25–26

RENEWED DAY BY DAY

DO WE EVER stop to consider what we are doing with our time? Do we wonder what time is doing to us? One strategy used to avoid these questions is to schedule every waking hour, leaving little time for reflection and thought. It is as if we need a framework for pushing away the anxiety that would rush in if we were faced with a moment to ourselves. But super-structuring our time succeeds in keeping our anxious feelings at arm's length for only so long; then like a relentless tide, our awareness of time, death, and eternity pours in, leaving our attempt at avoidance in ruins. Behind our walls erected against the reality of our situation, we try as best we can to relate to the truth of the words of the psalmist: "Each man's life is but a breath" (Psalm 39:5).

We could despair over the fact that "My days are swifter than a weaver's shuttle . . ." (Job 7:6), but we could also respond with courage and faith that behind the reality of the temporal is the promise of the eternal.

To those who have placed their life in God's hands, there is a quiet confidence that is echoed by Paul: "We do not lose heart. Though outwardly we are wasting away, yet inwardly we are being renewed day by day" (2 Corinthians 4:16).

How long, O men, will you turn my glory into shame?
How long will you love delusions and seek false gods?
Know that the Lord has set apart the godly for himself;
the Lord will hear when I call to him.

—PSALM 4:2–3

DRIFTING AWAY

HOW DIFFICULT IT is to stay on the right path. Our mind drifts, our hearts drift, and just as often, we find our life adrift in a swarm of competing objectives. The author of the letter to the Hebrews reinforces the reality of our tendency to drift away from the task at hand when he says, "We must pay more careful attention, therefore, to what we have heard, so that we do not drift away" (Hebrews 2:1).

As in the parable of the lost sheep, God is ever mindful that we have an inclination to wander into uncharted territory. The good news of the gospel is that God is ever seeking us. We may be miles from the path He lit for us, and we may have arrived at a dead end or worse, but He knows all about our propensity to stumble into dangerous regions of this sometimes dark and crooked world. To be truly safe, we are to turn back to the safety of God's protective arms. "In my distress I called to the LORD; I cried to my God for help." And God answered that call for help: "He reached down from on high and took hold of me; he drew me out of the deep waters. He rescued me from my powerful enemy, from my foes, who were too strong for me" (Psalm 18:6, 16–17).

Our wandering away from the path of truth and light may not seem as extreme as David's dire situation, but any distance between God and us is dangerous. It is so easy to become lost, but it is the greatest joy to be found.

Can anyone teach knowledge to God, since he judges even the
highest? One man dies in full vigor, completely secure and at
ease, his body well nourished, his bones rich with marrow.
Another man dies in bitterness of soul, never having enjoyed
anything good. Side by side they lie in the dust,
and worms cover them both.

—JOB 21:22–26

HIS LIFE BLESSED MANY

THE BIBLE IS full of difficult passages that may not conform to our own idea of justice. When something bad happens, we immediately look to God and say, "How can this be! If God is love and if God is good, he would never let this happen."

When I was nineteen, my father died suddenly in an automobile accident. My father "was full of vigor, completely secure and at ease," but then one May morning in 1963, he was gone. Years have not erased the pain and shock of that day.

I remember my mother, only forty-two years old then, crying out in anguish, "Why did God let this happen?" I couldn't answer her then, nor has time helped bring more clarity to the mystery of my father's death. But one thing has changed: today I focus on the blessings that my father brought to so many people, blessings so strong that they live on to this very day.

When you consider every life as a gift from God, then the mystery of an early death is often mitigated by the blessings of the life. No one can remove the pain of death with easy words of solace, but our suffering should be seasoned with humility and gratitude for every blessing that is given by the Creator of all things. While my father's death had a deep impact on me and my family, I still thank God for the blessing of being the son of such a man as my father.

Do not put your trust in princes, in mortal men,
who cannot save. When their spirit departs, they return to the
ground; on that very day their plans come to nothing.

—PSALM 146:3–4

BELIEF

WHAT DO YOU really believe in? Some will say they do not believe in anything, but even in this case, the statement is a belief in non-belief. The issue is not so much about the existence of belief as an essential characteristic of all human beings; rather, it comes down to the foundational truth underlying our beliefs. Institutions are full of people who have strong beliefs, but in these instances, the believer's faith is often deeply singular and unconnected to a greater truth.

Some believe in the saving power of education or intelligence or of the goodness of government programs or their own physical prowess. But biblical wisdom warns us away, not from faith, but faith in something that cannot save. Stop a moment and ask: "What is my deepest belief?" If I have to choose to stake my life on something, where do I draw the line in the sand?

In the end, we walk on a path marked by our beliefs. If the belief that propels our life forward is unconnected to truth, then how will it lead to a place that in the end will prove to be good for us for those who have known us.

What is man, that he could be pure, or one born of woman, that
he could be righteous? If God places no trust in his holy ones, if
even the heavens are not pure in his eyes, how much less man,
who is vile and corrupt, who drinks up evil like water!

—JOB 15:14–16

SUBSTITUTING A LIE FOR THE TRUTH

THE MORE INSISTENT voices of the popular culture swell up in
unison against the wisdom of Job. Popular culture is built on the
fantasy that we can explore the outer reaches of personal freedom
without considering consequences. But isn't this nothing more
than the original lie repeating itself in modern dress, backed up
with the ancient promise of: "And you will be like God, knowing
good and evil" (Genesis 3:5). In our own time we are easily blinded
by the glare of our ubiquitous culture of freedom, purveying the
absurd idea that everyone can be a master of the universe, exempt
from the laws of God and nature.

If we were to look at ourselves through the eyes of God, we
would recoil in shame and rebel against what is invading our
homes every hour of every day. But we do not rebel; instead, we
"drink up evil like water" and lose the will to resist a power that is
eating away at our souls. We disregard the words of the prophet
Isaiah at our own peril: "Woe to those who call evil good and good
evil, who put darkness for light and light for darkness and who put
bitter for sweet and sweet for bitter" (Isaiah 5:20).

The wicked man flees though no one pursues,
but the righteous are as bold as a lion.

—PROVERBS 28:1

BE BOLD

AS ITS ROOT is the source of nourishment to the tree, so fear is fed by the hidden tentacles of guilt. To deal with fear and drive it out, we must first deal with the source that feeds it. Unhappily, though, we often go after the symptom without touching the cause. Or we attempt to abolish the feeling of guilt by expanding the definition of what constitutes acceptable behavior.

If we buy into this hopeless strategy, then we are forced to abandon the fact that God is a God of justice as well as the God of love. If we say He is only a God of love and disregard justice, then we transform Him into a God who approves of everything we might do.

The problem is that this limited view of God runs counter to the character of His nature, and this leads us into the trap of relative truth. But rationalization is not truth, and denial is not reality. When we steal, we know it; when we cheat, we know it; when we commit sexual sins, we know it; and it is futile to try to deny the truth of our petty crimes. In reality, our transgressions give birth to pathological behaviors, and soon we are fleeing when no one pursues.

In contrast, the righteous man is bold because he has nothing to fear. He has not betrayed God but rather has embraced Him and now lives for Him.

*By the rivers of Babylon we sat and wept when we remembered
Zion. There on the poplars we hung our harps, for there our
captors asked us for songs, our tormentors demanded songs of
joy; they said, "Sing us one of the songs of Zion!" How can we
sing the songs of the Lord while in a foreign land? If I forget
you, O Jerusalem, may my right hand forget its skill.*

—PSALM 137:1–5

THE WARNINGS WERE UNHEEDED

HOW BEAUTIFUL AND how melancholy! Jerusalem has been invaded and sacked, and its people have been led as captives into exile. Jeremiah, the prophet, warned the people of Jerusalem of the impending invasion, but his cries were unheeded. Instead, death and destruction descend on David's city. The entire book of Lamentations, written by Jeremiah, focuses on the downfall of Jerusalem: "How deserted lies the city, once so full of people! How like a widow is she, who once was great among the nations! She who was queen among the provinces has now become a slave" (Lamentations 1:1).

When we survey the landscape of our own times, we seem to live as if the tragedy described by Jeremiah could never happen to us, but are we right? The citizens of Jerusalem believed that God would protect them from their enemies, but a sense of invulnerability led to their casual abandonment of honoring God with their lives. In the end, Jerusalem was fatally weakened by its corruption: "There is no one who does good, not even one" (Psalm 14:3). Catastrophe came upon the people not because God abandoned them but because the leaders and the people abandoned God.

His wife said to him, "Are you still holding on to your integrity?
Curse God and die!" He replied, "You are talking like a foolish
woman. Shall we accept good from God, and not trouble?"

—JOB 2:9–10

PERSEVERING IN THE FACE OF SUFFERING

JOB IS A righteous everyman: he is prosperous, respected, and generous. He is a good father and a good husband, and he is exemplary in the eyes of God. If this were all, then the story of Job would have been lost. But in the midst of his good life, Job is visited with troubles that all of us quietly fear for ourselves. Job loses everything, and the losses cannot be attributed to anything Job has done. The visitation of pain and deep suffering comes in an instant, and if the story of Job had not revealed to the reader the existence of a heavenly war that initiated the action on Earth, we would remain as dumbfounded as Job by the apparent injustice of it all.

Some of Job's friends tell him that his suffering is the result of some wrong he had committed against God or man. They believe they understand what is going on, but we are privileged to see a larger picture. The real drama of this story is being worked out in the heart of Job. Will this once prosperous man maintain his integrity of heart in the face of suffering? Or will he follow the admonition of his wife and curse God for all his troubles?

In heaven, Satan had made a similar argument: "A man will give all he has for his own life. But stretch out your hand [he is speaking to God] and strike his flesh and bones, and he will surely curse you to your face" (Job 2:4–5).

Will Job turn against God and blame Him for his troubles, or will he remain steadfast? Job answers his wife with a question: "Shall we accept good from God, and not trouble?" Faced with the same situation, how would we answer? Will we remain faithful, trusting God in the deepest depths of darkness, or will we abandon our faith because we have come to the conclusion that God has left us to suffer in darkness?

Hear my prayer, O Lord; let my cry for help come to you.

Do not hide your face from me when I am in distress.

Turn your ear to me; when I call, answer me quickly.

—PSALM 102:1–2

ON THE EDGE OF A PRECIPICE

IF WE FEEL prosperous, we often believe we are protected and safe. Walls of brick and mortar insulate us from strong winds and winter storms. It is disconcerting, therefore, to read David's poetic words that even he can be in danger of falling forever into the abyss with no hope of survival. Elsewhere in the same psalm, he says, "I am reduced to skin and bones. I am like a desert owl, like an owl among the ruins" (Psalm 102:5–6).

David's words serve to remind us that safety is provisional. We all walk through the "valley of the shadow of death," and the human bulwarks we erect to stave off the dangers of darkness are nothing without God's grace: "If I rise on the wings of the dawn, if I settle on the far side of the sea, even there your hand will guide me, your right hand will hold me fast" (Psalm 139:9–10).

As with David, there will come a time when we may fall the terror of the precipice. If we have arrived at the edge alone, then we will become overwhelmed by the fear of falling. But David, as well as each one of us, has a God who cares for our well-being because he loves us: "The angel of the Lord encamps around those who fear him, and he delivers them" (Psalm 34:7).

Can you raise your voice to the clouds and cover yourself
with a flood of water? Do you send the lightning bolts on their
way? Do they report to you, "Here we are?" Who endowed the
heart with wisdom or gave understanding to the mind? Who has
the wisdom to count the clouds? Who can tip over the water jars
of the heavens when the dust becomes hard and the clods
of earth stick together?

—JOB 38:34–38

WHO, INDEED?

IN ORDER TO avoid hard questions, we often construct our own intellectual and emotional cocoons, or we build ourselves up by miniaturizing the world around us, reducing it to bite-sized pieces that are easy to digest and explain.

We do this with the Bible all the time. We reduce it to a few sound bites in order to make it fit into our own personal definitions of God and reality. We reduce the beauty, majesty, and complexity of the Old Testament to the story of an angry God and of His wandering and wayward people. The New Testament is marginalized by reducing Jesus to fit the latest scholarly fad. And none of this addresses the question of God to Job: "Who endowed the heart with wisdom or gave understanding to the mind?" Who, indeed?

You rule over the surging sea; when its waves mount up,

you still them . . . The heavens are yours, and yours also

the earth; you founded the world and all that is in it . . .

Your arm is endowed with power; your hand is strong, your right

hand exalted. Righteousness and justice are the foundation of

your throne; love and faithfulness go before you.

—PSALM 89:9, 11, 13–14

A FURIOUS STORM

JESUS HAD BEEN performing miracles throughout the day, healing the demon-possessed and the sick. Matthew writes that, "This was to fulfill what was spoken through the prophet Isaiah: 'He took up our infirmities and carried our diseases'" (Matthew 8:17). But apparently His own disciples did not understand who this healer was.

Then Jesus bid His followers to join Him in a boat to cross the Sea of Galilee. Suddenly, as they were crossing, "a furious storm came up on the lake, so that the waves swept over the boat" (v. 24). The disciples were overcome with fear, and they cried out to Jesus: "Lord, save us! We're going to drown" (v. 25).

Jesus rebuked the winds and the waves, and the sea became calm. The disciples were bewildered and asked, "What kind of man is this? Even the winds and the waves obey him" (v. 27).

David, speaking of God, says, "You rule over the surging sea; when its waves mount up, you still them" (Psalm 89:9). When the disciples ask what kind of man is this, David provides the answer: *He is the holy one of God, the Messiah, the one who has been sent to crush sin, fear, and death.*

Then I realized that it is good and proper for a man to eat and
drink, and to find satisfaction in his toilsome labor under the sun
during the few days of life God has given him—for this is his lot.
Moreover, when God gives any man wealth and possessions, and
enables him to enjoy them, to accept his lot and be happy in his
work—this is a gift of God. He seldom reflects on the days of his
life, because God keeps him occupied with gladness of heart.

—ECCLESIASTES 5:18–20

A DEFINING MOMENT

THE DAY WAS Ash Wednesday, February 13, 1991. My family and I were on an island in the Caribbean, which was not a well-traveled place because the U.S. Navy had reserved large sections of the island for practice bombing runs. The bombs were no longer falling, and the house we were renting was situated near the top of a hill, providing panoramic views of the Atlantic and Caribbean oceans. It was in that house on that day that I unexpectedly came across a two-year lectionary hidden deep in the pages of the *Book of Common Prayer*. When I discovered this lectionary, it was if I heard a voice telling me that this was exactly what I needed as a way to come to know the whole Bible. So on that day many years ago, I quietly committed myself to following this biblical road map every day of the year no matter where I was or what I was doing.

And thus began my response to God's call. I would honor God by coming to know His Word by setting aside time every morning of every day. This journey would be slow, and it would require perseverance. But if I was going to truly honor God with my life, I would have to be equipped with a deeper understanding of God's Word. And through an everyday encounter with the Old and New Testaments, I began to understand what it meant to walk on God's ancient pathways.

You are a garden locked up, my sister, my bride;
you are a spring enclosed, a sealed fountain.
Your plants are an orchard of pomegranates with choice fruits,
with henna and nard, nard and saffron, calamus and cinnamon,
with every kind of incense tree, with myrrh and aloes
and all the finest spices. You are a garden fountain,
a well of flowing water streaming down from Lebanon.

—SONG OF SONGS 4:12–15

A COPY OF THE ORIGINAL

SONG OF SONGS is an extended love poem. It describes the passion a man has for a woman: "How beautiful you are, my darling! Oh, how beautiful!" (Song of Songs 4:1), as well as the love a woman has for a man: "Let him kiss me with the kisses of his mouth—for your love is more delightful than wine" (Song of Songs 1:2).

But Solomon is speaking of something beyond physical desire. The lover is compared to a garden fed by a spring of "flowing water," a garden abundantly provided with every kind of fruit and sustenance. This place, so fair and plentiful, resembles the original garden, Eden, where the first man and woman lived in harmony with God and with nature. It was a place created in love and for love, the love between God, the Creator, and Man, the one he created.

The love of a man for a woman should be understood as a copy of the original. We long to be in a place where love and abundance abide; this garden is "an orchard of pomegranates with choice fruits, with henna and nard, nard and saffron, calamus and cinnamon, with every kind of incense tree, with myrrh and aloes and all the finest spices."

Love is a garden where peace, joy, and intimacy exist. We may have lost our place in the original garden long ago, but that does not mean that we have lost the longing to return.

Good and upright is the Lord; therefore he instructs sinners in
his ways. He guides the humble in what is right and teaches
them his way. All the ways of the Lord are loving and faithful
for those who keep the demands of his covenant.

—PSALM 25:8–10

AN OPEN INVITATION

JESUS IS ALWAYS commanding, but He never demands. He often prefaces an instruction with an all-important "if." He says, "If you believe in me . . ." or "if you will follow me . . ." then "all the ways of the Lord are loving and faithful . . ." (v. 10).

The commandments of God always imply that we have a choice. We can follow the way provided by God through His Son and His Word, or like so many of Jesus' own disciples, we can turn aside to go our own way to follow the demands of our own mercurial hearts. Without God, all people are prone to "gratifying the cravings of our sinful nature and following its desires and thoughts" (Ephesians 2:3).

Jesus calls out to us to follow Him, but the decision is ours. It is false to think of God as an enforcer of a series of impossibly complex laws. God is the lawmaker, but the most important law of God is love. When we live within the orbit of God's love, then the choice to follow Him will be natural and straightforward—and because of God's merciful nature, the invitation always remains wide open for every one of us. Like the Prodigal Son, we too need to turn back and choose to accept the glorious gift being offered.

Why are you downcast, O my soul?

Why so disturbed within me? Put your hope in God,

for I will yet praise him, my Savior and my God.

—PSALM 42:11

A SINNER LIKE YOU AND ME

WHEN WE THINK of King David, we often think of the great warrior king who dispatched enemies near and far and who united two kingdoms and succeeded beyond measure.

But David was more than a powerful political figure; he was the poet king, a composer of songs who could search the deepest depths of the human heart. It is through his songs that we discover the man behind the crown. And to our surprise we find a man with the same fears, guilt, doubts, and anxieties of ordinary men. This is not what we might have expected.

He asks, "Why are you downcast, O my soul? Why so disturbed within me?" David, the king, the anointed one of God, the slayer of giants and the builder of cities and kingdoms, has a heart very much like yours and mine. For David is a sinner who turns away from God at the very pinnacle of his earthly powers; he forsakes God for a momentary temptation; but God does not forsake him. He receives forgiveness from the Lord, and he is restored to a new life by the grace of God. He is then freed to "teach transgressors your ways" (Psalm 51:13) and help sinners turn back to the Lord. "Put your hope in God," he says, "for I will yet praise him, my Savior and my God."

There is no wisdom, no insight, and no plan that can succeed
against the LORD. The horse is made ready for the day of battle,
but victory rests with the LORD.

—PROVERBS 21:30–31

THE SOURCE OF WISDOM

THERE WAS A time when I believed, truly believed, that wisdom, insight, and success came from . . . ME. And so, it is not totally surprising that eventually I would run off the road and end up in a ditch.

When you are blinded by self-regard, it is hard to steer a straight course. The sad thing is that I was quite typical of my generation. We were swerving all over the place when we thought we were plowing straight ahead.

Ironically, the disastrous experience of bankruptcy eventually restored my sight and my sanity. And with the restoration came the realization that victory of any kind can never rest with the singular possessive. "This is what the LORD says: 'Let not the wise man boast of his wisdom or the strong man boast of his strength or the rich man boast of his riches, but let him who boasts boast about this: that he understands and knows me, that I am the LORD, who exercises kindness, justice and righteousness on earth, for in these I delight,' declares the Lord" (Jeremiah 9:23–24).

The proverbs of Solomon: A wise son brings joy to his father,
but a foolish son grief to his mother . . . He who gathers
crops in summer is a wise son, but he who sleeps during
harvest is a disgraceful son.

—PROVERBS 10:1, 5

FATHERS AND SONS

WHILE WE MAY be alternately proud and troubled by the behavior of our own children, there is a biblical example of the perfect father-son relationship. We know that the Father loves the Son because He says, "You are my Son, whom I love; with you I am well pleased" (Mark 1:11). Later, the same Father says: "This is my Son, whom I love. Listen to him!" (Mark 9:7).

As a student is not above his teacher, so the son does not strive to be greater than the father. Instead, he does what his father asks of him. And in His moment of greatest crisis, the Son prayerfully humbled Himself and submitted to the will of His Father: "Father, if you are willing, take this cup from me; yet not my will, but yours be done" (Luke 22:42).

This is the picture of perfect love between a loving and worthy Father and His loving and obedient Son. Of course, it is the picture of God, the Father, and His Son, Jesus Christ, but what applies to God and His own Son also applies to each one of us as fathers and sons. This relationship modeled by God, the Father, and Jesus Christ, His Son, is the new standard, replacing the old norm that had been riddled with sin, conflict, and discord: "I reared children and brought them up, but they have rebelled against me" (Isaiah 1:2). That is the old pattern of rebellion which Jesus has replaced with the new pattern built on the solid foundation of love.

Your righteousness reaches to the skies, O God, you who have
done great things. Who, O God, is like you? Though you have
made me see troubles, many and bitter, you will restore my life
again; from the depths of the earth you will again bring me up.
You will increase my honor and comfort me once again.

—PSALM 71:19–21

THE POWER TO RESTORE

THERE IS MORE than a hint of the resurrection in this verse: "You will restore my life again; from the depths of the earth you will again bring me up." The reality of resurrection is not limited to the New Testament. Job says in a famous passage, "I know that my Redeemer lives, and that in the end he will stand upon the earth. And after my skin has been destroyed, yet in my flesh, I will see God" (Job 19:25–26).

Jonah is buried in the sea for three days but returns, and Hosea, the prophet, says, "After two days he will revive us; on the third day he will restore us, that we may live in his presence" (Hosea 6:2). So Jesus is standing on familiar ground when He says, "The Son of Man must suffer many things and be rejected by the elders, chief priests and teachers of the law, and that he must be killed and after three days rise again" (Mark 8:31). All of Scripture tells us that God not only has the power to create life; He also has the power to restore life.

How can a young man keep his way pure? By living according
to your word. I seek you with all my heart; do not let me stray
from your commands . . . Do good to your servant, and I will live;
I will obey your word. Open my eyes that I may see wonderful
things in your law. I am a stranger on earth;
do not hide your commands from me.

—PSALM 119:9–10, 17–19

SPENDING THE GIFT

"I SEEK YOU with all my heart." It is one thing to say "I seek the Lord," but it is another thing to live it. When the sun rises on a new day, we are given the choice of how we plan to dedicate our time. Time is a gift given freely by God, but this gift must be grasped and used or it will sift away like water through your fingers. "For I am a sojourner with you, a guest, like all of my fathers." (Psalm 39:12)

God gives us the gift of choice. We can choose to spend the gift of time on the Giver, or we can spend it on ourselves. "Open my eyes that I may see wonderful things in your law." Ask God to open your eyes so that your heart may discern how He would have you spend His precious gift today.

Do not fret because of evil men or be envious of the wicked,
for the evil man has no future hope, and the lamp of the
wicked will be snuffed out.

—PROVERBS 24:19–20

THE HOPE OF THE CROSS

Do you believe that "the evil man has no future hope"? Don't we complain that evil seems to be an overwhelming force in the world and nothing good seems to be found anywhere? This seems to be true not only of our time but of all time: "Everyone has turned away, they have together become corrupt; there is no one who does good, not even one" (Psalm 53:3).

It would seem to be a hopeless situation, for evil is pervasive. But wait! Paul tells us that there is hope, real hope, in the person of Jesus Christ "who gave himself for our sins to rescue us from the present evil age, according to the will of our God and Father" (Galatians 1:3–5). The hope is not in us because, left to our own devices, we cannot help but sin. Our hope lies with the cross and Jesus Christ who stepped in the path of that which would destroy. He died that we might live: "For our sake he made him to be sin who knew no sin, so that in him we might become the righteousness of God." (2 Corinthians 5:21)

To you I call, O LORD my Rock; do not turn a deaf ear to me.

For if you remain silent, I will be like those who have gone down

to the pit. Hear my cry for mercy as I call to you for help,

as I lift up my hands toward your Most Holy Place.

—PSALM 28:1–2

A LIGHT IN THE RUINS

AN AMERICAN MISSIONARY who once lived in Ukraine told me a story about an encounter he had with a friendly atheist. This young woman was giving him a tour around the city of Odessa. As they walked from place to place, she began to open up, and at one point, she told him that believing in God was ridiculously irrational. How could any educated person believe that God existed? She was not belligerent; she just stated her belief as a proven fact. She indicated that she was doing fine without God in her life.

As they were talking, they came to a blighted intersection that was nothing more than a ruin left over from the devastation of World War II. The empty, decaying structures were fragmented shells. Rubble rather than trees created an impression of a wasteland. Even flowers and weeds seemed to avoid this desolate place.

It was at that moment that my missionary friend turned to the woman and observed: "Look around. If you want to know what the world looks like without God, here it is right before us." She gazed at the wretched scene and seemed to make the link between a war-torn world and mankind's banishment of God from this modern and enlightened world. Did she see the relationship between famine, disease, and war, and our fractured relationship with the God who created us and nurtured us? Can love even exist in such a place? My missionary friend believes he touched her by using that desolate scene as a way of introducing God back into her life. He did not make his point with words or with arguments or talking points. He just revealed the obvious, and he let that do its work in her heart.

Teach us to number our days aright,

that we may gain a heart of wisdom.

—PSALM 90:12

THE INCLINATIONS OF THE HEART

IN OUR OWN times, wisdom has been relocated from the heart to the head. This is based on the idea that an accumulation of information will somehow lead to wisdom if we can just sort through the mass of facts and figures free-floating through our daily lives. But are we right to somehow link "knowing" to wisdom?

David Mamet sees right through the "knowledge conceit" when he points out that to maintain illogical belief systems, the believers themselves "have to pretend not to know a lot of things."

Adam and Eve changed the very nature of the love of God in their hearts when they fell for the promise that they "will be like God, knowing good and evil" if only they would eat of the fruit of that tree. (Genesis 3:5) It was that tragic act that turned the human heart away from the fullness of the love of God to darker inclinations. By the time of Noah, the infection of the heart had become so severe that God decided to "blot out man who I created from the face of the earth....The Lord saw that the wickedness of man was great in the earth, and that every inclination of the thoughts of the heart was only evil continually." (Genesis 6:5-6)

After the fall in the Garden, the human heart became overwhelmed with conflicting inclinations. The heart's natural love of God became corrupted by competing loves that drove out our primary love. Wisdom comes through a deep preference to love God first above everything else, even if that love causes the world to place itself (in small and large ways) in opposition to a believer in Christ. Jesus came into the world to transform the corrupted inclinations of our hearts by restoring the desire "to love the Lord your God with all your heart and with all your soul and with all your mind." (Matthew 22:37)

When you sit to dine with a ruler, note well what is before you,

and put a knife to your throat if you are given to gluttony.

Do not crave his delicacies, for that food is deceptive.

—PROVERBS 23:1–3

THE COST IS GREATER

WHY ARE THE delicacies of the king deceptive? This passage does not elaborate on the exact nature of the danger, though common sense might lead us to an appropriate interpretation. Rather, another passage in Psalms helps to pinpoint the meaning with great clarity: "Let not my heart be drawn to what is evil, to take part in wicked deeds with men who are evildoers; let me not eat of their delicacies" (Psalm 141:4).

The warning here relates to rulers who are evildoers. For we may be tempted to eat at their table because of their position and power even though there is danger for anyone who might fall under such a ruler's control. So we stand warned: the temptation to eat the delicacies at the table of a powerful but wicked leader is great, but the cost could be even greater.

With persuasive words she led him astray;
she seduced him with her smooth talk.
All at once he followed her like an ox going to the slaughter,
like a deer stepping into a noose till an arrow pierces his liver,
like a bird darting into a snare,
little knowing it will cost him his life.

—PROVERBS 7:21–23

FORBIDDEN FRUIT

SEDUCTION WITH EVIL intent is not love. Seduction is built on the foundation of deception and lust. In this passage from Proverbs, the woman leads the man astray; her weapon is persuasion and smooth talk promising irresistible delights.

Of course, men have their own methods of seduction, which are just as cruel and deadly. But no matter who is intent on seduction, their objective is self-gratification. The other person becomes a mere object of desire to be discarded once they are no longer needed.

Lust is a perversion of love. Whereas lust uses others for its purpose, love gives sacrificially and rejoices in the other person. Love "always protects, always trusts, always hopes, always perseveres" (1 Corinthians 13:7). Love is God's most amazing gift to each one of us.

Hear, O Lord, my righteous plea; listen to my cry.

Give ear to my prayer—it does not rise from deceitful lips.

—PSALM 17:1

POWERFUL AND EFFECTIVE

DAVID'S PRAYER IS not a plea but a "righteous" plea. His lips are not "deceitful." If the Lord probes to the very depths of his heart, He will find nothing detestable there.

This is the point: When we pray, we should come to God with a sincere heart; to be half-hearted means that we are not to engage with God on our terms. If we hold back part of ourselves, we are showing that there is something in us that we either do not want to be rid of or something that we do not want to reveal. James says, "Therefore confess your sins to each other and pray for each other so that you may be healed. The prayer of a righteous man is powerful and effective" (James 5:16).

I, wisdom, dwell together with prudence;
I possess knowledge and discretion . . . I walk in the way of
righteousness, along the paths of justice, bestowing wealth on
those who love me and making their treasuries full.

—PROVERBS 8:12, 20–21

HIS HUMAN FACE

WE OFTEN THINK of wisdom in the abstract—as if it represents a human philosophy constructed by the hand of man with little that we can apply to everyday life. But according to Scripture, wisdom preexisted the creation of the world and comes from the heart of God (Jeremiah 10:12). For us, therefore, living wisely means that we are living in harmony with the character of God. And that character is perfectly reflected in the Son He loves, Jesus Christ.

As with Christ, the wise person embodies the values of prudence, knowledge, and discretion. He is humble in all things, and he chooses his words with care because he knows that words are powerful and, when used carelessly, can wound. The wise person is sought out by others because he exhibits sound and fair judgment. Most importantly, love is at the very center of who he is. He is patient and kind. He neither envies nor boasts. He is not proud or rude. The wise person is not self-seeking, is not easily angered, and does not keep a record of wrongs. He takes no delight in evil but rejoices with the truth. He always protects, always trusts, always hopes, always perseveres (1 Corinthians 13:4–7).

When we live in harmony with God, as Christ did, we reflect all the wisdom of God who, from the beginning, has always wanted to share with His children. The face of God is the face of love, and it is the wise man who allows love to wash over him and through him and be transferred from himself to others who have not yet seen or fully experienced the beauty of that face, which is "the glory of God in the face of Christ" (2 Corinthians 4:6).

If you make the Most High your dwelling—even the Lord,
who is my refuge—then no harm will befall you, no disaster
will come near your tent. For he will command his angels
concerning you to guard you in all your ways.

—PSALM 91:9–11

THE FULL ARMOR OF GOD

A LIE IS often most persuasive when it is wrapped in a package that appears to be the truth. In the third chapter of Genesis, set in the Garden of Eden, Satan makes his first appearance disguised as a serpent, and he asks the woman a simple question: "Did God really say, 'You must not eat from any tree in the garden'?" (Genesis 3:1).

The question prompts a response which then provides Satan the opening he is looking for: "If you eat the fruit from the forbidden tree, you will not die; rather you will become like God, knowing good and evil." This simple declaration initiates a train of events that become the basis for the entire biblical narrative. Satan insinuates doubt that leads to temptation, which prompts the woman to act in defiance of the original prohibition. She has rebelled, and she quickly acts to create a co-conspirator with her mate.

But rather than becoming like God, the man and the woman find their actions have created division and separation from God, which was the plan of the serpent all along. For the first time, the man and the woman experience shame and guilt. They hide from God and then lie to Him and blame Him for something they in fact did.

The proverbs of Solomon son of David, king of Israel:
for attaining wisdom and discipline; for understanding words of
insight; for acquiring a disciplined and prudent life, doing what
is right and just and fair; for giving prudence to the simple,
knowledge and discretion to the young—let the wise listen and
add to their learning, and let the discerning get guidance—
for understanding proverbs and parables, the sayings
and riddles of the wise.

—PROVERBS 1:1–6

A DISCERNING HEART

SOLOMON WAS RENOWNED for his great wisdom, but that's not all: he was one of the most powerful rulers on earth, the son of King David, and a man of tremendous wealth. Yet King Solomon prized wisdom above everything else, for when he became king upon his father's death, God favored him by granting him whatever he might ask for. Here is how Solomon responded: "So give your servant a discerning heart to govern your people and to distinguish between right and wrong. For who is able to govern this great people of yours?" (1 Kings 3:9).

And here is how God replied: "Since you have asked for this and not for long life or wealth for yourself, nor have asked for the death of your enemies but for discernment in administering justice, I will do what you have asked" (1 Kings 3:11–12).

He makes springs pour water into the ravines;

it flows between the mountains. They give water to all the beasts

of the field; the wild donkeys quench their thirst. The birds of

the air nest by the waters; they sing among the branches.

He waters the mountains from his upper chambers;

the earth is satisfied by the fruit of his work.

—PSALM 104:10–13

MARCH MADNESS

IN THE SPRING of each year, hundreds, if not thousands, of enthusiastic hikers take their first steps on a 2,193-mile journey on the Appalachian Trail. Months of preparation have led to this moment. They have read guidebooks, bought equipment, packed food, and talked to those who have hiked before them. They have diligently studied every aspect of the journey to come, and now they stand under the stone portal as they prepare to ascend Springer Mountain, the true starting point of the trail.

Yet no amount of study can prepare these hikers for what lies ahead. Nature is beautiful and alluring and very hard. Hikers can expect sore knees, turned ankles, persistent thirst, lonely nights, and lingering doubts. They will be slowed by blizzards in the Smokies, startled by lightning strikes in Virginia, exhausted by searing summer heat in Pennsylvania, drenched by chilling downpours in New Hampshire, and tested by everything in Maine.

But as they walk the trail and become hardened by its challenges, hikers will experience a change of heart and mind. With time and miles, a veteran slowly emerges; the novice at Springer becomes the confident and knowledgeable Thru-Hiker who will keep on striving to achieve victory over every large and small adversity. The postcard landscape of the armchair hiker has given way to a deeper understanding of living outside of the normal comforts of civilized life. What began as toil and trouble has become something akin to joy.

The seasoned hiker overcomes through endurance and perseverance. He has encountered unexpected obstacles time and again, but he forges on because he has a defined purpose, an endgame that over time draws ever closer. And as he closes in on the last peak, the last big challenge, a new energy flows into and through his body as the final pinnacle finally comes into sight. He has reached the summit ... and tomorrow is another day.

Do not fret because of evil men or be envious of those who do wrong;
for like the grass they will soon wither, like green plants they
will soon die away. Trust in the LORD and do good; dwell in the
land and enjoy safe pasture. Delight yourself in the LORD and
he will give you the desires of your heart.

—PSALM 37:1–4

SEEK FIRST HIS RIGHTEOUSNESS

DAVID IS RIGHT when he admonishes us not to fret, but how can we stop when the world presents us with so many reasons to worry? At the top of the list is money: Do we have enough? Where will the next dollar come from? Can we afford our house and our lifestyle? Then there's the children: Do they have everything they need? Are their grades good enough, and where will they go to college? And did they make the team, and will they rise up the ladder of success as doctors or lawyers or executives? Finally, don't forget the worries brought on by the job: Does my boss appreciate me? Will I be promoted or fired? Will the company survive?

Yes, daily life can provide an overabundance of worries, but what should we do about it? When we descend into worrying about every little thing, our fretting becomes indicative of someone who insists on controlling the uncontrollable. It is a sign that we have substituted a genuine faith in God for a faith in our own efforts to bring everything under our own desire to determine all outcomes. In the Sermon on the Mount, Jesus speaks to the futility of needless and obsessive worry: "If that is how God clothes the grass of the field, which is here today and tomorrow is thrown into the fire, will he not much more clothe you, O you of little faith? So do not worry, saying, 'What shall we eat?' or 'What shall we drink?' or 'What shall we wear?' . . . But first seek his kingdom and his righteousness, and all these things will be given you as well" (Matthew 6:30–33).

Jesus is saying that we must keep God in our line of sight first and always. When we lose sight of God, our daily life becomes a jumble of worries, that pulls us away from God. Over time worry reduces us to being ineffective disciples in a world that may need of our faith and our lives.

Save me, O God, for the waters have come up to my neck.
I sink in the miry depths, where there is no foothold. I have come
into the deep waters; the floods engulf me. I am worn out calling
for help; my throat is parched. My eyes fail, looking for my God.
Those who hate me without reason outnumber the hairs of my
head; many are my enemies without cause, those who seek to
destroy me. I am forced to restore what I did not steal.

—PSALM 69:1–4

NO GREATER LOVE

THE MOVIE *The Passion of the Christ* opens in the depth of night. A full moon hangs ominously in the sky, creating a supernatural light of dark blue streaked with silver. The place is the garden of Gethsemane, and Jesus is the man fervently praying. Quietly, a shadowy figure emerges from the background, looking on with a cool curiosity. Jesus has already begun to suffer, and some of His words are preserved in the four Gospels; but many words are not recorded, and so we can only imagine all the words Jesus may have been praying.

The words of this psalm, beginning with "Save me, O God," could easily reflect the words that Jesus uttered alone in that garden: "I am worn out calling for help . . . Those who hate me without reason outnumber the hairs of my head."

Jesus knows what is in store for Him; He knows why He has come to earth, and He knows that the shadowy figure as portrayed in the movie wants Him to give in to temptation by escaping from what is about to happen. Satan would appeal to Jesus' human nature, but as the Gospels show, Jesus' God nature prevails. Though He knows what is to come, Jesus submits to the will of the Father in order to reverse the tragic choices made in Eden: "Not as I will, but as you will." And so the way is cleared for our own redemption and ultimate salvation.

Let us examine our ways and test them,

and let us return to the Lord. Let us lift up our

hearts and our hands to God in heaven, and say:

"We have sinned and rebelled and you have not forgiven."

—LAMENTATIONS 3:40–42

AFTER THE REBELLION

BY THE TIME the prophet Jeremiah wrote Lamentations, the unthinkable had taken place. Jerusalem had been attacked by invading armies, the walls had been breached, the temple destroyed, and many of the inhabitants, including the leaders and priests, had been led away into exile in chains.

Jeremiah had warned the leaders and people of their impending doom, but no one took heed. Instead, they continued in their godless way, worshipping idols and reveling in degrading and corrupt behavior: "Jerusalem has sinned greatly and so has become unclean . . . Her filthiness clung to her skirts; she did not consider her future. Her fall was astonishing; there was none to comfort her" (Lamentations 1:8, 9).

In 1917, the communists took control of Russia and named the new empire "The Soviet Union." The communist leaders expelled God, tore down churches and cathedrals, and persecuted Christians. Seventy-two years later, that same Soviet empire crumbled of its own corrupt weight, and the country once again became Russia. The experiment in a godless progressive society failed utterly. It remains to be seen, however, whether Russia and many other countries in the West will see the biblical parallels between the fate of ancient Jerusalem and the modern progressive society. Can any society that abandons the centrality of God in its life and culture expect anything different from the fate experienced by Jerusalem twenty-five hundred years ago?

In the beginning you laid the foundations of the earth,
and the heavens are the work of your hands. They will perish,
but you remain; they will all wear out like a garment.

—PSALM 102:25–26

HE WILL REMAIN

THE VERY FIRST words of the Bible are: "In the beginning God created the heavens and the earth" (Genesis 1:1). The word "beginning" might suggest to some that everything began with the creation, but it is clear from this passage that God predates the creation of the heavens and the earth. Before time, before molecules and atoms, before the sun and the moon, and before the planets and the solar system, God was. And when everything we see and experience this very day vanishes and time itself disappears, God will be: "Lift up your eyes to the heavens, look at the earth beneath; the heavens will vanish like smoke, the earth will wear out like a garment and its inhabitants die like flies" (Isaiah 51:6).

When we are tempted to focus all our energies on the little emergencies of life, perhaps it is useful to keep the big picture occasionally in view. While change permeates every aspect of our life here and now, God was, is, and will be forever. He is the great "I AM" (Exodus 3:14).

...Thus you will walk in the ways of good men
and keep to the paths of the righteous.

—PROVERBS 2:20

A READJUSTMENT OF THE HEART

SEVERAL YEARS AGO, a small group of people met at my office in New York City to launch an informal Bible discussion group. During the discussion, one young man expressed his frustration with the book of Proverbs.

"I read it," he said, "but all I came across was 'righteousness this' and 'righteousness that' without ever learning what righteousness is."

The young man posed a good question, "What is righteousness?" Let's start with what it is not. The rich ruler in Luke 18:18 lived by many of the commandments given to Moses, but Jesus told him that he still lacked one thing: to sell all his worldly wealth and "then come, and follow me" (Luke 18:22). The rich ruler refused because his wealth had a greater hold on him than God did.

But this is not the case with Abraham. At God's command, Abraham left everything, including his family and his home: "Abraham believed the Lord, and he credited to him as righteousness" (Genesis 15:6).

Righteousness is not self-righteousness; it is not bragging rights about what a great person you are, even if you are a very good person. Rather, it is a total readjustment of the heart so that you can move from doubt and detachment to a condition where you are willing not to be unwilling. Jesus summarizes it in a very straightforward way: "The work of God is this: to believe in the one he has sent" (John 6:29).

Righteousness is a willingness to subordinate your will, your needs, and your concerns to the Lord; "Worship the Lord your God, and serve him only" (Matthew 4:10).

"It's no good, it's no good!" says the buyer;
then off he goes and boasts about his purchase.

—PROVERBS 20:14

⟶ ∞ ⟵

GOD'S UNDIVIDED ATTENTION

WHY ARE MANY of the common matters of everyday life built into the fabric of the biblical narrative? After all, isn't the Bible about God and higher spiritual concerns? Yes, it is, but it is also about you and me. So the words are about our generation and all the countless generations that have come before us. It is about our highest aspirations and our lowest desires. It is about feeding and being fed. It is about wanderers and wayfarers, and it is about those who seek God in the city and those who seek to flee from him.

The study of man cannot be man alone; if it was just about us, it would be an incomplete and unsatisfactory story. The biblical narrative from creation to the cross and from the cross to this very day is about the complex relationship between God, the creator, and man, the creator he created. The surprise is that God is ever present. We may try to banish him from our lives, but that does not work: "What is man that you make so much of him, that you give him so much attention, that you examine him every morning and test him every moment?" (Job 7:17–18). God is near if we will only open our eyes and our hearts.

He reached down from on high and took hold of me;

he drew me out of deep waters. He rescued me from my powerful

enemy, from my foes, who were too strong for me. They confronted

me in the day of my disaster, but the Lord was my support.

He brought me out into a spacious place; he rescued me

because he delighted in me.

—PSALM 18:16–19

SALVATION COMES FROM THE LORD

AFTER DAVID HAD been anointed by Samuel and before he was named King, he became the object of King Saul's concentrated, jealous rage. Saul was enraged because the people sang praise to David for defeating the Philistine, Goliath, and the people praised him by singing: "Saul has slain his thousands, and David his tens of thousands" (1 Samuel 18:7).

Now David, alone and without resources, is being hunted down by the full force of King Saul's army. In his darkest moment when "the cords of death" were overwhelming him, he "called to the Lord; (he) cried out to . . . God for help" (Psalm 18:6). We know that David was saved that day; he says in the same psalm that God "reached down from on high and took hold of me; he drew me out of deep waters. He rescued me from my powerful enemy; from my foes who were too strong for me" (v. 16, 17).

David, with his battles, suffering, and close relationship to God, becomes for us a precursor to Jesus, who will enter a hostile world to "save the people from their sins" (Matthew 1:21). But for Jesus the nature of the enemy is far more powerful and crafty than any Philistine warrior or wayward king. Jesus has come to conquer the enemy of all mankind who would separate us from God through temptation and sin. "For our struggle is not against flesh and blood, but against the rulers, against the authorities, against the powers of this dark world and against the spiritual forces of evil in the heavenly realms" (Ephesians 6:12). Against forces such as this, mankind has needed and still needs a very great Savior. God did provide.

If you have played the fool and exalted yourself,
or if you have planned evil, clap your hand over your mouth!
For as churning the milk produces butter, and as twisting the
nose produces blood, so stirring up anger produces strife.

—PROVERBS 30:32–33

QUICK TO LISTEN, SLOW TO SPEAK

BEHIND THE ERUPTION of anger is a real or imagined feeling of injustice. Sometimes anger can be truly righteous, but we should be careful not to confuse our own sense of justice with God's. If there is impurity within our own hearts, then there is a high probability that our holy righteousness will be compromised by our own unrighteousness. Rather, we should remember that God Himself is "gracious and compassionate . . . slow to anger and abounding in love" (Jonah 4:2).

As children of God, we "should be quick to listen, slow to speak and slow to become angry, for a man's anger does not bring about the righteous life that God desires" (James 1:20).

But I will sing of your strength, in the morning I will
sing of your love; for you are my fortress, my refuge in times
of trouble. O my Strength, I sing praise to you; you,
O God, are my fortress, my loving God.

—PSALM 59:16–17

THE ENEMY IS AT THE GATES

THE CITY IS under attack. The enemy is swarming at the gates, and all may be lost. This passage can certainly be read as historical fact, but with David, there is often a spiritual analogy to be gleaned. For every one of us, both then and now, is under assault from the enemy trying with all of his power and craftiness to gain a foothold in the citadel of the human heart.

God warns us of the threat, but just as often as we hear it, we turn away, letting our guard down. He tells Cain, for example, that "sin is crouching at the door; it desires to have you" (Genesis 4:7). Peter says the same thing: "Your enemy the devil prowls around like a roaring lion looking for someone to devour" (1 Peter 5:8).

The wars and battles of the Old Testament are historical, but we should also see the spiritual backstory behind the conflict: "For our struggle is not against flesh and blood, but against the rulers, against the authorities, against the powers of this dark world and against the spiritual forces of evil in the heavenly realms" (Ephesians 6:12). Conflict in this life is real; it is the outgrowth of a much greater battle in the spiritual realms.

There are those who rebel against the light, who do not know its
ways or stay in its paths. . . . For all of them, deep darkness is
their morning; they make friends with the terrors of darkness.

—JOB 24:13,17

———❧———

IN THE SHADOWS

WHY IS IT that we seem to have a perverse desire to dwell in darkness even when we clearly have a choice to move into the light? Here is the biblical explanation: "This is the verdict. Light has come into the world, but men loved darkness instead of light because their deeds were evil" (John 3:19–20).

This attraction to darkness began in the original Garden when the man and woman disobeyed God's simple command: "But you must not eat from the tree of the knowledge of good and evil, for when you eat of it you will surely die" (Genesis 2:17). From there with the introduction of knowledge of evil came the spread of a plague that corrupted mankind almost beyond recognition, casting us in the role of "rebel[s] against the light." As a result, "all have turned aside, they have together become corrupt; there is no one who does good, not even one" (Psalm 14:3). Jesus has not only come to save sinners, but to provide us with a diagnosis of the disease: "For from within, out of men's hearts, come evil thoughts" (Mark 7:21), and so, "in the night [we] steal forth like a thief . . . and [we] make friends with the terrors of darkness" [Job 24:14, 17].

If we are living without God, then we have chosen to live under the tyranny of our compulsion to rebel against God. We have chosen to live in the shadows and away from the light that is the way to true life.

Blessed are all who fear the LORD, who walk in his ways. . . .
Thus is the man blessed who fears the LORD.

—PSALM 128:1,4

ETERNAL VALUE

SOME BELIEVE THEY are blessed when they are prosperous; others believe that their prosperity is an outward sign of their inward goodness. But the Bible links blessings and prosperity only incidentally. The opening line of this verse has it just right: "Blessed are all who fear the LORD." In other words, you are blessed by your right relationship to the Lord; little counts beside that because God's blessings link you to Him, even when the whole world may be lined up against you.

Jesus says in the Sermon on the Mount: "Blessed are those who are persecuted because of righteousness, for theirs is the kingdom of heaven" and "blessed are you when people insult you, persecute you and falsely say all kinds of evil against you because of me" (Matthew 5:10–11). God's blessings can come at a great cost, but they are always of eternal value.

The sayings of King Lemuel—an oracle his mother taught him:
"O my son, O son of my womb, O son of my vows, do not spend
your strength on women, your vigor on those who ruin kings."

—PROVERBS 31:1–3

SAMSON

SAMSON IS AN Old Testament superhero apparently brought low by a fatal flaw. He is mighty in power, vanquishing entire armies, terrifying the enemies of Israel, but his weakness for women saps him of his supernatural strength, and he is led away in defeat and humiliation. Or so goes the conventional reading of this story.

On another level, we might reduce the tale of Samson to a morality play where the son, gifted with great strength, fails to cleave to the admonition not to "spend your strength on women, your vigor on those who ruin kings." But this version neglects the role that God plays in the story, for the actual account of Samson begins with the visitation of an angel to a barren and aging woman. The angel tells her that she will give birth to a son who will "be a Nazirite, set apart to God from birth, and he will begin the deliverance of Israel from the hands of the Philistines" (Judges 13:5). The story progresses along expected lines until an act of folly delivers Samson into the hands of his enemies. He is bound, blinded, tortured, and humiliated, but then, unexpectedly, he returns and triumphs through a redeeming act that brings about his own death as well as the destruction of his enemies.

The annunciation, the miraculous birth, the great triumphs, the capture, torture, death, and final victory foreshadow a pattern of events God will use at a later time. But whereas Samson's mission is to "begin" to deliver Israel, Jesus will complete God's purpose by liberating not only Israel but *all* peoples from the bondage of sin. The story of Samson is intriguing, but it is more intriguing when read in light of the birth, life, death, and resurrection of Jesus Christ.

There are those who curse their fathers and do not bless their mothers; those who are pure in their own eyes and yet are not cleansed of their filth; those whose eyes are ever so haughty, whose glances are so disdainful; those whose teeth are swords and whose jaws are set with knives to devour the poor from the earth, the needy from among mankind.

—PROVERBS 30:11–14

SOMETHING OUT THERE

SOME MODERN THINKERS like to think of the existence of evil in our world as something beyond oneself or one's immediate circle of friends. Instead of seeing the problem as a primal impulse that grows within an individual, they are more likely to identify the problem of evil as something associated with groups or classes or even nations. And they are just as likely to ascribe naturalistic causes or reasons for evil in the world.

It is uncomfortable to think of evil as so close that it could be inside rather than outside of oneself. Who wants to think of themselves as being capable of being evil or doing wrong? Even the symbol of all evil in the modern world, Adolph Hitler, undoubtedly believed that he himself was right in his quest to destroy this or that group or nation. He undoubtedly believed he was a progressive agent of righteousness rather than a diabolical instrument of darkness. Who willingly recognizes that they are susceptible to inclinations from the heart that can lead to mass murder and mayhem?

Solomon says that people can curse their fathers and not bless their mothers and still they remain pure in their own eyes, yet he also says they are "not cleansed of their filth." When it comes to determining our own purity, are we to be trusted? Or are we blind to the nature of what might lurk within our own hearts? And how do we think God is judging us? Would God agree that we are "really good people"? We need to be wise in our humility when it comes to pointing our fingers at others.

I denied myself nothing my eyes desired; I refused my heart no
pleasure. . . .Yet when I surveyed all that my hands had done
and what I had toiled to achieve, everything was meaningless, a
chasing after the wind; nothing was gained under the sun.

—ECCLESIASTES 2:10, 11

HOW SHOULD WE LIVE

SOLOMON HAD ACCESS to every material advantage known to man.
He ruled over a powerful kingdom, and he denied himself nothing
his eyes desired; however, it added up to nothing in the end. He felt
a hunger for something more, but nothing in this world, absolutely
nothing, could satisfy his persistent and lingering hunger and thirst.

What was true for Solomon is true for each one of us. Instead
of being surprised by Solomon's conclusion that "everything was
meaningless," we should try to step back and see what it is we are
actually doing. Do we have eternal matters in mind as we maneuver
through our daily lives, or are we allowing "the worries of this life,
the deceitfulness of wealth and the desires for other things" (Mark
4:19) to deflect us from God's purposes for us?

Blessed is he who has regard for the weak;
the LORD delivers him in times of trouble.
The LORD will protect him and preserve his life.

—PSALM 41:1–2

THE REWARD IN HEAVEN IS GREAT

IN HIS TEACHING, Jesus expands on David's description of the blessed among us. The poor in spirit are blessed, as are those who mourn. The meek are blessed, and so are those who hunger and thirst for righteousness. The merciful, the pure in heart, the peacemakers, all are blessed. Then Jesus tells us that being blessed also means we may be opposed by powerful forces in this world who may persecute us because of righteousness. More specifically, they may persecute us because we have given our lives over to Jesus Christ. So, almost counterintuitively, Jesus says, "Rejoice and be glad, because great is your reward in heaven" (Matthew 5:12).

The reward for righteousness may not be what we anticipated for this life, but great is the reward in heaven for those who love and follow the Lord.

For in his own eyes he flatters himself too
much to detect or hate his sin.

—PSALM 36:2

❦

FROM HEAVENLY TO HELLISH

WHEN EVIL IMPULSES are incubating deep within the human heart, it is often hard for us, as well as others, to detect it. The Psalmist says we flatter ourselves and become experts at self-justification. And as we become consumed by the evil desires within, outwardly we engage in lies and deceit. The progress of wickedness is often slow and plodding at first, but with time it consumes the whole person, toppling the entire edifice.

In his book, *Mere Christianity*, C. S. Lewis wrote, "Every time you make a choice you are turning the central part of you, the part that chooses, into something a little different from what it was before. And taking your life as a whole, with all your innumerable choices, all your life long you are slowly turning this central thing either into a heavenly creature or into a hellish creature; either a creature that is in harmony with God, and with other creatures, and with itself, or else into one that is in a state of war and hatred with God, and with its fellow creatures and with itself. To be the one kind of creature is heaven; that is, it is joy and peace and knowledge and power. To be the other means madness, horror, idiocy, rage, impotence, and eternal loneliness. Each of us at each moment is progressing to the one state or the other."

Why is life given to a man whose way is hidden,
whom God has hedged in? For sighing comes to me instead of food;
my groans pour out like water. What I feared has come upon me;
what I dreaded has happened to me.

—JOB 3:23–25

A TREASURED COMPANION

IT IS COMMON to grow up with real as well as imagined fears. With time and experience, some of these childhood fears will dissolve, but others will stick and be carried into adult life. One of my own persistent fears was the fear of failure. I had built my life on the assumption of success, and so, when a major failure of my business stared me straight in the face, I panicked because the thing I feared was becoming an insidious reality.

In the midst of these troubles, I needed to overcome the inertia of depression; I needed to regain my balance, and I needed to take action. But by myself, my resources were totally inadequate. It was during this time of stress and danger that I began to read the Bible. Soon enough, it became a needed companion, a resource for hope and perspective and life. As time passed, reading the Bible wove itself into the very fabric of my being, bringing equilibrium to a life "blown and tossed by the wind" (James 1:6). And with this newfound balance came hope, and with hope, confidence that I was on the right path even if I had no idea exactly where I was going or where I was being led. I had traded in my fear of financial loss and humiliation for a peaceful joy because I finally had discovered a purpose that outweighed anything I had ever known.

Starting a quarrel is like breaching a dam; so drop the matter
before a dispute breaks out. He who loves a quarrel loves sin;
he who builds a high gate invites destruction.

—PROVERBS 17:14, 19

GENTLY INSTRUCT

WE ARE NOT called by God to enter into endless controversies and arguments; rather, we are called to demonstrate the power of the Holy Spirit, not through words alone but with our lives.

Here is Paul speaking to the young church in Corinth: "I came to you in weakness and fear, and with much trembling. My message and my preaching were not with wise and persuasive words, but with a demonstration of the Spirit's power, so that your faith might not rest on men's wisdom, but on God's power" (1 Corinthians 2:3–5).

If we believe that religion is an institution founded by men for men, then our preaching can be nothing more than quarrels dressed up as high-sounding truth. We lose the power to change lives and instead serve the purpose of preserving particular traditions. It is good to remember that God is not impressed with our intelligence, knowledge, or earthly accomplishments.

Rather, He wants us to open our hearts to His Holy Spirit so that we can share our faith with those who have not heard the truth. Paul instructs Timothy in the way of being God's servant: "Don't have anything to do with foolish and stupid arguments, because you know they produce quarrels. And the Lord's servant must not quarrel; instead, he must be kind to everyone, able to teach, not resentful. Those who oppose him he must gently instruct, in the hope that God will grant them repentance leading them to knowledge of the truth . . ." (2 Timothy 2:23–25).

It is good to remember that Paul placed his emphasis on the Holy Spirit's power and not his own. The power of Paul's letters comes through his conviction of the truth of God's Word. Paul's humility and steadfastness should be a model for all disciples.

Do not eat the food of a stingy man, do not crave his delicacies;
for he is the kind of man who is always thinking about the cost.
"Eat and drink," he says to you, but his heart is not with you.

—PROVERBS 23:6–7

CONSIDER THE SOURCE

PEOPLE OFTEN OFFER us things; they may seem to be very generous and helpful and they may seem to care about our every need, but can we discern what is motivating them? In this proverb, the act of generosity and hospitality is contradicted by a stingy and possessive heart. The man gives reluctantly and bitterly and will later demand a very high price for what he originally gave.

Consider the source; know who it is who gives, because if you receive a gift that is given for reasons other than love, you may learn to your surprise and regret that the cost in the end is extremely dear.

Praise the Lord from the earth . . . lightning and hail,

snow and clouds, stormy winds that do his bidding,

you his mountains and all hills, fruit trees and all cedars. . . .

Let them praise the name of the LORD.

—PSALM 148:7–9, 13

FORECAST: SNOW ON FLOWERS

IT WAS APRIL in Tennessee, and in the valleys budding trees, emerging flowers, and fields blanketed in green all heralded the warmth and joy of spring. But up on the ridge of the Appalachian range, winter clutched the white and gray wooded landscape with a relentless grip.

Before setting out on my twenty-two mile day trip, I kept imagining the valley picture of a warm sunlit walk in the woods, but at the trailhead, all I could see were gray clouds moving ominously across the skies from west to east. The wind was cold and sustained. This was not what I expected.

I started out with the hope of covering about three miles each hour. This was possible because elevation gain and loss on this section of the trail was moderate. So if I could maintain this pace, I would be able to finish before 5 p.m. However, the game plan did not include 30 mph winds sweeping across the mountain ridges.

And the plan did not allow for blizzard conditions that worsened throughout the day. I had envisioned a clear path, but the snow came hurling at me from all angles; after three arduous hours, I had covered a disappointing seven miles with fifteen miles still to go. The terrain had become clothed in white.

Occasionally, a northbound hiker would emerge out of the whiteness. We would stop and trade information and then quickly go our separate ways because, without movement, the cold would begin to penetrate through the layers of gear. The real benefit of meeting other hikers was the path they left providing me for a time with a marked way forward through the accumulating snow.

Eventually though, the wind would erase any evidence of the hiker's existence. I had to be careful not to lose my way.

Just after nightfall, I arrived at Vandeventer Shelter, located about three thousand feet above Watauga Lake. A few hikers were inside their tents near the shelter, but they did not bother to emerge, nor did I bother to stick around. By then, the storm had relinquished its firm grip on the mountains. Occasionally, the full moon peered out from behind passing clouds. Lights flickered around the lake, giving me the strong desire to keep trekking toward the warmth and safety below. But I still had over four miles of steep downs before reaching my car.

So I journeyed forward toward my destination, even though getting there had been fraught with unexpected twists and turns. Snow, wind, and cold kept trying to divert or turn me but I persisted toward the destination I had set out for earlier that day when I had been surrounded with intimations of a quiet and gentle Spring ridge walk in the Appalachian mountains.

Your throne, O God, will last for ever and ever;
a scepter of justice will be the scepter of your kingdom.
You love righteousness and hate wickedness;
therefore God, your God, has set you above your
companions by anointing you with the oil of joy.

—PSALM 45:6–7

A PROMISE KEPT

GOD IS THE God of promises kept. Even though Abraham was an old man and his wife Sarah was well beyond childbearing age, God promised them this: "Through your offspring all nations on earth will be blessed, because you have obeyed me" (Genesis 22:18). Abraham's role in God's great narrative began as a step taken in faith, or as Paul tells us, "He believed God, and it was credited to him as righteousness." (Galatians 3:6).

Through Abraham's son Isaac; through Jacob and Joseph; through Moses, who delivered the Israelites out of bondage in Egypt; and Joshua, who led God's people into the promise land, God kept His Word. And when David sat on his throne in Jerusalem, God made another promise that would be fulfilled a thousand years later in the tiny city of Bethlehem: "When your days are over and you rest with your fathers, I will raise up your offspring to succeed you, who will come from your own body, and I will establish his kingdom . . . . and I will establish the throne of his kingdom forever" (2 Samuel 7:12–13).

That promise has reverberated through the centuries and has blessed millions of lives up to this very hour. I pray that the promise that began with Abraham's journey of faith touches your life today and will extend through your own faith to others and to people not yet even born.

You are God my stronghold. Why have you rejected me?
Why must I go about mourning, oppressed by the enemy?
Send forth your light and your truth, let them guide me;
let them bring me to your holy mountain,
to the place where you dwell.

—PSALM 43:2–3

I WILL NEVER DISOWN YOU

IT IS TEMPTING in times of trouble to cry out against God, saying, "Why have you abandoned me?" Sometimes the circumstances seem so dire and frightening that it appears as if we have been cast away. But David is a model of how we should handle adversity because he remains faithful to God under terrible conditions. He does not turn against God; quite the opposite; he calls out for help and guidance: "Send forth your light and your truth, let them guide me. . ."

David's distress is not caused by God but by "deceitful and wicked men." David's faithfulness might be contrasted to the more common response to adversity seen in Peter and the disciples when Jesus is betrayed and arrested in the Garden of Gethsemane. Right before that hour, Peter said, "Even if I have to die with you, I will never disown you" (Mark 14:31). Shortly after saying this, "Everyone deserted him [Jesus] and fled" (Mark 14:50).

When we feel most abandoned and in greatest peril, that is the time when we are called to be steadfast, putting our hope in God, saying, "I will yet praise him, my Savior and my God." God's promise to us is that He'll never leave us or forsake us. That promise should engender hope, as it did with David. "You are God my stronghold."

Let love and faithfulness never leave you; bind them around
your neck, write them on the tablet of your heart. Then you will
win favor and a good name in the sight of God and man.

—PROVERBS 3:3–4

A MASQUERADE

WHEN THE FATHER says to his son, "bind love and faithfulness around your neck," he is making a reference that lends power to his words. This reference was known by every child of Israel because he was required to memorize the most important commandment found in Scripture: "Hear, O Israel: The LORD our God, the LORD is one. Love the LORD your God with all your heart and with all your soul and with all your strength." Then the boy would be told to "tie them as symbols on your hands and bind them on your foreheads" (Deuteronomy 6:8).

The love and faithfulness referred to by the father is not some vague generalization; it is the love of the commandment. Our love must be for the Lord before everything else. Love that exists apart from a love of God is a mere shadow of authentic love, a masquerade. Authentic love begins with our relationship with God and then filters through our relationships with family, friends, and neighbors. When love focuses only on things we want or things we want to do and we leave out the love of God, then we are assuredly setting for a counterfeit of love and not the real thing.

Listen to this, Job; stop and consider God's wonders. . . .

Tell us what we should say to him; we cannot

draw up our case because of our darkness. . . .

Out of the north he comes in golden splendor;

God comes in awesome majesty. . . . Therefore, men revere him,

for does he not have regard for all the wise in heart?

—JOB 37:14, 19, 22, 24

BARRIER BUILDERS

EVEN THOUGH GOD comes in "awesome majesty" and "golden splendor," He cares for each one of us. God seeks us out one by one, but we often respond by putting up our own defenses in order to hide behind them. We often hear how men long for a relationship with God, but the opposite is just as true; we can be very adept at building barriers. We either magnify ourselves through pride, or we miniaturize ourselves by saying that God is way too big and important to care about us. Either way, God is saying, "Tear down that wall; tear down the barrier you have built between us." God is calling out to each one of us: "Open the door, let me come in!" Are we listening? Can we hear? Will we open the door?

But I am a worm and not a man,
scorned by men and despised by the people.
All who see me mock me; they hurl insults,
shaking their heads: "He trusts in the Lord;
let the LORD rescue him. Let him deliver him,
since he delights in him."

—PSALM 22:6–8

ONE FOR ALL

HOW SOMEONE RESPONDS to the fact of the crucifixion of Jesus depends very much on how the Gospels are read. If Jesus is looked at as only a mere man caught up in the religious and political turmoil of the time, then it will be hard to fathom the purpose behind the suffering.

To many, the punishment of Christ is R-rated violence, which appears to be gratuitous and meaningless. However, if we believe that Jesus is the Son of God, who came to take away the sin of the world, then the punishment exacted on Him shows how grave our situation really is.

The weight of the evidence in all of Scripture clearly indicates that the passion of Christ is not a story of mortals; this is the story of spiritual warfare at its highest pitch. The suffering of Jesus was not only foreshadowed by the description of crucifixion in Psalm 22 but also by Isaiah who spoke of the suffering servant who was "pierced for our transgressions . . . crushed for our iniquities" (Isaiah 53:5). He died so that we might live. He died a perfect sacrifice, one for all that all might once again experience a relationship with God.

The length of our days is seventy years—or eighty,
if we have the strength; yet their span is but trouble and sorrow,
for they quickly pass, and we fly away.

—PSALM 90:10

THE GOSSAMER MOMENT

IT IS STARTLING to read that "the length of our days is seventy years or eighty if we have the strength," because it is humbling to realize how the facts of life have changed over the course of time. This verse was written one thousand years before Christ, and yet the average life span is generally the same today.

The truth is that we are propelled forward each and every day with greater momentum, and we say with the Psalmist that our years "pass quickly away." We are no longer impatient schoolchildren looking at the slow-paced clock ticking away each minute. Now we do everything in our power to slow this down by metaphorically digging in our heels, trying in vain to capture and hold the gossamer moment. But while time may be ceaselessly pouring through our fingers every day, Isaiah the prophet takes comfort in this: "The grass withers, the flower fades But the word of our God will stand forever." (Isaiah 40:8)

Does not wisdom call out? Does not understanding raise
her voice? . . ."I, wisdom, dwell together with prudence;
I possess knowledge and discretion. To fear the Lord is to hate evil;
I hate pride and arrogance, evil behavior and perverse speech."

—PROVERBS 8:1, 12–13

GOD NEVER FAILS

ACCORDING TO SCRIPTURE, wisdom and love come from the same source. Love "does not envy, it does not boast, it is not proud. It is not rude, it is not self-seeking, it is not easily angered, it keeps no record of wrongs. Love does not delight in evil but rejoices with the truth" (1 Corinthians 13:4–6).

Likewise, wisdom declares that "to fear the Lord is to hate evil; I [wisdom] hate pride and arrogance, evil behavior and perverse speech." Genuine wisdom for man is to love God and hate everything that stands in the way of our relationship with Him. Wisdom calls us to see with the eyes of our heart that God and love for His children are one and the same: God is patient, God is kind . . . He always protects, always trusts, always hopes, always perseveres. God never fails. To believe this opens the way to living for God and through God and this is the beginning of wisdom.

Where were you when I laid the earth's foundation?
Tell me, if you understand.

—JOB 38:4

EXPLAINING CREATION

GOD MAKES IT clear to Job that it is not possible for man to understand the full mystery of creation: "Where were you when I laid the earth's foundation? . . . On what were its footings set, or who laid its cornerstone—while the morning stars sang together and all the angels shouted for joy?" (vv. 4, 6–7).

The power of God's questions stand in poetic contrast to the self-assured claims of the disciples of the natural sciences to answer every question that touches on the mystery of creation. Whereas Job is taught to abide in great humility in the questions at the center of the mystery of creation, many modernists slavishly adhere to a new naturalistic literalism that can be reductive and constrained. Exploring the universe is one thing; explaining it, absent of God, is another.

If you say, "But we knew nothing about this,"

does not he who weighs the heart perceive it?

Does not he who guards your life know it?

Will he not repay each person according to what he has done?

—PROVERBS 24:12

MOTIVES OF THE HEART

MOTIVES OF THE heart often contradict explanations of the head. We speak with confidence about the reason why someone acted in a certain way, but are we as confident when we examine the motives behind our behavior?

Usually we default to convoluted self-justifications and self-serving rationalizations because the truth might be too hard to bear. There is precedent for this which can be found in the third chapter of Genesis. Immediately after they defy God's single prohibition, Adam and Eve cover their nakedness and go into hiding. And instead of admitting to their fatal act, they fall into using the convenient tools of the guilty: They lie and blame, shift the attention away from their own culpability. They have turned against God because the corruption of sin has entered into their hearts. The prophet Jeremiah warns each one of us that "the heart is deceitful above all things and beyond cure. Who can understand it?" (Jeremiah 17:9).

"Does not he who weighs the heart perceive it?" The answer is this: No motive of the heart can be hidden from God, and no explanation of the head can mask the truth buried deep within.

Jerusalem has sinned greatly and so has become unclean.
All who honored her despise her, for they have seen her
nakedness; she herself groans and turns away.

—LAMENTATIONS 1:8

JERUSALEM

As JESUS APPROACHES Jerusalem for the last time, He looks out upon what was once the Holy City of God and says, "O Jerusalem, Jerusalem, you who kill the prophets and stone those sent to you, how often have I longed to gather your children, as a hen gathers her chicks under her wings, but you were not willing!" (Luke 13:34).

Jesus looks at the sacred place where Abraham had taken his son Isaac in obedience to God's command. He looks at the city of David and the city of Solomon who built the first temple. But now it is an occupied city, a place where "all the splendor has departed . . ." (Lamentations 1:6) and where "the faithful city has become a harlot" (Isaiah 1:21). It has become a place where "your rulers are rebels, companions of thieves; they all love bribes and chase after gifts" (Isaiah 1:21–23). The once holy city of Jerusalem has come to represent the tragic condition of the city of man where all have turned away from God.

But Jesus does not turn back, for His purpose is one of restoration—not of a city or of a people or race but of all mankind from the tragedy of sin. As God provided Abraham a substitute for his son Isaac, so God provided His one and only Son as a substitute for all of us. And through that act of absolute love, God provides each one of us with a way back to Him. "But be glad and rejoice forever in what I create, for I will create Jerusalem to be a delight and its people a joy. I will rejoice over Jerusalem and take delight in my people; the sound of weeping and of crying will be heard in it no more" (Isaiah 65:18–19).

My lover spoke and said to me, "Arise, my darling,
my beautiful one, and come with me. See! The winter is past;
the rains are over and gone. Flowers appear on the earth;
the season of singing has come, the cooing of doves is
heard in our land . . . Arise, come, my darling;
my beautiful one, come with me."

—SONG OF SONGS 2:10–13

THE WORLD IS AWAKENING

THE WORLD IS awakening. The hard, gray ground has softened and shoots are pushing through the soil as if they have sensed the growing warmth of the spring sun. Buds are emerging on the branches of bushes and trees; and the robins are everywhere looking for twigs and dried leaves to build their nests. Finally, "The winter is past; the rains are over and gone," and the joy of new life can be seen in everything.

The blast of winter winds now is becoming a distant memory; and as the world awakens, and we are beckoned to emerge from our season of hibernation. The new season calls us to "sing to the Lord with thanksgiving; make music to our God on the harp. He covers the sky with clouds; he supplies the earth with rain and makes grass grow on the hills"(Psalm 147:7-8). God's blessings are new every morning! The earth itself cries out for us to praise the Lord.

*I know that my Redeemer lives, and that in the end he will
stand upon the earth. And after my skin has been destroyed,
yet in my flesh I will see God; I myself will see him with my own
eyes—I, and not another. How my heart yearns within me!*

—JOB 19:25–27

WILL WE HAVE A DEFENDER?

IMAGINE WHAT IT would be like to be hauled into a court of law to stand before a judge without understanding the charges being lodged against you. A gentleman, full of confidence, sits to your right and is thumbing through a huge file of papers. Obviously, he is the Prosecutor. He is your Accuser, and while you may want to declare your innocence, you know better. He has the dossier, and in it is everything you have ever done from the day you were born up to the present moment. You don't stand a chance unless . . . unless you can find a Defender who will take on your case.

When Job says, "I know that my Redeemer lives," he is saying that he has such a Defender and that when he stands before the Ultimate Judge, he will receive justice. But in order to destroy the Accuser's case against you, you must have someone who will care about you and represent you. Without his help, your case is hopeless. Job's statement of faith resonates with Christians because it is foundational to our belief that one day all of us will stand before the Judge of the universe and our Defender will be standing by our side to tell our story of faithfulness.

O righteous God, who searches minds and hearts, bring to an
end the violence of the wicked and make the righteous secure.

—PSALM 7:9

WHEN THE UNGODLY ARE IN COMMAND

DAVID'S PRAYER ENDS with a plea to God to "bring an end to the violence of the wicked and make the righteous secure." But what would the world look like if the righteousness of God were absent altogether?

Thomas à Kempis, writing on the passion of the Christ, paints an unwelcoming picture: "To what lengths is justice eviscerated when the ungodly are in command! Behold how the Just One perishes and there is none to free him. The One who is true is given over to the fraudulent, and the Holy One is scourged by the unholy. The Innocent is handed over rather than the guilty; a thief is chosen over Christ, and Barabbas is released from his bonds in place of Jesus of Nazareth. The Lamb is exchanged for a wolf, a saint for a criminal, the best for the worst, a desperado acquitted rather than true God. Darkness is preferred to light, vice to virtue, death to life, scum for gold, shell to pearl, and he who is infamous is favored over him who is noble."

Anger is cruel and fury overwhelming,
but who can stand before jealousy?

—PROVERBS 27:4

PLAGUED BY JEALOUSY

JEALOUSY IS THE stepchild of anger. Both are related through the passion of hatred, but whereas anger often has a specific object as the focal point, jealousy is built on doubt, suspicion, and fear. The fury generated by jealousy is often the by-product of doubt.

When the seed of doubt is planted, it is then watered and nurtured by a devious imagination, and soon what was merely the appearance of a wrong becomes a whole cause for war. Many marriages have shattered because of jealousy; much suffering has resulted from imagined slights and betrayals fed not by knowledge but rather by the mere suspicion of faithlessness. Marriages have often disintegrated through the distrust brought on by an overheated imagination rather than a real act of betrayal. When Paul says, "Husbands, love your wives, just as Christ loved the church and gave himself up for her" (Ephesians 5:25), he is offering men and women in marriage a balm that can lead to reconciliation through a love that mirrors the love of Christ for all His children: "My command is this: Love each other as I have loved you. Greater love has no one than this, that he lay down his life for his friends. You are my friends if you do as I command" (John 15:12–14).

Teach me your way, O Lord, and I will walk in your truth;
give me an undivided heart, that I may fear your name.

—PSALM 86:11

A HEART OF FLESH

WHEN DAVID PRAYS for an undivided heart, he is speaking of the central conflict in each of our lives: I want to do the right thing, but as a moth to a candle, I am drawn to the very thing that will hurt me and hurt the people I love.

If we have no understanding of the motives of the divided heart, we will never understand the attraction of so many harmful and destructive tendencies within us. It is only when we put God first that we begin to heal from so much of what afflicts us. It is then that we experience the promise of new life found in the book of Ezekiel: "I will give you a new heart and put a new spirit in you; I will remove from you your heart of stone and give you a heart of flesh" (Ezekiel 36:26).

This is the prophecy fulfilled in Jesus Christ. It is the reality of miraculous healing available to every divided heart, if we will only accept it by praying for the Holy Spirit to come and dwell within.

[M]y lips will not speak wickedness,
and my tongue will utter no deceit.
I will never admit you are in the right; till I die,
I will not deny my integrity.

—JOB 27:4–5

FEARFUL TO BEHOLD

JOB IS ANSWERING the accusations of his three friends who are "comforting" him with their explanations for the terrible suffering their friend is experiencing. Job does not say that he is without sin; he knows that all sin. But he is saying that an injustice has been done him because he has lived as a good and righteous man. He has lived as one who fears and praises God in everything he does. He has not lived as a hypocrite, covering up secret wrongdoing. Job knows his own heart, and even though God seems to have abandoned him and has allowed him to taste extreme bitterness of soul, his lips will not speak wickedness by cursing God. Job's suffering is terrible, but he maintains his integrity by not turning against God despite his suffering.

Be still before the LORD *and wait patiently for him;*
do not fret when men succeed in their ways,
when they carry out their wicked schemes.

—PSALM 37:7

BE STILL

"BE STILL BEFORE the Lord and wait patiently for him. . . ." These are words to live by, yet we find them almost impossible to put into practice. Instead of stillness, we often run around in a state of high distraction, rarely pausing to listen to anyone or anything. We run rather than walk. If we are involved in business, we go to our office with the intention of accomplishing specific tasks but often end up distracted in a hundred ways.

How can we build a relationship with God if we always keep Him out in the waiting room while we busily go bouncing around from one distraction to the next? "Be still," says the Psalmist. When God appears before Elijah on Mount Horeb, God comes as a "gentle whisper" (1 Kings 19:12). Have we built so many noisy distractions into our lives that we cannot hear the "gentle whisper?" Be still. Wait patiently. Do not fret. God is calling you. Be still so that His Word may be heard. "Be still and know that I am God" (Psalm 46:10).

You have made known to me the path of life;
you will fill me with joy in your presence,
with eternal pleasures at your right hand.

—PSALM 16:11

———— ∞ ————

EXPOSED

ONCE IN A while it is a good thing to be reminded of one's own vulnerability. Not that we should risk danger unnecessarily, but neither should we pretend that we can permanently insulate ourselves from the tempest and the storm. For "man is born to trouble" (Job 5:7), and to try to live a bubble existence outside the perimeter of that reality is to stake one's life on the premise that trouble will never knock at our own door.

One early spring day, I set out on the Appalachian Trail in southwestern Virginia. I planned to cover 56 miles over three days; I packed under the assumption that I would spend each night in a shelter, which meant I would not need to carry the extra weight of a tent. After a late start and many miles of relatively flat walking, I reached the base of Chestnut Knob, a 4,400-foot peak with an open summit ridge.

I ascended without much difficulty, but the weather deteriorated as I approached the long ridge. Strong winds and rain swirled around me. I quickly changed into rain gear and set out for the shelter still 2.5 miles ahead. I walked as fast as I could because time suddenly was not on my side; dusk was setting in, turning the open, wet landscape into a lonely and somewhat forbidding place. Soon I reached some woods where the path seemed to begin to descend. I checked the guidebook, which suggested the warden's shelter was near the summit. Suddenly doubt entered my mind: Could I have walked past the shelter in my rush to get there?

Soon the gray of dusk became the darkness of night. If I turned back to hunt for the shelter on the exposed ridge, I could easily lose the trail. And if I had missed the shelter, pushing ahead would have left me no better off. My expectations of sleeping in a dry shelter quickly evaporated. I was without my tent; I had lost my bearings, and I needed to make a decision. Experience and intuition told me to stay put until the morning. And that is what I did. I placed my sleeping bag on the wet ground, got in, and tried to fall asleep. I worried throughout the night that the rain would soak through my bag, but for the most part the bag stayed dry on the inside. Still, the wind did not relent, often sounding like an advancing freight train as it slammed into the western side of the ridge. But eventually morning broke, and I emerged to resume my trek north.

Sometimes our choices are reduced to what is the least bad thing to do. That night, I lost the usual comforts that can often dull our awareness of the nature of the world we live in. Sometimes, our one option is to stay put. And that is what I did. The night was lonely, wet and uncomfortable and it once again reminded me of the thin line between danger and well-being.

The stone the builders rejected has become the capstone;
the LORD has done this, and it is marvelous in our eyes.
This is the day the LORD has made;
let us rejoice and be glad in it.

—PSALM 118:22–24

THE NEW DAY

HOW WE ENTER a new day is generally how we will experience the entire day. For over twenty-eight years I have begun the day by reading and reflecting on the passages provided in the "Daily Service," a two year lectionary found toward the back of the *Book of Common Prayer.*

Jonathan Aitken had reached the pinnacle of a political career in Great Britain that put him in contention to become the next prime minister. Then his world fell apart; he was arrested for various crimes and he found himself in a jail cell with the lowest of the low. He had fallen from the top to the bottom, losing everything, but in the midst of his despair, he discovered the Bible, and soon enough discovered a lectionary that put him in touch with the Word of God for the first time in his life.

In an article on "the Lectionary Life," Aitken quotes Thomas Cranmer from the 1662 *Book of Common Prayer:* "Blessed Lord who has caused all holy scripture to be written for our learning: Grant that we may in such wise hear them, read, mark, learn, and inwardly digest them…"

Aitken goes on to say, "the point of the lectionary is that it guides readers through well-trodden paths of Scripture with unseen companions, conservatively numbered in the hundreds of millions, from all parts of the body of Christ around the world."

This is exactly what happened in my own life; on February 13th, 1991, I joined millions of Christians on a journey of joy in discovering daily that indeed "all Scripture is breathed out by God and (is) profitable for teaching, for reproof, for correction, and for training in righteousness." (2Timothy 3:18). I had entered not only a new day; I had discovered, along with Jonathan Aitken and millions of others, a new world and a pathway to a better one.

They reeled and staggered like drunken men;
they were at their wits' end. Then they cried out to the LORD
in their trouble, and he brought them out of their distress.
He stilled the storm to a whisper; the waves of the sea
were hushed. They were glad when it grew calm,
and he guided them to their desired haven.

—PSALM 107:27–30

I WAS LIFTED OUT OF MY DISTRESS

WHEN WE FACE serious trouble, we often lose heart and sink into despair over the apparent hopelessness of our situation. We cannot escape the grip of whatever it is that is overwhelming us. Whatever originally caused the problem has become more and more irrelevant because nothing seems to heal us or make us whole. Doubt and fear turn into despair and hopelessness, but as this psalm shows, there is a way to change all of this: "They reeled and staggered like drunken men; they were at their wits' end. Then they cried out to the Lord in their trouble, and he brought them out of their distress."

Are you at your wits' end? Have you run out of the common answers? Call out to God with all of your heart, and He will answer you: "To the LORD I cry aloud, and he answers me from his holy hill. I lie down and sleep; I wake again, because the LORD sustains me. I will not fear the tens of thousands drawn up against me on every side" (Psalm 3:4–6).

Set a guard over my mouth, O LORD;

keep watch over the door of my lips.

Let not my heart be drawn to what is evil,

to take part in wicked deeds with men who are evildoers;

let me not eat of their delicacies.

—PSALM 141:3–4

A SMALL SPARK—A BIG FIRE

THE PSALMIST PRAYS to the Lord to guard over his speech because he knows that words can be used as weapons. Words can kill. James warns that the "tongue" is a small but exceedingly powerful instrument and, therefore, must be controlled. He says, "Likewise the tongue is small, but it makes great boasts. Consider what a great forest is set on fire by a small spark. The tongue also is a fire, a world of evil among the parts of the body. It corrupts the whole person, sets the whole course of his life on fire, and is itself set on fire by hell" (James 3:5–6).

What comes out of the mouth reflects the condition of the heart. James concludes, "With the tongue we praise our Lord and Father, and with it we curse men, who have been made in God's likeness. Out of the same mouth come praise and cursing" (vv. 9–10). We need to remember that we were made to praise and not to curse. We should pray for a generous heart.

My son, keep your father's commands and do not forsake
your mother's teaching. Bind them upon your heart forever;
fasten them around your neck. When you walk, they will
guide you; when you sleep, they will watch over you;
when you awake, they will speak to you.

—PROVERBS 6:20–22

THE GREATEST COMMANDMENT

JESUS WAS ASKED, "Teacher, which is the greatest commandment in the Law?" (Matthew 22:36). He simply replies that love is the greatest commandment: Love God first over everything else, and love your neighbor. This is the same supreme law of God given to Moses to pass on to the people of Israel: "Hear, O Israel: The LORD our God, the LORD is one. Love the LORD your God with all your heart and with all your soul and with all your strength" (Deuteronomy 6:4–5).

But the commandment to "love the Lord your God" was so much more than just a teaching to be memorized and then lived out in the breach. Moses was speaking of a way of being. This commandment was certainly meant to be curriculum for school children, but it was also meant to be a life work as children moved into adulthood and into the world.

The commandment the Father gave His Son is the same commandment God gave Moses to give to Israel and the same commandment Jesus gave the teachers of the law and to the entire world. It is the commandment that found its fullest and most profound realization on the cross on Calvary.

*He determines the number of the stars and calls them
each by name. Great is our Lord and mighty in power;
his understanding has no limit.*

—PSALM 147:4–5

THE EMPTY TOMB

NO STORY BETTER illustrates the power and purpose of God than the story of the resurrection of Jesus Christ. The story of the crucifixion would have been lost in the mists of time if the followers of Jesus had not found the tomb empty and witnessed the presence of the living Lord for many days after His death. This story was so powerful to first century Christians that many chose to die rather than deny the truth of the living Lord.

Today many skeptics consider the resurrection to be pure fiction, and they never tire of providing reasons to explain why Christ could never have risen from the dead. But others, including millions of people in our own time, have staked everything on the truth of the gospel and on the power and might and love of God.

Ultimately, each one of us must deal with the biblical accounts of the resurrection of Jesus Christ. If we side with the skeptics, then we must consider the implications of Jesus dying a brutal death with nothing else but the burial and empty tomb. That would mean the biblical accounts were made up and would throw into question the veracity of the New Testament itself: "For if the dead are not raised, then Christ has not been raised either. And if Christ has not been raised, your faith is futile; you are still in your sins" (1 Corinthians 15:16–17).

Thomas, one of the apostles, famously doubted until he came face to face with the risen Lord. Jesus said this to Thomas and to us: "Because you have seen me, you have believed; blessed are those who have not seen and yet have believed" (John 20:29).

A word was secretly brought to me, my ears caught
a whisper of it. Amid disquieting dreams in the night,
when deep sleep falls on men, fear and trembling seized
me and made all my bones shake.

—JOB 4:12–14

A DESCENT INTO HELL

LISTEN TO WHAT Eliphaz, a friend of Job, is saying: "Amid disquieting dreams in the night . . . a spirit glided past my face. . . . A form stood before my eyes and I heard a hushed voice" (Job 4:15,16). He is filled with fear, making his bones shake. Eliphaz came face to face with spiritual reality, which reminded me of Howard Storm and his story as it is recounted in his bestselling book, *My Descent into Death: A Second Chance at Life.*

One summer day in Paris in the mid-1980s, Howard Storm became violently ill and was taken to a hospital where he appeared to die. He tells of rising from his own body and looking around the room and hearing voices beckoning him to follow. He is persuaded to leave the hospital room but begins to feel a desire to turn back. However, the voices become insistent, then vicious, and finally violent. They start devouring him, but deep within he has enough strength to call out in desperation to Jesus with a prayer, begging for help. Suddenly, light appears, and Howard returns to his bed and life.

Howard began that hot summer day as an atheist; he emerged shaken and changed forever. The modern mind refuses to consider the reality of both heaven and hell, but Howard's compelling story of death and miraculous rebirth should prompt the skeptics to reconsider their assumptions.

Wisdom, like an inheritance, is a good thing and benefits those who see the sun. Wisdom is a shelter as money is a shelter, but the advantage of knowledge is this: that wisdom preserves the life of its possessor.

—ECCLESIASTES 7:11–12

IT DIDN'T NEED TO END THIS WAY

CAIN LACKS WISDOM when he disregards God's warning that he should not submit to the promptings of his envious heart. God says, "Sin is crouching at the door; it desires to have you" (Genesis 4:7).

Instead, Cain foolishly submits to his darker inclinations by turning against his brother and kills him, and as a consequence of his crime, he is condemned by God to become "a restless wanderer of the earth" (Genesis 4:12). Cain's sinful desire separates him (as it separates every man) from God and the wisdom that comes from God. He is condemned to wander through the earth, but it did not need to end this way.

In the parable of the lost son, the younger son goes off to foolishly waste his inheritance. After he squanders everything, he repents and returns home to be embraced by his father. The father says, "Let's have a feast and celebrate. For this son of mine was dead and is alive again; he was lost and is found" (Luke 15:23–24).

If we choose to wander with Cain, we will live lives that seem to promise good things, but in fact are artful traps that ensnare and destroy. But if we turn to the Father and ask for forgiveness, we can say with John Newton, "I once was lost, but now am found; was blind, but now I see."

I call to the LORD, who is worthy of praise, and I am saved from
my enemies. The cords of death entangled me; the torrents of
destruction overwhelmed me. The cords of the grave coiled
around me; the snares of death confronted me. In my distress
I called to the LORD; I cried to my God for help.

—PSALM 18:3–6

WAR

WHEN WE READ about the early battles of David, beginning with his victory over the giant Goliath and the Philistines, we are reminded that war is the rule and peace the exception: "Here they come swift and speedily! Their arrows are sharp, all their bows are strung; their horses hoofs seem like flint, their chariot wheels like a whirlwind. Their roar is like that of the lion, they roar like young lions; they growl as they seize their prey and carry it off with no one to rescue. In that day they will roar over it like the roaring of the sea. And if one looks at the land, he will see darkness and distress; even the light will be darkened by the clouds" (Isaiah 5:26, 28).

War has always been part of the human experience, but over the years, some have come to believe that in our own times we are exempt from the awful forces of history so evident in earlier times. That is, until September 11, 2001, when we were awakened from our slumber and reintroduced to an aspect of history we would prefer to deny.

Whether we experience war as Isaiah described it, or we experience battles of a more private sort, David called out to God for help in his time of trouble and that should point the way for each of us. For when everything else fails, David has a "rock, a fortress and a deliverer" who will not fail him.

A man can do nothing better than to eat and drink and find
satisfaction in his work. This too, I see, is from the hand of God,
for without him, who can eat or find enjoyment? To the man
who pleases him, God gives wisdom, knowledge and happiness,
but to the sinner he gives the task of gathering and storing up
wealth to hand it over to the one who pleases God. This too is
meaningless, a chasing after the wind.

—ECCLESIASTES 2:24–26

FEEDING THE WHOLE MAN

WHO ARE WE bringing up our children to be? It seems most schooling aims at educating children not so much for life but for work. After all, both parents often work to earn enough in hopes that their children may be accepted at a better college, which will provide a means to enter the workforce at a higher level, whereupon the cycle begins all over again.

If the purpose of life is to get a job and earn more and more money, then all we will be doing is "gathering and storing up wealth to hand it over." If we do not consider ourselves children of God, made in God's own image, then work will simply be its own reward, and we will live day to day saying, "Let us eat and drink, for tomorrow we die" (1 Corinthians 15:32).

In essence, this is the philosophy behind many modernist political philosophies—feed the body and you feed the whole man. What a diminished world this venture turned out to be! The Word of God speaks to the whole man, and that makes all the difference: "Man does not live on bread alone but on every word that comes from the mouth of the LORD" (Deuteronomy 8:3).

He who is pregnant with evil and conceives trouble gives birth
to disillusionment. He who digs a hole and scoops it out falls
into the pit he has made. The trouble he causes recoils on
himself; his violence comes down on his own head.

—PSALM 7:14–16

THE NATURE OF EVIL

THE REALITY OF the existence of sin as the key to understanding the mystery of our human nature is hard for many to accept. David says, "Surely I was sinful at birth, sinful from the time my mother conceived me" (Psalm 51:5). And Paul says, "For all have sinned and fallen short of the glory of God" (Romans 3:23).

What this means is that we should not delude ourselves into underestimating the capacity for evil in any man who has not been saved. "For the sinful nature desires what is contrary to the Spirit. . . . The acts of the sinful nature are obvious: sexual immorality, impurity and debauchery; idolatry and witchcraft; hatred, discord, jealousy, fits of rage, selfish ambition, dissensions, factions and envy; drunkenness and orgies, and the like" (Galatians 5:17, 19–21).

Much of the world would prefer to believe that sin is imposed upon us by various outside forces, rendering us victims of a society built primarily on money and greed, but is this true? If this view is right, then the truth of the power of the cross of Jesus Christ must be wrong, and if that is true, then if Jesus did not die to deal with sin once and for all, and if he was not raised from the dead, then as Paul wrote, if Christ has not been raised, our faith is futile and we are still in your sins. (1 Corinthians 15:17)

Oh, for the days when I was in my prime,
when God's intimate friendship blessed my house.

—JOB 29:4

INTIMACY

THE THING TO remember about Eden is that it was an intimate place. There was no division between God, the Creator, and man, the creature He created. There was no division between the man and the woman; they lived intimately. And the first man and first woman were one with their environment. It was the perfect place for them to worship God and enjoy His blessings. But paradise was lost, and when that happened, mankind lost the intimacy that God created us for; we have yearned to recover ever since.

As a child, my own little corner of paradise was a lake in New Hampshire that I lived on every July for three years. When I think of that place, the memory in my heart takes me instantly back, and there I am on my cot in a small cabin on the lake's shore. Outside, moths and other insects, drawn by the light of my reading lamp, buzz against the screened windows. I can smell the scent of pine that permeates the soft summer evening air. And behind the nocturnal sounds of crickets and frogs, I hear the rhythmic lapping of gentle waves as they softly touch the rocks near where I am resting my head.

And I remember how, early in the morning, my father would invite his boys to join him on a walk up Bean road to a small local farm. As we walked along the road, we could feel a mountain chill in the air, and we could see the mist suspended like a blanket above the green fields. The farm itself rested between the road and the lower reaches of Red Hill, and so we gathered up some strawberries or raspberries and thick heavy cream to take back to our cottage for the family breakfast.

Of course, in this idealized setting, I suffered the normal worldly intrusions of fights, skinned knees, hurt feelings, and the rest, but as I now think back to my time on that lake in New Hampshire, I am reminded that the intimacy I experienced there is but a shadow of the intimacy that God wants to experience with all of His children.

I went past the field of the sluggard, past the vineyard of
the man who lacks judgment; thorns had come up everywhere,
the ground was covered with weeds, and the stone wall was in
ruins. I applied my heart to what I observed and learned a
lesson from what I saw: A little sleep, a little slumber, a little
folding of the hands to rest—and poverty will come on you
like a bandit and scarcity like an armed man.

—PROVERBS 24:30–34

INACTION BREEDS POVERTY

THE SLUGGARD IS plagued by inaction; he is pathologically passive. He lets life happen to him. He waits for his chances. He puts off until tomorrow what could be done today. The problem for anyone afflicted by laziness is that life is cumulative; what began as something small becomes large and overwhelming if action is not taken.

Even much of business life is processing information efficiently and effectively. If systems break down, then information backs up, and soon it crushes those who stand in the way.

Life has to be rigorously taken care of each and every day. If we put off our necessities for another day, we are only adding to the number of actions we will need to take later. And soon enough the sheer weight of inaction will become an insurmountable barrier to any action, compromising our well-being and happiness.

Let those who love the LORD hate evil, for he guards the lives
of his faithful ones and delivers them from the hand of the
wicked. Light is shed upon the righteous and joy on the upright
in heart. Rejoice in the Lord, you who are righteous, and
praise his holy name.

—PSALM 97:10–12

A PASSION FOR THE LIGHT

IN THE PROLOGUE to his Gospel, John explains that being a child of God is very different than being a child of the world: "Yet to all who received him, to those who believed in his name, he gave the right to become children of God—children born not of natural descent, nor of human decision, or a husband's will, but born of God" (John 1:12–13).

According to John, this is the testimony of God: "God has given us eternal life, and this life is in his Son. He who has the Son has life; he who does not have the Son of God does not have life" (1 John 5:11–12). He who does not have the Son lives in darkness. Jesus, the Son of God, says, "This is the verdict: Light has come into the world, but men loved darkness instead of light because their deeds were evil. Everyone who does evil hates the light and will not come into the light for fear that his deeds will be exposed" (John 3:19–20).

As a child of God, born of the Spirit, your greatest desire will come to serve the Lord and him only. It is when your heart is transformed by the Holy Spirit that the inclination of the heart shifts from a desire to live in darkness to a passion for the light.

By wisdom a house is built, and through understanding
it is established; through knowledge its rooms are filled
with rare and beautiful treasures.

—PROVERBS 24:3–4

LIKE LIVING STONES

THE HOUSE BUILT on a rock is more than a metaphor. Jesus constructs an edifice of hope built on the most solid foundation possible: "Everyone who hears these words of mine and puts them into practice is like a wise man who built his house on the rock." (Matthew 7:24). Paul elaborates by showing us how this house or temple is furnished: "Do you not know that your body is a temple of the Holy Spirit, who is in you, whom you have received from God?" (1 Corinthians 6:19).

Peter builds even further on the same rock, the church: "As you come to him, the living Stone—rejected by men but chosen by God and precious to him—you also, like living stones, are being built into a spiritual house to be a holy priesthood, offering spiritual sacrifices acceptable to God through Jesus Christ" (1 Peter 2:4–5).

So what is this house built by the wisdom of God? It is the body of Christ, a temple of the Holy Spirit built with living stones, offering spiritual sacrifices acceptable to God. This is the church, the temple built on the living stones of the children of God.

Do not move an ancient boundary stone or encroach
on the fields of the fatherless, for their Defender is strong;
he will take up their case against you.

—PROVERBS 23:10–11

A PERVERSE IMPULSE

EVEN THOUGH WE hear the warning, we often feel strangely compelled to ignore the danger in defiance of the obvious consequence. When we hear someone say, "Don't touch the hot plate!" we touch the plate anyway.

Why does a warning cause us to want to defy the rules? Why do we irrationally embrace risk when we know better? Edgar Allen Poe called this darker impulse "the imp of the perverse." Dostoyevsky says that we have within our makeup an "underground man" who acts as a double, nudging us away from the good life to ruin and despair. The Bible calls this subterranean prompt sin, which is a desire to do the wrong thing when we know it is wrong.

The ancient boundary stone is the signpost that keeps us from wandering far afield. Jesus invites us to follow him on his path, but we often demur and set off on what appears to be a far easier way.

He who conceals his sins does not prosper, but whoever confesses
and renounces them finds mercy. . . . A man tormented by the
guilt of murder will be a fugitive till death; let no one support
him. He whose walk is blameless is kept safe, but he whose ways
are perverse will suddenly fall.

—PROVERBS 28:13, 17–18

MY BURDEN IS HEAVY— HIS BURDEN IS LIGHT

IF WE HAVE any doubt about what sin looks like, Paul gives a definitive description in his letter to the Galatians: "The acts of the sinful nature are obvious . . ." (Galatians 5:19), and then he delves into a catalog of actions that should appall the sensibilities of most people.

The truth is, none of us are exempt from the temptation to indulge in sinful acts. And what is worse, we often move from temptation to action through a momentary compulsion, as if we were not in our right minds. The inevitable consequence is a burden of guilt that becomes impossibly heavy. We try to bury our secrets or flee from them as if we were being pursued by a demon.

Here is the difficulty. Sin will not let go unless we recognize and accept the one way out. Covering up our sins will not work, nor will we benefit by attempting to unload our burdens on a friend.

The only way to remove the burden of past sins is to turn to Christ. Jesus asks us to turn our life over to Him: "Come to me, all you who are weary and burdened, and I will give you rest. Take my yoke upon you and learn from me, for I am gentle and humble in heart, and you will find rest for your souls. For my yoke is easy and my burden is light" (Matthew 11:28–30).

The leech has two daughters. "Give! Give!" they cry. There are
three things that are never satisfied, four that never say,
"Enough!": the grave, the barren womb, land, which is never
satisfied with water, and fire, which never says, "Enough!"

—PROVERBS 30:15–16

NEVER ENOUGH

WHEN THE PURPOSE of life is reduced to only attempting to satisfy the appetites of the body, we ultimately discover that the appetites are insatiable, and like a rapacious beast, they can never have enough. Solomon explains how futile it is to strive only after things of this world: "I denied myself nothing my eyes desired; I refused my heart no pleasure. My heart took delight in all my work, and this was the reward for all my labor. Yet when I surveyed all that my hands had done and what I toiled to achieve, everything was meaningless, a chasing after the wind; nothing was gained under the sun" (Ecclesiastes 2:10–11).

Looking back over the course of his long life, Solomon realized that he had lost his way when he turned to pursue pleasure as the primary principle of life. For no matter how much wealth he accumulated, no matter how much he built or possessed, the thirst could never be quenched nor the appetite ever satisfied. The leech does have two daughters, and they do cry, "Give, Give!" and the fire within will never say, "Enough!"

O God, you are my God, earnestly I seek you;

my soul thirsts for you, my body longs for you,

in a dry and weary land where there is no water.

—PSALM 63:1

WORDS TAUGHT BY THE SPIRIT

EVERY ONE WHO finds himself lost in a "dry and weary land" will experience physical thirst. But what about the soul? Is the Psalmist speaking about our physical need for water only?

When Jesus was passing through the parched land of Samaria, He came upon a woman at a well near the town of Sychar. While resting there, He asked this woman for water. When she questioned Him, He begins to speak figuratively about a different kind of "living water" that will become "a spring of water welling up to eternal life" (John 4:14).

At first, the woman is confused, but soon she realizes to whom she is speaking and goes away to tell her townspeople to "come, see a man who told me everything I ever did. Could this be the Christ?" (John 4:29).

Jesus uses figurative language to reveal a spiritual truth that remains the same in all places and times. We need to satisfy the thirst of the heart with the living water of the Spirit that is freely offered by God to all who will ask to drink it. The language of this world cannot adequately express the spiritual truth behind Jesus' words, which is why he uses figurative speech when revealing a spiritual truth.

Paul, speaking about the power of the Holy Spirit, says, "The Spirit searches all things, even the deep things of God. . . . This is what we speak, not in words taught us by human wisdom but in words taught by the Spirit, expressing spiritual truths in spiritual words. The man without the Spirit does not accept the things that come from the Spirit of God, for they are foolishness to him, and he cannot understand them, because they are spiritually discerned" (1 Corinthians 2:10, 13–14).

But I pray to you, O LORD, in the time of your favor;
in your great love, O God, answer me with your sure salvation . . .
Answer me, O LORD, out of the goodness of your love;
in your great mercy turn to me.

—PSALM 69:13, 16

AMAZING GRACE

WHAT ARE WE to do when trouble comes our way? Years ago in my own case, I found myself facing bankruptcy, multiple threats of lawsuits, and financial ruin. With blinding speed, my naive self-confidence was blown away and I was rendered defenseless. Against an onslaught of troubles, fear filled every corner of my life. But when the chips were down and there was absolutely nowhere to turn, something unexpected happened: I turned to God in my distress and asked Him to help me.

Trouble is a common denominator in everyone's life. Sometimes it is subtle and sometimes dramatic, but trouble always seems to be lurking on the fringe ready to pounce. When I found that I could not save myself, I called out to God, not knowing what to expect. What I received was undeserved beyond measure, and ultimately, the experience drew me back to Jesus Christ.

My encounter with business failure turned out to be a "fortunate fall." Sometimes we need to be stripped of the pretensions and conceit that cause us to claim all the glory for ourselves. Sometimes we need to start afresh in order to learn to walk through this world with God rather than without Him.

Great is the Lord, and most worthy of praise,
in the city of our God, his holy mountain.
It is beautiful in its loftiness,
the joy of the whole earth.

—PSALM 48:1–2

"O JERUSALEM"

JERUSALEM IS A holy place. Jerusalem is the city where David took the Ark of the Covenant and where Solomon built the first temple. "Jerusalem is built like a city that is closely compacted together. That is where the tribes go up, the tribes of the LORD, to praise the name of the LORD according to the statutes given to Israel. There the thrones for judgment stand, the thrones of the house of David" (Psalm 122:3–5).

Jerusalem is the holy city of God, but after the reign of King David, the leaders of Israel began to fall into corruption and sin until no one could discern right from wrong: "The visions of your prophets were false and worthless; they did not expose your sin to ward off your captivity" (Lamentations 2:14).

Over the centuries, the leaders and priests of Jerusalem oscillated "between sin and repentance, but by the time of Christ, it was a city held captive under the iron yoke of Rome. As Jesus approached the holy city for the last time, He spoke of God's deep sorrow at what Jerusalem had become: "O Jerusalem, Jerusalem, you who kill prophets and stone those sent to you, how often I have longed to gather your children together, as a hen gathers her chicks under her wings, but you were not willing. Look, your house has left you desolate" (Matthew 23:37–38). God grieves when we fall away from Him, whether it be just you or me or a whole city. Our waywardness grieves God.

Though he slay me, yet will I hope in him; I will surely defend
my ways to his face . . . Now that I have prepared my case,
I know I will be vindicated.

—JOB 13:15, 18

DIVINE JUSTICE

JOB'S FRIENDS HAVE been inquiring into why he might be experiencing such terrible suffering. Just as we can never know any story completely, Job's friends have assumed that he must have done something to offend God and that he is now paying the price for his wrongs. They claim to have knowledge where they, in fact, have none. Job will have none of it: "Though he slay me, yet will I hope in him; I will surely defend my ways to his face."

Job claims a great injustice has been done him and yet is able to say, "I know I will be vindicated." He has faith that, in the end, divine justice will prevail and that God will vindicate him. But the friends have a very different view. They claim to know the reasons for Job's suffering; they believe that human reason is sufficient to understand the causes behind what has happened. But their vision is too earthbound, and while Job cannot fully understand the ways of God, he is completely confident that God is always and will restore him in the end.

Why, O LORD, do you reject me and hide your face from me? . . .
You have taken my companions and loved ones from me;
the darkness is my closest friend.

—PSALM 88:14, 18

SEEK AND HIDE

Is GOD HIDING from you . . . or are you hiding from God? The common complaint is that God has left us to fight our own fight. It is as if we are claiming to be like lost children who frantically search everywhere but cannot find our parents anywhere. And sometimes this is how we feel about God, too.

But how hard are we really looking? Are we just repeating in our own time a pattern that has existed from the very beginning? In the Eden story, Adam and Eve transgress and immediately feel shame and, as a result, go into hiding. God calls out to them, but they hide from Him at the very time when God is searching them out. In the time of the prophets, Isaiah identifies the intractable persistence of this problem of who is seeking and who is hiding: "We all, like lost sheep, have gone astray, each of us has turned to his own way" (Isaiah 53:6).

What causes us to hide from God? Is it us, or is it Him? And what might cause us to hide in the first place? In the Genesis story, the man and woman flee from the presence of a searching God because of shame and fear. If they had nothing to hide, they would not have taken cover. But they did have something very real to hide, which was their act of utter unfaithfulness. After the man and the woman are cast out of Eden, they seem to pass on to their own child Cain the same inclinations of faithlessness and rebellion. Cain murders his brother, and when he is found out, he cries out that his punishment is more than he can bear. He rejected God and became not a seeker but rather a "restless wanderer of the earth." From then until now, that is the condition of despair that many of us suffer each and every day.

Many today claim to be "seekers" and many churches are "seeker friendly," and that is a very good thing. But we should also keep in mind that God is never far away; He is near, and He is ready to embrace us if only we will turn to Him. We should always ask ourselves: are we running toward God, or are we running away? And if we are running away, why are we running away?

Come, my lover, let us go to the countryside, let us spend the
night in the villages. Let us go early to the vineyards to see if
the vines have budded, if their blossoms have opened, and if the
pomegranates are in bloom—there I will give you my love.

—SONG OF SONGS 7:11–12

SOUNDS OF MUSIC AND LAUGHTER

SPRING IS FINALLY in full bloom. Gentle breezes summon up fond pastoral memories of green pastures, rolling hills, and tree-lined lakes that invite children to take one last swim before the fireflies announce the slow advance of twilight. Men, women, and children come out to celebrate the warmth of the season, and lovers walk hand-in-hand as the sounds of music and dancing and laughter fill the air. This is the season when children allow the relentless tide of time to pause momentarily in its relentless flow. They play and sing and dance as if the joy of the moment can be held onto forever. But night will not be denied and so they play on as if the revelries will never end.

But even children know that the long summer days will flicker out, that the days will grow slowly shorter and that the family automobile must soon be packed up to return home to another sort of world. But the children can still dream of soft breezes, lightning bugs, laughter and new adventures still to come.

To the faithful you show yourself faithful, to the blameless you
show yourself blameless, to the pure you show yourself pure,
but to the crooked you show yourself shrewd.

—PSALM 18:25–26

THE EYES OF THE LORD

WE OFTEN HEAR that God is faithful and pure, but do we ever think of God as shrewd? To many of us, this comes as a surprise because it is so unexpected and uncharacteristic.

But should it be? The reference here is to those who have departed from the way to pursue a fraudulent and dishonest living; God is shrewd with them because He cannot be fooled. They attempt to shield themselves by working under cover of darkness and secrecy, but God can penetrate any darkness and sees everything: "The eyes of the LORD are everywhere, keeping watch on the wicked and the good" (Proverbs 15:3).

To try to deceive God is vain and foolish because it is an impossibility; every attempt to deceive God will only be an exercise in self-deception.

O LORD, you will keep us safe and protect us from such people
forever. The wicked freely strut about when what is vile is
honored among men.

—PSALM 12:7–8

PANDEMONIUM

PANDEMONIUM IS THE region ruled by Satan. It is a corrupted replica of heaven, built on discord and disorder, war and suffering, horror and despair. It is where everything that is vile is honored and where Satan rules over those condemned to serve him as prisoners of sin and despair. And it is Satan's chief desire to establish this counterfeit of God's kingdom here on earth.

No one should doubt, given the state of the world at any given moment, that he has made serious inroads. It was into such a place that God sent "the Lord Jesus Christ, who gave himself for our sins to rescue us from the present evil age" (Galatians 1:3–4).

When we pray the Lord's Prayer, saying "your kingdom come, your will be done on earth as it is in heaven," we are asking God to rescue us from a place that looks very much like Satan's Pandemonium, where what is vile is honored, and what is pure, righteous, and godly is hated. When we become Kingdom builders, we acknowledge a King who will "destroy the shroud that enfolds all peoples, a sheet that covers all nations; he will swallow up death forever" (Isaiah 25:7–8).

Enter his gates with thanksgiving and his courts with praise;
*give thanks to him and praise his name. For the L*ORD *is good*
and his love endures forever; his faithfulness continues
through all generations.

—PSALM 100:4–5

FOR THE LORD IS GOOD

I WAS NINETEEN and within a week of completing my freshman year in college. It was 1963, and only a promising future seemed to lie before me. I remember sitting outside the school dining hall with a group of friends planning the weekend and discussing course work and exams. I was oblivious to what was about to happen only a few hours hence. For that night in a place far away, my father's life came to a sudden violent end on the road home.

Early that morning, the police arrived at my mother's home with the shattering news that my father was dead. From that moment on, my mother and her children began to live in the aftermath of unfathomable loss. When I got the phone call, I went to a nearby church and I prayed. I don't remember the prayers, but I prayed. It was the only thing I thought of doing.

I hope my prayer was one of thanksgiving for the extraordinary life of my father. I hope that I praised God, asking that His will be done, whatever that meant for my family and me. I know, though, that my first response to the news was to instinctively turn to prayer to fill the void that had invaded my heart.

Remember your Creator in the days of your youth, before the
days of trouble come and the years approach when you will say,
"I find no pleasure in them"... when the doors to the street are
closed and the sound of grinding fades; when men rise up at the
sound of birds, but all their songs grow faint; when men are
afraid of heights and of dangers in the streets; when the almond
tree blossoms and the grasshopper drags himself along and desire
no longer is stirred. Then man goes to his eternal home and
mourners go about the streets.

—ECCLESIASTES 12:1,4–5

THE OLD MAN AT THE WINDOW

THOUSANDS OF YEARS have passed since Solomon wrote this description of old age, but there is nothing old about it. It is immediate and contemporary, and we can see and feel the dusty street "where the grasshopper drags himself along." Even if we are young, we can imagine, through this verse, what old age feels like.

The poet transports us back in time to an old man, and there we are, sitting in the shaded room by that same window, unable to hear the sounds of children playing in the street or the music of the organ grinder. It is not hard to imagine that old man was once like one of the little children playing in the street outside of the window. And one day at some point in the future the child playing outside the window will one day become the old man who looks out at the world where "songs grow faint."

If I had cherished sin in my heart, the Lord would not
have listened; but God has surely listened and heard my voice
in prayer. Praise be to God, who has not rejected my prayer
or withheld his love from me!

—PSALM 66:18–20

WHAT PASSION WILL RULE?

THE HUMAN HEART is a big place, but not so big where sin and the Holy Spirit can co-exist. Jesus illustrates this in the Sermon on the Mount: "No one can serve two masters. Either he will hate the one and love the other, or he will be devoted to the one and despise the other" (Matthew 6:24).

We are born into conflict and we thirst for resolution, but the greatest struggle most of us will ever experience is the struggle over what passion will rule our hearts. Will it be a passion for sin, or will it be a passion for Christ? If we cherish sin in our hearts, if we love darkness instead of light, then we cannot have fellowship with God through Christ: "God is light; in him there is no darkness at all. If we claim to have fellowship with him yet walk in the darkness, we lie and do not live by the truth" (1 John 1:5–6). A genuine love of Christ opens the door for the Holy Spirit, but opening that door will be the cause of struggle and pain as we begin to shed the old while simultaneously growing through the new.

Drink water from your own cistern, running water from your
own well. Should your springs overflow in the streets, your
streams of water in the public squares? Let them be yours alone,
never to be shared with strangers. May your fountain be blessed,
and may you rejoice in the wife of your youth. A loving doe, a
graceful deer— may her breasts satisfy you always, may you
ever be captivated by her love. Why be captivated, my son, by an
adulteress? Why embrace the bosom of another man's wife?

—PROVERBS 5:15–20

MEN AND MARRIAGE

IN THE MID-1980S, George Gilder wrote a controversial book called *Men and Marriage*. In it, he argues that marriage is the glue that holds civilization together because, without marriage, many men would generally be little more than "barbarians at the gates." Since marriage has been central to our everyday experience, we tend to accept the arrangement without thinking much about the dynamic behind it. Gilder seems to enjoy troubling our normal perceptions by arguing that marriage permits women to transform the barbarian into the prince who then becomes the protector of the community for this and the generation to come. In short, Gilder argues that women civilize men and that marriage is the structure through which this happens.

Gilder explains that young men are characteristically dreamers, warriors, and adventurers. Without the self-limiting relationship fostered by marriage, young men would be content to do whatever they want whenever they want. Though the institution of marriage itself has changed over the past fifty years, marriage still generally defines the role of men as provider and protector; he has willingly allowed his own freedom to be circumscribed for the sake of love and mutual interest. And this bond creates the context for commitment that is the essential building block underpinning the next generation.

While marriage may seem to some men like a sacrifice and a loss of freedom, it would be more accurate to describe the marriage bond as a transition into a new stage of life through a new kind of freedom. The dreamer does not vanish under a mountain of new domestic responsibilities; rather, the new purpose behind the dreams changes by including others as part of the new dream narrative. A man's instinct for adventure is a good thing and it needs to stay alive, but devoting one's life to the well-being of the family and the generation to come is of greater value because our entire civilization depends upon it. The adolescent boy may dream great dreams and he may yearn to become some kind of superhero, but in most respects, these dreams find their most powerful expression in the form of a committed and attentive husband and an involved and loving father.

*Where then does wisdom come from? Where does understanding
dwell? . . . then he looked at wisdom and appraised it; he
confirmed it and tested it. And he said to man, "The fear of the
Lord—that is wisdom, and to shun evil is understanding."*

—JOB 28:20, 27–28

ETERNAL WISDOM

WHEN WE SPEAK of wisdom, we are often referring to knowledge.
We have an almost insatiable desire to know, but knowing is not
enough unless we have an understanding of the dimensions of
God's word, the Bible. "Where is the one who is wise? Where is
the scribe? Where is the debater of this age?" For the foolishness
of God is wiser than men and the weakness of God is stronger
than men.

The biblical narrative is not about human power or knowledge;
it is about God's eternal power that runs through everyone and
everything. The wisdom of the Bible is a gift that we can accept or
reject, but whatever our choice, we should realize that all our
actions, both good and not good, will be measured by the only true
standard: God's justice tempered by his mercy.

He draws up the drops of water, which distill as rain to the
streams; the clouds pour down their moisture and abundant
showers fall on mankind. Who can understand how he spreads
out the clouds, how he thunders from his pavilion? See how he
scatters his lightning about him, bathing the depths of the sea.
This is the way he governs the nations and provides food in
abundance. He fills his hands with lightning and commands it
to strike its mark. His thunder announces the coming storm;
even the cattle make known its approach.

—JOB 36:27–33

A FLEETING MOMENT

MANY YEARS AGO, during my first long hike on the Appalachian Trail in New Hampshire, I witnessed a fleeting moment of beauty that I have never forgotten. Late one day, after an easy ten miles of walking on mostly flat ground, I began to search for a place to rest for the night. About a mile or so beyond a small town, I happened upon a cabin about fifty yards off the trail. Inside, the uninviting shelter was cold and dark. I dropped my gear and settled in resigning myself to a night in the woods alone.

After a light dinner, I felt an urge to get away from the gloom of the shelter, and so I left it to take a walk toward an open field on a hillside that was surrounded by thick woods. As I approached the field, the light from the declining sun drew contrasting shadows against the bright yellows and greens of the long, uncut grass. It was a picture of tranquility, and I was glad to bask in it.

As I stood in the midst of this natural still-life, I became aware of three deer grazing above me on the hillside. They did not notice me, and so I quietly gazed on that scene of tranquil beauty. Time seemed to suspend itself: even the wind briefly stood still. Just as quickly, though, a soft breeze cut across the scene, and the deer lifted their heads in unison, sensing an intruder. They hesitated a moment and then vanished into the shadows of the surrounding woods. Once again, I was in what had been a bright place; now, though, dusk was transforming the soft summer scene into something more ominous as the waning colors of the fields turned gray.

Now, all these years later, I remember that scene as if it were an image painted by God Himself. I felt the warmth of God's peace that day, but I had to turn back to the cold embrace of the lonely cabin. I did not know then that the journey ahead would often be long and hard. Yet, wherever life would lead me, I carried with me that image of momentary grace as sustenance for the journey ahead, regardless of the conditions, whether easy or difficult.

The sea looked and fled, the Jordan turned back; the mountains
skipped like rams, the hills like lambs . . . Tremble, O earth, at the
presence of the Lord, at the presence of the God of Jacob, who
turned the rock into a pool, the hard rock into springs of water.

—PSALM 114:3–4, 7–8

MIRACULOUS POSSIBILITIES

HAVE WE BEEN diminished by our obsessive pursuit of the literal? Have we strained the possibility of the miraculous through the filter of the factual?

It is a fact that the earth moves around the sun at a speed of almost 67,000 miles per hour. And it is a fact that the earth, with a circumference of 24,902 miles, rotates on its axis at approximately 1,038 miles per hour to create the 24-hour day. And it is a certainty that a slight change in any of these physical facts would mean for us instant death, extreme heat or extreme cold.

How did these life-friendly facts come to be without a creator? How would we have any facts at all without the miracle of creation? If we look at this wondrous creation through the filter of the Spirit of God, we come to a very different and much more fertile interpretation of the "facts" of the miracle of the created universe.

Oswald Chambers, in his book *Biblical Psychology*, had this to say on the reasonableness of miracles: "The miracles which our Lord performed (a miracle simply means the public power of God) transcend human reason, but not one of them contradicts human reason. For example, our Lord turned water into wine, but the same thing is done every year all over the world in process of time: water is sucked up through the stem of the vine and turned into grapes. Why should it be considered more of a miracle when it is done suddenly by the same Being who does it gradually?" Opening the eyes of our hearts and unfettering our minds to the reality of the miraculous opens our lives to miraculous possibilities.

There is a time for everything, and a season for every activity
under heaven: a time to be born and a time to die, a time to
plant and a time to uproot, a time to kill and a time to heal, a
time to tear down and a time to build, a time to weep and a
time to laugh, a time to mourn and a time to dance, a time to
scatter stones and a time to gather them, a time to embrace and
a time to refrain, a time to search and a time to give up, a time
to keep and a time to throw away, a time to tear and a time to
mend, a time to be silent and a time to speak, a time to love and
a time to hate, a time for war and a time for peace.

—ECCLESIASTES 3:1–8

THE GOD OF NEAR AND FAR

ONE OF THE advantages of age is the perspective that the accumulation of time and experience can give. When Solomon wrote Ecclesiastes, he was an older man. When we read his words, it feels as though we are being guided to the top of a large mountain to be shown a view of earthly existence with all the patterns that make up the varied heights and depths of human life. But the advantages of perspective must be weighed against the disadvantages of missing the taste and texture of existence. If we choose to look at things from a vast distance, then we lose the details that add to the substance and meaning of our lives.

Being mortals, we humans must often decide which view to take, the near or the far. But God is different, for He can do both simultaneously. And herein lies a paradox. God is so big, so powerful, and so vast in scope that He can create the entire universe. But at the same time, he never loses sight of the smallest, most seemingly insignificant details of everyday life. He is the God of the vast and the microscopic. He brought the whole universe into being, yet He cares intimately and intensely about the well-bring of each of us.

My son, do not despise the LORD's discipline and do not resent

his rebuke, because the Lord disciplines those he loves,

as a father the son he delights in.

—PROVERBS 3:11–12

WAKE-UP CALL

FREQUENTLY WE HEAR people speak about receiving a "wake-up call," but rarely do they imply that the call has a supernatural caller at the other end of the line. Instead, they mean that some change in circumstance or fortune forced them to rethink what they were doing and may have helped them out of a tight situation.

Many years ago, I received one of those calls. I was being buffeted by a financial storm that had grown out of control. In the end, I found a safe harbor, but by then, I knew that my own efforts would never have been enough to save me. I was saved from ruin at that time, but I was not quite ready to admit that I had witnessed a supernatural act of God in my own life. Eventually, though, my eyes opened to the host of angels that had led me through the danger (2 Kings 6:17). Finally, I could see that the crisis had a divine purpose behind it.

Sometimes God's love feels like pain, but in reality, it is nothing more than an opening to get back the life He desires for us. "One thing God has spoken, two things have I heard: that you, O God, are strong, and that you, O Lord are loving" (Psalm 62:11–12).

My heart is not proud, O LORD, my eyes are not haughty;
I do not concern myself with great matters or things too
wonderful for me. But I have stilled and quieted my soul;
like a weaned child with its mother,
like a weaned child is my soul within me.

—PSALM 131:1–2

GOD OPPOSES THE PROUD

WHEN WE STEP out in front of God, we ignite a desire to be great in the eyes of the world; at the same time, we damp down our ability to live in genuine humility. We unleash pride, which is lethal to our ability to maintain our relationship with God. We substitute a love of God with a near reverence for ourselves.

Self-love puffs up and distorts our relationship not only with God but also with other people. Self-love is exclusionary. It interferes with our ability to see clearly and relate appropriately to others. It also obstructs our ability to relate to God. It might be helpful to remember that Jesus did not say: "Blessed are the powerful, and pompous and important." Instead He said, "Blessed are those who mourn, who are meek, who are merciful and who are pure in heart." Perhaps the leadership model Jesus gives the world should be considered as a mandatory course at our top business schools. Then again, perhaps some of the world's great business and religious leaders are already following Jesus' servant leadership model but without acknowledging the source of their wisdom.

Consider what God has done: Who can straighten what he has made crooked? When times are good, be happy; but when times are bad, consider: God has made the one as well as the other. Therefore, a man cannot discover anything about his future.

—ECCLESIASTES 7:13–14

RISK IT

FOR MANY, TOO much of our time is spent attempting to control every aspect of our existence, from the upbringing of our children to the next five-year plan for our business. We try to control our time, our environment, our future, and our health, as if our desire for an outcome is the same as reality itself. Much of the impulse for control is based on a fear-driven life; we fear the worst and therefore try to design our actions and behavior in a way that will avoid risk.

There is a balance between living a life built around risk avoidance and a life built around risking it all. It is good to plan and to order your life accordingly, but there are times when plans need to be scrapped and risks need to be taken. The truth is, none of us control the future. We can spend our time trying to fathom what tomorrow will bring, but it probably is more fruitful to focus our energy on today because it is today, and only today, where we might have some level of influence.

For I am about to fall, and my pain is ever with me.
I confess my iniquity; I am troubled by my sin.
Many are those who are my vigorous enemies; those who
hate me without reason are numerous. Those who repay my
good with evil slander me when I pursue what is good.

—PSALM 38:17–20

THE REALITY OF EVIL

THE SECULAR MIND has a problem with "evil." And this may explain why they have a major problem with the Old and New Testaments. For them, evil is external and easily identifiable. Evil can be reduced to class warfare where one group rapaciously preys on another. It is called colonialism or racism or bigotry and on and on. Notice that in secular terms, evil is most often found in other groups, exempting the observer from any culpability. In fact, the observer places himself or herself in the role of savior who will finally rid the world of pernicious blights once and for all. If this sounds familiar, it is because many of the twentieth century tragedies grew out of this view of evil in the world. Stalin built his gulags to rid his world of "evil" Cossacks and other groups within the Soviet Union, as Hitler built his death camps to exterminate the Jews.

The Bible exempts no one from the temptations that can lead to all kinds of evil. Even King David says he is troubled by his sin, and he confesses his iniquity because he knows that the temptation to sin against God and man resides inside the human heart. Evil does exist, but unlike the secular thinkers, we need not search "out there" to find it. The real transformative discovery is when we finally look to our own hearts for the source of so much of our troubles and sorrows.

The path of the righteous is like the first gleam of dawn,
shining ever brighter till the full light of day.
But the way of the wicked is like deep darkness;
they do not know what makes them stumble.

—PROVERBS 4:18–19

THE LANGUAGE OF GOD

SOLOMON COMPARES "RIGHTEOUSNESS" to the first light of morning, and in contrast, he compares the deeds of the "wicked" to deep darkness. The light and dark imagery point to our relationship with God in a language that speaks to our spiritual longing for holiness.

The language of Scripture has beauty and truth embedded within its very core, and it is through the power of its language that it reveals the presence and the power of God. The Bible opens with God saying, "Let there be light" (Genesis 1:3). Before there was light, the universe was void and without life and form.

And here is how John describes the second creation story, the birth of God's one and only Son: "In him was life, and that life was the light of men. The light shines in the darkness, but the darkness has not understood it" (John 1:4–5).

And here is Jesus during His three-year ministry: "I am the light of the world. Whoever follows me will never walk in darkness, but will have the light of life" (John 8:12). John echoes this in his first letter: "God is light; in him there is no darkness at all" (1 John 1:5).

When reading Scripture, look for patterns of imagery within the written word, for within these patterns is revelation. The power of the language of Scripture is the presence of the Holy Spirit embedded in the language. This language transcends time and place, for the Holy Spirit speaks to the deepest longings of the human heart, which yearns to shuck the things that would harm and destroy and to recover the righteousness that comes from God.

Do not withhold discipline from a child;
if you punish him with the rod, he will not die.
Punish him with the rod and save his soul from death.

—PROVERBS 23:13–14

DISCIPLINE

DISCIPLINE IS A fact of life. If we are not disciplined early in life by a loving parent, then it is likely we will be disciplined later by an indifferent world. Today parents often think that punishment is equivalent to harm, but children require direction. If they do not learn at a young age that certain actions will have adverse consequences, then they will be defenseless against temptations when they are old enough to make up their own minds.

The parent's purpose is to raise godly children who are aware that Satan does not discriminate by age.

The purpose of parenting has been mostly lost in our own times, partly because in our pursuit of the good life, we have neglected the spiritual life. Solomon tells us that God put eternity in the hearts of men and women (Ecclesiastes 3:11). The book of Genesis tells us that we are made in the image of God (Genesis 1: 27) and the psalmist writes, "For you formed my inward parts, you knitted me together in my mother's womb. I praise you, for I am fearfully and wonderfully made. Wonderful are your works, my soul knows it very well."(Psalm 139:13-14)

The Bible says that we are not an accident of nature. God, the creator of the heavens and the earth, had an intention in mind when we were conceived. Our children should become abundantly aware of this. We, as parents, form the spiritual bond to the next generation through our own children. If the link is broken, then, as we learned in the twentieth century, anything is possible.

*Praise be to the L*ORD, *for he has heard my cry for mercy.*
*The L*ORD *is my strength and my shield; my heart trusts in him,*
and I am helped. My heart leaps for joy and I will give thanks
*to him in song. The L*ORD *is the strength of his people,*
a fortress of salvation for his anointed one.

—PSALM 28:6–8

I AM THE GOOD SHEPHERD

WHEN DAVID WAS called by Samuel to be anointed, he was tending sheep for his father Jesse. David was a shepherd, foreshadowing the shepherd to come who would claim, "I am the good shepherd. The good shepherd lays down his life for the sheep. The hired hand is not the shepherd who owns the sheep. So when he sees the wolf coming, he abandons the sheep and runs away" (John 10:11–12).

Jesus, the good shepherd, has "heard my cry for mercy." He is my strength; "my heart trusts him" and "leaps for joy" when I hear His voice. The Good Shepherd is "a fortress of salvation," and He will save us from the wolf that has come to attack and devour. David, the good shepherd of Israel, prepared the way for the Good Shepherd of all the people.

Turn to me and be gracious to me, for I am lonely and afflicted.
The troubles of my heart have multiplied; free me from my anguish.
Look upon my affliction and my distress and take away all my
sins . . . for I take refuge in you. May integrity and uprightness
protect me, because my hope is in you.

—PSALM 25:16–18, 20–21

MY HOPE IS IN YOU

WHEN WE FINALLY admit to being lonely and afflicted, we often try to medicate our way back to health. But at the heart of this distress and shame is a word that has been nearly banished from our contemporary vocabulary: sin.

The Bible tells us that it is the sinful nature that separates us from God and leaves us vulnerable to the vagaries of this world. Sin afflicts us with the weight of guilt and regret from the accumulated memories of past acts. Alone, we cannot bear the burden. We feel that we must unload this crushing burden but we do not know how. We fear the future, and we anguish over what is to come. Our days become crowded with worries, and we lose all sense of joy. This is why David turns to One who can bring real healing and says, "I take refuge in you . . . my hope is in you." And it is why Paul cries out, "Wretched man that I am! Who will deliver me from this body of death? Thanks be to God through Jesus Christ our Lord! (Romans 7:24-25)

One man pretends to be rich, yet has nothing;

another pretends to be poor, yet has great wealth.

A man's riches may ransom his life,

but a poor man hears no threat.

—PROVERBS 13:7–8

RICH AND POOR

A MAN CAN be rich and have nothing, and a poor man can want for everything and yet be rich. When we open our hearts to the Holy Spirit, God pours into our whole being, releasing us from the prison of circumstance and freeing us to experience the presence of God in our commerce with a sometimes resistant world: "As servants of God we commend ourselves in every way . . . through glory and dishonor, bad report and good report; genuine, yet regarded as impostors; known, yet regarded as unknown; dying, and yet we live on; beaten, yet not killed; sorrowful, yet making many rich; having nothing, and yet possessing everything" (2 Corinthians 6:4, 8–10).

The world cannot begin to comprehend this paradox; it evaluates riches and richness as merely the one-dimensional accumulation of things of this life. The frustration experienced by the worldly man grows out of the fleeting nature of time and the awareness of mortality. Yet we would do well to cleave to the wisdom of Jesus in dealing with everyday living: "Do not store up for yourselves treasures on earth, where moth and rust destroy, and where thieves break in and steal. But store up for yourselves treasures in heaven, where moth and rust do not destroy, and where thieves do not break in and steal. For where your treasure is, there your heart will be also" (Matthew 6:19–21).

At the window of my house I looked out through the lattice. I
saw among the simple, I noticed among the young men, a youth
who lacked judgment. He was going down the street near her
corner, walking along in the direction of her house at twilight,
as the day was fading, as the dark of night set in.

—PROVERBS 7:6–9

GUIDE ME, LORD

HERE THE YOUNG man departs the company of his friends and opens the way for temptation: "As the day was fading, as the dark of night set in," he moves away from the safety of the town square to the intrigue of stealing pleasure under the cover of night.

The inclination to stray is ever-present and no one is exempt. For the young man is being tempted away from God. There is a short prayer in the traditional St. Augustine's *Prayer Book* that is helpful in reminding us of the real responsibilities of living as followers of Jesus Christ. We have *God to glorify / Jesus to follow / A soul to save / A body to mortify / Sins to repent of / Virtues to acquire / heaven to gain / hell to avoid / Eternity to prepare for / Time to profit by / Neighbors to edify / The world to despise / Devils to combat / Passions to subdue / Death, perhaps, to suffer / Judgment to undergo.*

I lift up my eyes to you, to you whose throne is in heaven.

As the eyes of slaves look to the hand of their master,

as the eyes of a maid look to the hand of her mistress,

so our eyes look to the LORD our God, till he shows us his mercy.

—PSALM 123:1–2

THE STUDENT AND HIS TEACHER

WHEN WE THINK of our relationship with God, do we really think of a slave's relationship to a master or a maid's to her mistress? It is hard to imagine that we would because contemporary thought finds such ideas repugnant. For many, nothing less than being equal is unacceptable, even if there is no reality to back up our claim. So we transform God into something that fits our diminished idea of him.

But in reality, it is God who calls us to transformation, asking us to relinquish love of self for the love of God. Jesus defines a right relationship with God this way: "A student is not above his teacher, nor a servant above his master" (Matthew 10:24). Furthermore, He says, "Whoever wants to become great among you must be your servant, and whoever wants to be first must be your slave—just as the Son of Man did not come to be served, but to serve, and to give his life as a ransom for many" (Matthew 20:26–28).

My son, pay attention to what I say; listen closely to my words.
Do not let them out of your sight, keep them within your heart;
for they are life to those who find them and health to a
man's whole body. Above all else, guard your heart,
for it is the wellspring of life.

—PROVERBS 4:20–23

A PARENT'S WISDOM

OH, HOW WE wish our wise words could penetrate the hearts of our children so that they might walk a straighter and narrower path than we did in our own youth. As parents, we desire that our children will avoid our mistakes, but if we are wise to the ways of this world, we know that they will invent new pitfalls we could not have imagined during the time of our own youth exuberance.

In this verse, the father is commanding attention, but he is not demanding strict compliance. The father has great wisdom and knows it is important to warn his son of the dangers that lie hidden on the left and the right. If we refrain from warning our children of the real dangers of life, they will blindly proceed and discover too late that they have not guarded their hearts and have not kept their feet from evil.

Pray for your children. Guard their steps with persistent prayers and ask for good guidance as parents.

Does not man have hard service on earth? Are not his
days like those of a hired man? Like a slave longing for
the evening shadows, or a hired man waiting eagerly for his
wages, so I have been allotted months of futility,
and nights of misery have been assigned to me.

—JOB 7:1–3

A CROOKED AND EVIL TIME

IF WE REMOVE the Christianity of Christ from life and describe raw existence as it really is, we will inevitably come up with the picture Job paints here. Without Christ, life is much like the hard service of a hired hand.

In a world where Jesus never existed, one would be forced to adopt a strategy based on either stoicism or its reverse, hedonism. Life in such a world would indeed be nasty, brutish, and short, as it often proves to be. But in a world where Christ lives through the power of the Holy Spirit, the issue of hard service and suffering is transformed into joyful and willing service no matter the cost. Christ asks those who serve to be strong and persevere, whatever the circumstance. He tells us that to suffer as Christians in a crooked and evil time is a blessed honor that will reap rewards for all eternity: "Blessed are you when people insult you, persecute you and falsely say all kinds of evil against you because of me" (Mathew 5:11).

And He then gives the reason for hope: "Rejoice and be glad, because great is your reward in heaven, for in the same way they persecuted the prophets who were before you" (Matthew 5:12).

Out of the depths I cry to you, O LORD; O Lord,

hear my voice. Let your ears be attentive to my cry for mercy.

If you, O LORD, kept a record of sins, O LORD, who could stand?

But with you there is forgiveness; therefore you are feared.

—PSALM 130:1–4

THE PROMISE FULFILLED

THE PSALMIST UNDERSTANDS that his dilemma has been caused by a "record of sins." He knows that he cannot cure himself but must rest his case on the mercy of God. And then he says, "My soul waits for the Lord more than watchmen wait for the morning, more than watchmen wait for the morning" (v. 6)

Repeating the last line puts a special emphasis on his longing for a Savior who will provide the way for the forgiveness of sins and new life through God's grace. It is almost as if he is waiting for the One who "will save his people from their sins" (Matthew 1:21).

And now the Savior has come and has washed away all our sins through the cross; all we need to do is respond as Nathanael did when he realized who Jesus was: "Rabbi, you are the Son of God; you are the King of Israel" (John 1:49). The wait is over; new life is the promise fulfilled.

A scoundrel and villain, who goes about with a corrupt mouth,
who winks with his eye, signals with his feet and motions with
his fingers, who plots evil with deceit in his heart—he always
stirs up dissension. Therefore disaster will overtake him in an
instant; he will suddenly be destroyed—without remedy.

—PROVERBS 6:12–15

OUT OF MEN'S HEARTS

THIS PASSAGE MAY remind us of those early movies where the villain would wear black, leaving little doubt about who the bad guy really is. It is as if the movie makers took their cue from Proverbs as they created their villains for the moviegoing audiences.

But there is a serious dimension to this passage that should not be overlooked. The scoundrel might speak with a corrupt mouth, wink his eye, and signal with his feet as external signs of malicious intent. But evil is not so easy to explain in the actual world. The Bible, though, provides a deeper understanding of why evil exists in the first place. It is Jesus who provided the diagnosis of the chronic condition that grows out of the damaged and corrupted human heart: "For from within, out of men's hearts, come evil thoughts, sexual immorality, theft, murder, adultery, greed, malice.... All these evils come from inside and make a man 'unclean'" (Mark 7:20–23).

Have you journeyed to the springs of the sea or walked in the
recesses of the deep? Have the gates of death been shown to you?
Have you seen the gates of the shadow of death? Have you
comprehended the vast expanses of the earth?
Tell me, if you know all this.

—JOB 38:16–18

A SHIPWRECK

IN HIS INTRODUCTION to G. K. Chesterton's *Orthodoxy*, Philip Yancey writes that the world we live in is "a sort of cosmic shipwreck. A person's search for meaning resembles a sailor who awakens from a deep sleep and discovers treasure strewn about, relics from a civilization he can barely remember. One by one he picks up the relics . . . and tries to discern their meaning." He goes on to compare the scattered remnants washed ashore from a shipwreck to "bits of Paradise extended through time."

When I am out hiking, I find it easier to see myself as just another restless wanderer of the earth. I walk through unfamiliar landscapes, up one side of a mountain and down the other where my identity is not defined by job, or education or home. I am stripped of these layers of identity. I am liberated to see the world through a more poetic imagination, marveling at the mystery and beauty of what I am encountering.

Walking the ridges of the Presidential Range in New Hampshire, I come across huge boulders, some the size of small houses, lying scattered everywhere, with some resting precariously at the edge of deep ravines. This vast, improbable stone-strewn landscape prompts all kinds of responses from a sense of natural grandeur to how did this strange arrangement of rocks happen in the first place? In the end I am left with a sense of the strange improbability of it all. It is perhaps the Psalmist who understands the mystery of creation best: "O Lord, how manifold are your works! In wisdom have you made them all; the earth is full of your creatures. Here is the sea, great and wide, which teems with creatures innumerable, living things both small and great. There go the ships, and Leviathan, which you formed to play in it." (Psalm 104: 24-26)

The highway of the upright avoids evil; he who guards his way
guards his life. Pride goes before destruction, a haughty spirit
before a fall . . . There is a way that seems right to a man,
but in the end it leads to death.

—PROVERBS 16:17–18,25

IN EVERY CORNER OF THE WORLD

A FATHER OFTEN will express pride in his son or daughter and a worker will be proud of a task well done, but this is not the pride of "a haughty spirit," nor is it the pride that "goes before destruction." The seeds of the pride that kills can be found in the earliest chapters of Genesis where the serpent persuades Eve to defy God's warning not to eat of the tree of the knowledge of good and evil. The serpent tells her that if she eats of this tree, she "will be like God" (Genesis 3:5). Both Adam and Eve make themselves number one by defying God. By wanting to be like God, they deny their own human nature as created by God and fall into the self-consciousness of self-love.

The pattern was set at the very beginning of human history: with man's disastrous tendency to deny God by exalting self. The so-called agnostics may not be certain about the existence of God, but they surely put a huge emphasis on themselves. They repeat the self-destructive mistake of our earliest ancestors.

When you defy God, you deny God and thereby make yourself into a false god to fill the void. It is hard to miss this, for evidence abounds on every street in every city in every corner of the world.

My son, if you accept my words and store up my commands
within you, turning your ear to wisdom and applying your
heart to understanding . . . then you will understand the fear of
the LORD and find the knowledge of God.

—PROVERBS 2:1–2, 5

A JOURNEY

WHEN WE HEAR people say that life is a journey, they are almost always implying that the journey will be from darkness to light, from bad to good, and from sin to salvation. This, of course, can be true, but my own experience would suggest that life is more like a very bumpy road, filled with unexpected turns, strange dead ends, and ambiguous intersections. It is a journey where we often have no idea where we are going, and rather than admit to our own lack of knowledge, we fake it, pull out the map, and point authoritatively to a place that is nowhere near where we intended to be.

Fathers who have been on that uncharted road have experienced a thing or two, and they have a great desire to impart advice about right and wrong ways to their own sons. Will the son hear and avoid wrong turns, or will he behave like the lost son in Jesus' parable? "Not long after that, the younger son got together all he had, set off for a distant country and there squandered his wealth in wild living" (Luke 15:13). But, of course, his journey did not end in squalor, for he repented and returned home in humility and received forgiveness from his father. We should not assume that a wrong turn will always lead to a disastrous end. The son did squander his inheritance, but in the end he repented of his foolishness and returned to the father who loved him.

The righteous will see and fear; they will laugh at him,

saying, "Here now is the man who did not make God his

stronghold but trusted in his great wealth and grew strong by

destroying others!" But I am like an olive tree flourishing in the

house of God; I trust in God's unfailing love for ever and ever. I

will praise you forever for what you have done; in your name I

will hope, for your name is good. I will praise you in

the presence of your saints.

—PSALM 52:6–9

THE GIFT OF THE HOLY SPIRIT

PHILOSOPHER AND THEOLOGIAN Thomas Aquinas says, "For no one can truly love God, unless he has the Holy Spirit abiding in his soul, for we do not come to God before the grace of God, but it comes to us first."

Transformation comes when we accept the gift of grace and turn away from our natural disposition to worship ourselves. It is then that the depth and dimension of the revealed truth of Scripture begins to crystallize, and we begin to see and feel and understand with new eyes and a new heart: "I love those who love me, and those who seek me find me" (Proverbs 8:17).

Discerning the love of God comes from the Spirit of God that is placed within the heart as a deposit, which then allows us to say with Paul, "We have not received the spirit of the world but the Spirit who is from God, that we may understand what God has freely given us" (1 Corinthians 2:12).

When justice is done, it brings joy to the righteous but terror to
evildoers. A man who strays from the path of understanding
comes to rest in the company of the dead. He who loves pleasure
will become poor; whoever loves wine and oil will never be
rich . . . He who pursues righteousness and love finds life,
prosperity and honor.

—PROVERBS 21:15–17,21

GOD'S NORM

IT IS EASY to skim over words of wisdom because they seem so normal. Everyone is for justice, right? And we all know that straying from the right path can cause problems. But what if the entire culture begins to wander away from the norm, when "[T]he wicked freely strut about when what is vile is honored among men" (Psalm 12:8)?

God has a norm, and he places a longing for that norm in every human heart. When we are right with God, we understand and see connections which before did not seem to exist. We come to love justice, and we abhor injustice when we see it. We understand that there is a way that leads to death, and we avoid it. We plan and make provision for the future and try not to squander our wealth on foolish things. God's norm is a pathway that leads to life; when the reverse is honored, then we find ourselves enslaved in a culture of death.

God says this to the people of the promise as they prepare to cross the Jordan River to enter the new land: "This day I call heaven and earth as witnesses against you that I have set before you life and death, blessings and curses. Now choose life, so that you and your children may live and that you may love the LORD your God, listen to his voice, and hold fast to him. For the LORD is your life, and he will give you many years in the land he swore to give to your fathers, Abraham, Isaac and Jacob" (Deuteronomy 30:19–20).

What does the worker gain from his toil? I have seen the burden
God has laid on men. He has made everything beautiful in its
time. He has also set eternity in the hearts of men; yet they
cannot fathom what God has done from beginning to end.

—ECCLESIASTES 3:9–11

THIS IS ETERNAL LIFE

TO HAVE EVERYTHING is never enough. We strive and attain, but we are not satisfied, so we strive again, reaching ever higher, but never high enough. Solomon tells us that this persistent yearning is a gift from God, but we should be warned that the desire for the eternal can be corrupted when we take our focus off God by substituting a longing for worldly rewards.

Jesus speaks of this heart-centered inclination when He explains the meaning of His parable of the sower: "Still others, like seed sown among thorns, hear the word; but the worries of this life, the deceitfulness of wealth and the desires for other things come in and choke the word, making it unfruitful" (Mark 4:18–19).

God planted eternity in the hearts of men so that we could be his ambassadors in this world and "like seed sown on good soil, hear the word, accept it, and produce a crop—thirty, sixty or even a hundred times what was sown" (v. 20). The gift of a God-centered life has been offered to each of us; how we choose to use it is a question each one of us must answer.

*Come, let us sing for joy to the L*ORD;
let us shout aloud to the Rock of our salvation.
Let us come before him with thanksgiving
and extol him with music and song.

—PSALM 95:1–2

SING AND MAKE MUSIC

As a boy, I found church intimidating. It didn't start out that way, because I had asked my parents if I could please go to church. They agreed, and one Sunday a church school bus picked me up and transported me and my older brother to a nearby church for worship and Sunday School. Even though I wanted to like the experience of attending church, I found it intimidating. Perhaps it was the building with its high arched ceilings, its long rows of half-empty pews, and its distant altar with larger-than-life wooden carvings of Jesus and His apostles. If the architect had envisioned "grand" as his primary consideration, then he succeeded heroically: Grand and cold. For a young boy with an attraction to Jesus, this particular place failed to create any sense of intimacy and joy. Instead, this church was a beautiful rendition of the historic church at a particular moment in time.

The Psalmist speaks of worship in terms of joy, thanksgiving, music, and song. Paul speaks of worship in terms of being filled with the Holy Spirit, of singing hymns and giving thanks to God for the immeasurable blessings of Jesus Christ (Ephesians 5:18–20).

The early church, as given to us in Scripture, had it right. It isn't about money or buildings or perfectly crafted sermons. It is about a passionate love and belief in our Lord and Savior Jesus Christ.

In spite of all this, they kept on sinning; in spite of his wonders,
they did not believe. So he ended their days in futility and their
years in terror. Whenever God slew them, they would seek him;
they eagerly turned to him again. They remembered that God
was their Rock, that God Most High was their Redeemer.

—PSALM 78:32–35

GOD IS FAITHFUL

THE PEOPLE OF Israel had, by God's grace, been brought out of slavery in Egypt with the promise that they would be led to a land of "milk and honey." To get there, they needed to travel across the Sinai Desert. But as the hardships of the journey increased, they turned against Moses and his leaders and against God because "they did not believe." God in His graciousness had liberated them from the hardship and humiliation of bondage, but their unfaithfulness led them deeper into the desert wilderness where their "days ended in futility and their years in terror."

When we consider faithfulness, we should remember that God is always faithful; we, on the other hand, are the ones who are like adolescents "tossed back and forth by the waves, and blown here and there by every wind of teaching" (Ephesians 4:14). We should take heart that we have a merciful and loving God, but we, who have been delivered out of the bondage of sin, should remember that we are called to follow Him, even when it may seem hard to do so.

*Like a muddied spring or a polluted well is a righteous
man who gives way to the wicked.*

—PROVERBS 25:26

JUDAS

JUDAS WAS ONE of the twelve apostles who walked with Jesus. By
all appearances, he seemed like a man who loved and served the
Lord. But then in a moment of doubt and weakness, he gave way
to temptation, accepted money from the chief priests in Jerusalem,
and so he led guards to the Garden of Gethsemane to identify the
one whom the leaders wanted to capture and kill.

At the very moment that Jesus is taken prisoner, Judas must have
realized the enormity and irreversibility of his craven act of
betrayal. Instantly, he must have felt the awful darkness of despair
enter his soul. It did not take long for Judas to be overwhelmed
with hopelessness. He tried to return the thirty pieces of silver to
the priests, but they refused to accept the blood money, and so he
left. Soon his overwhelming despair led him to hang himself
(Matthew 27:3–5).

One of Solomon's proverbs says, "There is a way that seems
good to a man, but in the end it leads to death." Judas must have
justified his act of betrayal with all kinds of high-minded reasons
for taking the way he chose to go. But in reality, he betrayed the One
he loved, and that realization must have come upon him when he
felt there could be no forgiveness for what he had done. Sometimes
our own reasoning is not enough to save us from making fateful
decisions. It is dangerous to lean on our own understanding.
Depend on the Lord to show you the better path.

This is what the wicked are like—
always carefree, they increase in wealth.
Surely in vain have I kept my heart pure;
in vain have I washed my hands in innocence.
All day long I have been plagued;
I have been punished every morning.

—PSALM 73:12–14

ALL IN VAIN?

DOES IT MAKE any sense to say, "In vain have I kept my heart pure; in vain have I washed my hands in innocence?" If we look at events strictly from the world's point of view, we can sympathize with people who mourn the fact that the spoils seem to go to the wicked, the arrogant, and the powerful.

Referring to religious hypocrites who love to show off their power and position, Jesus gives us a different perspective: "I tell you the truth, they have received their reward in full" (Matthew 6:5). He makes a distinction that needs to be reiterated constantly: rewards in this life do not necessarily lead to the reward of eternal life; likewise, the reward of eternal life is often preceded by great suffering in this life. What appears to be victory for the wicked in this world may be a prelude to something very different in the next.

Like snow in summer or rain in harvest, honor is not fitting
for a fool. . . . Do not answer a fool according to his folly,
or you will be like him yourself.

—PROVERBS 26:1,4

A FOOL FOR GOD

A FOOL ENGAGES in self-destructive tendencies that seem irrational
to most people. Does the Bible tell us what causes people to act in
ways that are harmful to their own well-being?

In Psalm 14, it says, "The fool says in his heart, 'There is no
God'" (v. 1). The Psalmist tells us the fool begins his strange odyssey
by denying the existence of God. By rejecting God, the fool frees
himself to do anything he wants. He lives without boundaries even
as he comes up against boundaries every day.

The abuse of the gift of freedom leads us away from God.
Freedom in defiance of God's will for us is not freedom but a trap
for sin to take hold of our whole being. God does not want us to
use this gift of freedom to abandon Him. He wants us to choose to
follow in His way, thus becoming a fool (in the opinion of the
world) for God. "For the foolishness of God is wiser than man's
wisdom, and the weakness of God is stronger than man's strength"
(1 Corinthians 1:25).

The LORD will extend your mighty scepter from Zion; you will
rule in the midst of your enemies. Your troops will be willing on
your day of battle. Arrayed in holy majesty, from the womb of
the dawn you will receive the dew of your youth.

—PSALM 110:2–3

FRIENDS AT OUR SIDE

IN THE MIDST of the chaos of battle, the outcome often remains in doubt. We fight from minute to minute and depend upon split-second decisions that may lead to disaster or triumph. Looked at from another perspective, war is merely everyday life accelerated.

When life is lived at the normal pace, we seem to have time to deliberate in order to arrive at the right decision about the next move. In this condition, we also have the luxury of living within a pattern of repetitive experiences that allow us to makes many decisions as if we were on automatic pilot.

But we delude ourselves if we live as if tomorrow is predictable and certain. Whether we are at war or peace, the principles remain the same: we must choose to act on the information we have at that moment. We must turn to the right or to the left, aware that one way may lead us to the mountain while the other may lead us to the swamp. Therefore, we must depend on more than our own intuition and judgment.

We need reliable friends at our side because it is better that decisions not be made in isolation. And when we put our full trust in God, we have a friend at our side helping us in all our decisions. For without Him, the battle will be lost and the soldiers will be unwilling: "Therefore, you kings, be wise; be warned, you rulers of the earth. Serve the LORD with fear and rejoice with trembling" (Psalm 2:10–11).

As you do not know the path of the wind,
or how the body is formed in a mother's womb,
so you cannot understand the work of God,
the Maker of all things.

—ECCLESIASTES 11:5

CLEVERNESS WITHOUT COMPASS

WISDOM IS OFTEN thought of as a product of the intellect. If we can only come to know enough, we are told, then we will become wise. But often mere intellect is cleverness without compass. God did not call us to love Him only with our minds; He said, "Love the LORD your God with all your heart and with all your soul and with all your strength" (Deuteronomy 6:5).

To know God intellectually leads to futility because the mind can analyze and compute, but it cannot love. If we think of God only as an aspect of our theology, we are already in opposition to God's greatest commandment. God commanded us to love Him; He did not command us to think about loving Him. In *Biblical Psychology*, Oswald Chambers wrote, "The reason people disbelieve God is not because they do not understand with their heads—we understand very few things with our heads—but because they have turned their hearts in another direction." Man's pride may be seated in his intellectual prowess, but his righteousness grows out of a true, faithful, and loving heart.

Can you pull in the leviathan with a fishhook or tie down his

tongue with a rope? Can you put a cord through his nose or

pierce his jaw with a hook? ... If you lay a hand on him, you

will remember the struggle and never do it again!

—JOB 41:1–2, 8

FISHING FOR LEVIATHAN

LEVIATHAN, OR THE great whale, is not a fish you would try to catch with an ordinary fishing hook. Yet God tells Job that mankind has been doing just that by trying to capture God with our imagined idea of who God is.

We are fishing for leviathan when we try to explain God by defining him down to a size that will allow us to believe that we are in charge, thank you very much. We are surprised when we find leviathan at the other end of the line. But as with leviathan, so with God: "If you lay a hand on him, you will remember the struggle and never do it again!"

It is a very common temptation to try to bring God down to our own size, but the endeavor fails utterly every single time. Whether it is building a tower to heaven or inventing engines of war to end all wars, we fall short. "As the heavens are higher than the earth, so are my ways higher than your ways and my thoughts than your thoughts" (Isaiah 55:8–9).

Rather than the futility of fishing for leviathan, Jesus turned the tables completely around. In the early days of His three-year ministry, He called to some fishermen to be His followers, and He made them a promise: He would transform each of them into a different kind of fisherman. "'Come, follow me,' Jesus said, 'and I will make you fishers of men'" (Matthew 4:19). Man fishing for leviathan is foolishness. God fishing for men is the very embodiment of hope and love that flows through faith in the One who enlisted fishermen to transform the world.

Lord, who may dwell in your sanctuary?
Who may live on your holy hill? He whose walk is
blameless and who does what is righteous.

—PSALM 15:1–2

THE ARDUOUS JOURNEY

WE NEVER START the journey at the summit of the holy hill, nor are we parachuted in. Arriving there is a lifelong process. How are we to get there?

Jeremiah says, "Stand at the crossroads and look; ask for the ancient paths, ask where the good way is, and walk in it, and you will find rest for your souls" (Jeremiah 6:16). Jesus tells His disciples to travel light: "Do not take along any gold or silver or copper in your belts; take no bag for the journey, or an extra tunic or sandals or a staff . . ." (Matthew 10:9–10). And Paul says to be careful in everything you do on the way: "Become blameless and pure, children of God without fault in a crooked and depraved generation, in which you shine like stars in the universe as you hold out the word of life" (Philippians 2:15–16).

The journey is arduous; the path has many intersections, but staying on the ancient path, the good path, goes a long way in fulfilling the promise of your calling.

Rescue me, O LORD, from evil men; protect me from
men of violence, who devise evil plans in their hearts
and stir up war every day.

—PSALM 140:1–2

THE RIGHTEOUS WILL PREVAIL

HERE IS A prayer of a righteous man surrounded by those who desire to destroy him. Those opposing him "devise evil plans" and "stir up war every day;" their words are poisonous, and they lie in wait to snare their victim. It is uncomfortable to realize the prophet representing God's interest in this world often face treacherous opposition.

When Jesus embarked on His three-year ministry, He encountered strong resistance from religious and political authorities. From His first teaching in Nazareth where "all the people in the synagogue were furious" at what they heard (Luke 4:28) to the betrayal of Judas, Jesus experiences the brunt of a sinful generation that is in rebellion against God himself. But take heart, for the righteous will prevail: "Rejoice and be glad because great is your reward in heaven, for in the same way they persecuted the prophets who were before you" (Matthew 5:12).

The wicked lie in wait for the righteous, seeking their very lives;

but the Lord will not leave them in their power or let them be

condemned when brought to trial.

—PSALM 37:32–33

THE LORD WILL NOT ABANDON THEM

DOES THE PRESENCE of evil in the world invalidate the reality of the existence of God? Some would say so. Why does God permit evil and injustice to exist? Why do innocent people fall prey to violent men? God "causes his sun to rise on the evil and the good, and sends rain on the righteous and the unrighteous" (Matthew 5:45).

It is as if the questioners were surprised by the mere existence of evil in the world and, if they could, they could just wish it away. But the surprise should not be about the existence of evil; the surprise should be about how prevalent it is and how the best of men can be overcome and destroyed by its power to confuse and misdirect. In speaking to Cain, God speaks of evil as an entity that crouches ready to spring on its prey (Genesis 4:7). Peter compares it to a roaring beast that devours (1 Peter 5:8). But most frightening of all, Jesus tells us that evil already has broken down the barriers and now inhabits the human heart (Mark 7:30–33).

The good news is that Jesus came into this world to save us from the forces in the heavenly realms who wills to destroy us. Jesus is the one who was sent by God to "save his people from their sins" (Matthew 1:21).

My days are swifter than a weaver's shuttle,

and they come to an end without hope.

Remember, O God, that my life is but a breath;

my eyes will never see happiness again.

—JOB 7:6–7

THE WHOLE DUTY OF MAN

CONTEMPORARY CAREGIVERS MIGHT diagnose Job as being depressed and prescribe pills to relieve his symptoms. But do pills fix the problem, or do they just cover it up?

Job's lamentation is appealing because he describes a reality all people face: "You sweep men away in the sleep of death; they are like the new grass of the morning—though in the morning it springs up new, by evening it is dry and withered" (Psalm 90:5–6).

If this life is all there is, then where is the reason for hope? Solomon called such a life "meaningless." And Job summarizes the stark facts of such an existence this way: "For this is your lot in life and in your toilsome labor under the sun. Whatever your hand finds to do, do it with all your might, for in the grave, where you are going, there is neither working nor planning nor knowledge nor wisdom" (Ecclesiastes 9:9–10).

Yet neither Job nor Solomon falls into the trap of succumbing to the view that there is no God and that life is "full of sound and fury signifying nothing." The ways of God may not always seem brilliantly clear, but this is not cause for abandoning God. In the end, Job says, "I know that my Redeemer lives, and that in the end he will stand upon the earth. And after my skin has been destroyed, yet in my flesh I will see God" (Job 19:25–26). And Solomon says this: "Now all has been heard; here is the conclusion of the matter: Fear God and keep his commandments, for this is the whole duty of man" (Ecclesiastes 12:13).

Place me like a seal over your heart, like a seal on your arm;
for love is as strong as death, its jealousy unyielding as the grave.
It burns like blazing fire, like a mighty flame. Many waters
cannot quench love; rivers cannot wash it away.

—SONG OF SONGS 8:6–7

THE MEANING OF LOVE

WHEN WE DIG a little deeper beneath the normal niceties of everyday life, we often discover a vague foreboding residing somewhere within our hearts that seems to whisper that we are not good enough for God's love. Call it a spiritual insecurity complex, but we insist on remaining away from God for any number of personal and often secret reasons.

Yet the central truth of the entire Bible is love, God's love for each one of us. The other truth is that men and women often reject God's love for all kinds of secret reasons. We say, "How can God accept me when I have done this or that?" Or we say, "I am not good enough" or, "God is angry with me."

In reality, we are angry with ourselves, and so we block God at the closed door of our heart. We even reject the truth of Scripture just to keep God at bay.

It is odd how we talk about love in so many different ways but do not try to puzzle out where love actually originated. The Bible tells us from the beginning in Genesis through the Book of Revelation that love comes from God and that we thirst for love because God is love and He created us in His image which is the image of love. (1 John 4:19).

Give thanks to the LORD, call on his name; make known among
the nations what he has done . . . Remember the wonders he has
done, his miracles, and the judgments he pronounced.

—PSALM 105:1,5

SOME VERY RELIGIOUS PEOPLE

ONE WEEKEND SEVERAL years ago, I was invited to speak to a group of people who were very spiritual. They spoke of the "spirit," but the spirit they talked about seemed foreign to the Holy Spirit as given to us in the Bible. When they tried to explain their beliefs, they would ultimately default to the Almighty Self as the source of all their joy, their hopes, and their faith.

It was as if, in rejecting the religion of their youth and in pursuing the desires of their own hearts, they were afraid to reject God entirely, and so, hedging their bets, they made up a new faith that spoke to their individual needs and aspirations. In fact, the believers were so various in their beliefs that it seemed as if I had entered some kind of spiritual super market.

I was struck by the sense of sheer desperation underlying this spiritual mélange because their faith seemed to be built on subjectivity as if to say that: "God is real if he/she is real to me. I am the author of my own life, and it is my right to define God in any way that I want to. Furthermore, I love everyone, except those I believe are enemies."

I was reminded of Paul in Athens (all the Athenians and the foreigners who lived there spent their time doing nothing but talking about and listening to the latest ideas): "Men of Athens! I see that in every way you are very religious. For as I walked around and looked at your objects of worship, I even found an altar with this inscription: TO AN UNKNOWN GOD" (Acts 17:21–23).

Apparently, it is possible to be both religious and idolatrous. I witnessed it. I was gratified that so many people I met at that meeting were on a "spiritual journey," but I was troubled that so many of these same people had rejected the truth of Scripture for a very personal definition of spiritual reality and well-being.

Listen, my son, and be wise, and keep your heart on the right
path. Do not join those who drink too much wine or gorge
themselves on meat, for drunkards and gluttons become poor,
and drowsiness clothes them in rags.

—PROVERBS 23:19–21

REDEMPTION

AN UNREDEEMED WORLD is an arid place where the iron law of
inevitable consequences prevails. It is a world of predictable
outcomes, a place free of mystery and miracles, a world devoid of
hope. So when the father addresses the son in this proverb and
speaks of the consequences of deviating from the "right path," he
speaks of a standard that, without redemption, challenges the
abilities of even the best among us.

But, elsewhere, Job prophetically speaks of a redeeming God,
one who loves His lost children enough to care to restore them.
Ultimately, God cared enough to send his Son into the world to
"save the people from their sins." It is through the power of the
cross that the most unworthy criminal can break the chains of
inevitability to find new life and hope through the One who died
for all. "For he [God, the Father] has rescued us from the dominion
of darkness and brought us into the kingdom of the Son he loves,
in whom we have redemption, the forgiveness of sins" (Colossians
1:13–14).

You are not a God who takes pleasure in evil;
with you the wicked cannot dwell.
The arrogant cannot stand in your presence;
you hate all who do wrong. You destroy those who tell lies;
bloodthirsty and deceitful men the LORD abhors.

—PSALM 5:4–6

A GOD OF WRATH?

THE GOD OF the Old Testament has a reputation of being a wrathful God, but do we have the mirror pointed in the right direction? This verse does not say that God hates his children; rather, it points to those who have rejected God and have become wicked, arrogant, bloodthirsty, and deceitful. It is not God who has turned away. It is his children who have abandoned their inheritance for worthless things. They have become rebellious and treacherous to the One who loves them, forgetting all the while that God is also a God of judgment: "The Lord knows how to rescue godly men from trials and to hold the unrighteous for the day of judgment, while continuing their punishment. This is especially true of those who follow the corrupt desire of the sinful nature and despise authority" (2 Peter 2:9–10).

Oh, for the days when I was in my prime, when God's intimate
friendship blessed my house, when the Almighty was still with
me and my children were around me, when my path was
drenched with cream and the rock poured out for me streams
of olive oil.

—JOB 29:4–6

ADAM'S CHOICE

As WE TRAVEL through life, we seem to experience the loss of
something precious, yet we cannot quite put our finger on what it
is. Job says, "How I long for the days when God watched over me.
Oh, for the days when I was in my prime, when God's intimate
friendship blessed my house. . ."

This universal sense of loss was reversed on Calvary, but up
until that moment in history, the human story was written by the
choice of Adam, the first man. He too walked with God: "The
LORD God took the man and put him in the Garden of Eden to
work and take care of it" (Genesis 2:15), but "In the middle of the
garden were the tree of life and the tree of knowledge of good and
evil" (Genesis 2:9).

Adam was commanded not to eat of the second tree or he
would die and lose access to the tree of life. But he disobeyed, and
forever after, until the advent of Christ, we have all felt the sting of
Adam's sin. "So the LORD God banished him from the Garden of
Eden to work the ground from which he had been taken. After he
drove the man out, he placed on the east side of the Garden of
Eden cherubim and a flaming sword flashing back and forth to
guard the way to the tree of life" (Genesis 3:23–24).

From that time until Calvary, all men and women were born
exiles; all experienced the same sense of loss and all longed to find
a path "drenched with cream" and rocks that "poured out for [us]
streams of olive oil."

Let the sea resound, and everything in it, the world, and all who
live in it. Let the rivers clap their hands, let the mountains sing
together for joy; let them sing before the LORD.

—PSALM 98:7–9

MUSIC IN THE HEAVENLY SPHERES

IT IS TRAGIC when men attempt to reduce the world to a collection of "objective" facts. Can we really claim objectivity when we are so intimately dependent on the very world we wish to know? We breathe it, we feel it, we move in it as it relentlessly moves. The "objective" mind rejects this intimacy, depending instead on the selective power of reason to achieve understanding and knowledge.

Wisdom, though, requires the attention of our hearts as well as our heads. Our minds alone cannot hear "the rivers clap their hands," nor can the mind alone hear "the mountains sing together for joy." But if we walk in faith, trusting in the Lord as the creator of the very world we wish to know, then the whole world becomes a symphony making music before the Lord and all his creation, singing praise to his glorious name: "Sing to the Lord a new song, for he has done marvelous things . . ." (Psalm 98:1). When we include God in our consideration of the mysteries of life, then life itself becomes a daily act of worship.

You turned my wailing into dancing;
you removed my sackcloth and clothed me with joy,
that my heart may sing to you and not be silent.
O LORD my God, I will give you thanks forever.

—PSALM 30:11–12

ALWAYS THERE

JOY IS WHAT we experience when we are connected to God. God created us to worship Him, but we cannot worship God if we choose to live apart from Him. God desires that we turn away from danger; He wants us back and will search us out to the farthest ends of the earth to show His mercy and lead us away from self-destruction.

But we must turn to embrace him: we must believe in Him, follow Him, praise Him and speak to Him in prayer. He is always there, sorrowing at our wailing but delighting in our dancing.

A wife of noble character who can find? She is worth far
more than rubies. Her husband has full confidence in her
and lacks nothing of value. She brings him good,
not harm, all the days of her life.

—PROVERBS 31:10–12

THE POWER OF TWO

THE WIFE DESCRIBED here is of noble character because she knows that she is a partner in a joint venture and the success of the enterprise will very much depend on how well that partnership functions: "She is worth far more than rubies. Her husband has full confidence in her and lacks nothing of value." This is the way God intended it. "The LORD God said, 'It is not good for the man to be alone. I will make a helper suitable for him'" (Genesis 2:18).

And Paul reminds us how God wants the marriage to work: "In the same way, husbands ought to love their wives as their own bodies. He who loves his wife loves himself. . . . For this reason a man will leave his father and mother and be united to his wife, and the two will become one flesh" (Ephesians 5:28, 31). Joined together as one, we become stronger than if we stand alone: "Two are better than one, because they have good return for their work. . . . But pity the man who falls and has no one to help him up!" (Ecclesiastes 4:9–10).

I lift my hands to you in prayer.
I thirst for you as parched land thirsts for rain.

—PSALM 143:6

———∞∞∞———

GENUINE THIRST

I WAS HIKING in the Selway-Bitterroot Wilderness in Montana when I took a wrong turn. I thought I was on the right track, and I was comforted by the fact that the map showed a small body of water up ahead, so I continued on.

But as I climbed higher, the land grew drier; trees and vegetation gave way to dust and unrelenting heat, and my supply of water quickly dwindled to a few drops. I thought of turning back, but I foolishly made the decision to forge ahead to what became even drier and more isolated ground.

Within an hour, the water shown on the map became a longing, then an obsession, then an urgent necessity. With every step I was becoming more desperate. Then just when my hope was turning to despair, I stumbled upon a shallow pool of still water. Without hesitation, I drank it as if it were the sweetest water I had ever tasted. I experienced overwhelming relief and joy at something as common as water because my body desperately needed replenishment.

What is true for the body depleted of life-giving water is just as true for the soul of any person wandering in a spiritual wasteland. David says, "As a deer pants for streams of water, so my soul pants for you, O God. My soul thirsts for God, for the living God" (Psalm 42:1–2). And elsewhere, he says, "O God, you are my God, earnestly I seek you; my soul thirsts for you, my body longs for you, in a dry and weary land where there is no water" (Psalm 63:1).

Our physical nature mirrors a thirst dwelling deep within our heart. Will we find drink to quench this spiritual thirst, or will we continue farther into the dry land where there is no water to be found?

Take heed, you senseless ones among the people;

you fools, when will you become wise?

Does he who implanted the ear not hear?

Does he who formed the eye not see?

Does he who disciplines nations not punish?

Does he who teaches man lack knowledge?

The LORD knows the thoughts of man;

he knows that they are futile.

—PSALM 94:8–11

CONSIDER THE EYE

WE ARE OFTEN amazed by images created by cameras. We are mystified by the extraordinary power behind digital technology. We sit transfixed before high definition TV screens, often confusing the fleeting image with reality itself. But do we ever stop to consider the original technology that surpasses all the imagery generated by the genius of man?

Take a moment to consider the human eye with its stunning ability to translate trillions of particles of light into images instantly comprehensible to the human brain. We spent time explaining the function of the eye, but we have a tougher time dealing with its original construction itself. Worse, we tend to avoid the idea that the human eye had an inventor. We may marvel at the highly complex technology behind image making, but at the same time we assume that the far greater technology of the eye just somehow came into existence by chance or by the mysterious laws of nature. Perhaps it might be beneficial to consider the original design as it is far more astonishing than anything we have invented. Cameras can create amazing facsimiles of reality, but they do not hold a candle to the human eye.

Hope deferred makes the heart sick,
but a longing fulfilled is a tree of life.

—PROVERBS 13:12

—⚬⚬⚬—

I PRESS ON

IN WAR, WE long for peace; in sickness, we long for health; when we are lonely, we seek friends; and when we are away, we yearn for home and family. The present moment never seems to be enough; we are restless and wish to satisfy a powerful drive for something better. For many, this need expresses itself through the desire to recover something lost. In others, it translates into a quest for a better life here and now.

The Christian is also striving, but with a difference: as his faith grows stronger, his longing becomes a desire to know and follow Jesus as an intimate friend. "I want to know Christ and the power of his resurrection. . . . Not that I have already obtained all this, or have already been made perfect, but I press on to take hold of that for which Christ Jesus took hold of me. . . . One thing I do: Forgetting what is behind and straining toward what is ahead, I press on toward the goal to win the prize for which God has called me heavenward in Christ Jesus" (Philippians 3:10, 12–14).

You crown the year with your bounty,
and your carts overflow with abundance.
The grasslands of the desert overflow;
the hills are clothed with gladness.
The meadows are covered with flocks and
the valleys are mantled with grain;
they shout for joy and sing.

—PSALM 65:11–13

AN UNLIKELY SAVIOR

PICTURE THE SHIRE in Tolkien's *Lord of the Rings*: It is a gentle and bounteous place where "the hills are clothed with gladness. The meadows are covered with flocks and the valleys are mantled with grain." But right below the surface of this peaceful and pleasant image lies an ominous presence that threatens the very existence of the idyllic Shire. The gathering menace promises the desolation described by the prophet Jeremiah: "The ruined city lies desolate; the entrance to every house is barred. In the streets they cry out for wine; all joy turns to gloom, all gaiety is banished from the earth. The city is left in ruins, its gate is battered to pieces. So it will be on the earth and among the nations . . ." (Isaiah 24:10–13).

But Tolkien wrote an epic of salvation and hope where the peaceful Shire is saved through the quest of the most unlikely heroes. The prophets of Israel also tell of a Savior to come who will restore peace and joy to the land and who will invite us to join the battle in His name. And He too will be just as unlikely as the fictional hobbits: "He had no beauty or majesty to attract us to him, nothing in his appearance that we should desire him. He was despised and rejected by men, a man of sorrows, and familiar with suffering" (Isaiah 53:2–3). His name: Christ Jesus of Nazareth.

Some trust in chariots and some in horses,

but we trust in the name of the LORD our God.

They are brought to their knees and fall,

but we rise up and stand firm.

O LORD, save the king!

Answer us when we call!

—PSALM 20:7–9

TRUST IN THE LORD

LET'S START WITH the fundamentals: it is impossible to function successfully in life without a strong dose of trust. Think about it: If we were able to exist independently of everyone else, we might be able to achieve a state of total self-reliance.

But from the time we are conceived, we are intimately involved in the lives of other people, beginning with our own mothers and fathers. As we emerge from childhood, we become aware of our interdependence with the world at large. When we play sports, we join teams, and when we begin to work, we join organizations. Libraries are filled with books on "networking" and "teamwork."

But to live in this world without trust would inject us into a world of suspicion, intrigue, and paranoia. We would be incapable of acting because we would see threatening forces behind every tree and corner. Trust, therefore, is an essential component of our human condition. We need to trust to live effective, healthy lives, but even then, we need to discern who is and who is not worthy of our trust: "Some trust in chariots and some in horses, but we trust in the name of the Lord our God."

Pay attention and listen to the sayings of the wise;
apply your heart to what I teach, for it is pleasing when you
keep them in your heart and have all of them ready on your lips.
So that your trust may be in the LORD, I teach you today, even
you. Have I not written thirty sayings for you, sayings of counsel
and knowledge, teaching you true and reliable words, so that
you can give sound answers to him who sent you?

—PROVERBS 22:17–21

BE TEACHERS OF YOUR CHILDREN

PARENTS, DO NOT be discouraged. Though it often seems like our children are heading off to a distant country equipped only with a wild and unrestrained heart, they have heard your "sayings of counsel and knowledge" that have made an impression and that they will carry your wisdom with them wherever they go.

As parents, we are called to be teachers, and those teachings begin at home. And at the heart of everything is this: "Hear, O Israel: The LORD our God, the LORD is one. Love the LORD your God with all your heart and with all your soul and with all your strength. These commandments that I give you today are to be upon your hearts. Impress them on your children. Talk about them when you sit at home and when you walk along the road, when you lie down and when you get up" (Deuteronomy 6:4–7).

When you teach, teach with your life, not with mere words that are undermined by your own contradictory behavior. For it is by your good example that your children will learn the elementary principles of life: "...do not exasperate your children; instead, bring them up in the training and instruction of the Lord" (Ephesians 6:4).

I cried out to God for help; I cried out to God to hear me.

When I was in distress, I sought the Lord; at night I stretched

out untiring hands and my soul refused to be comforted.

I remembered you, O God, and I groaned; I mused, and my spirit

grew faint. You kept my eyes from closing; I was too troubled to

speak. I thought about the former days, the years of long ago;

I remembered my songs in the night. My heart mused and my

spirit inquired:"Will the LORD reject forever? Will he never

show his favor again? Has his unfailing love vanished forever?

Has his promise failed for all time? Has God forgotten to be

merciful? Has he in anger withheld his compassion?"

—PSALM 77:1–9

AN UNBEARABLE LOSS

IMPLANTED WITHIN THE soul of every person is a longing for something lost. This is true even of young people, but it becomes acutely evident as we move through the middle years and become dragged down by circumstance and trouble. We look over our shoulders, and with the Psalmist, we lament: "I thought about the former days, the years of long ago; I remembered my songs in the night."

It is as if the biblical story of the Garden of Eden is somehow intertwined with who we once were that now seems lost forever. It is when that feeling of loss becomes unbearable that we just may turn to God for help.

The Psalmist asks: When will God's favor, love, mercy, and compassion return? There are times when our world seems stripped of love and hope. We are tempted to despair, but in his anguish the Psalmist cries out to God: "Help me Lord; hear me Lord; save me Lord." Instead of languishing in despair, he takes action by calling upon God to intervene. There is nothing wrong with this. God does hear our call for help. Do not be afraid. Ask and you will be amazed at how caring and merciful God is.

Though the LORD is on high, he looks upon the lowly, but the proud he knows from afar. Though I walk in the midst of trouble, you preserve my life; you stretch out your hand against the anger of my foes, with your right hand you save me. The LORD will fulfill his purpose for me; your love, O LORD, endures forever— do not abandon the works of your hands.

—PSALM 138:6–8

IN THE MIDST OF TROUBLE

HAVE YOU EVER read a passage from a book and suddenly a line or word or phrase leaps right off the page and grabs you? Often the eye skims over the surface of the page, and the words fail to register on the mind and heart. You may be thinking of something else, or you find other passages more compelling. You read but do not absorb. Then, at another time, you reread the passage; and for no apparent reason, that same passage becomes electric, and now you see it and feel it for the first time ever.

That happened to me with this verse: "Though I walk in the midst of trouble, you preserve my life." With twelve short words, I finally felt the universal truth the words expressed and how it applied to a crucial moment in my own life.

It would be easy to say that when trouble befell me, I met the challenge and conquered the foe. I could have claimed victory for myself, but my heart told me that the victory wasn't mine at all. I had walked in the midst of very real trouble, but the trouble never wounded me in a mortal way. I walked through the greatest conflict of my life as if I were an observer rather than one of the battling soldiers. This verse finally revealed to me why I survived. It was not my will that saved at all; realizing the revelation of this truth has made all the difference.

This is the way of an adulteress:
She eats and wipes her mouth and says,
"I've done nothing wrong."

—PROVERBS 30:20

SELF-JUSTIFICATION

DENYING OUR OWN sinfulness is as old as human history itself. After succumbing to temptation, Adam and Eve come up with every unsupportable excuse in the book in an attempt explain why they recklessly betrayed God's commandment. Eve said, "The serpent deceived me, and I ate." And the man said, "The woman . . . gave me some fruit from the tree, and I ate" (Genesis 3:13, 12).

When we give way to temptation and indulge sinful inclinations, we respond with rationalizations, self-justifications and coverups. But behind the assertion that "I've done nothing wrong" is the uneasy knowledge that we, indeed, have done something wrong, and our weak claims of innocence cannot wash away our very real guilt and shame.

Sing joyfully to the LORD, you righteous; it is fitting for the
upright to praise him. Praise the LORD with the harp; make
music to him on the ten-stringed lyre. Sing to him a new song;
play skillfully, and shout for joy. For the word of the LORD is
right and true; he is faithful in all he does. The LORD loves
righteousness and justice; the earth is full of his unfailing love.

—PSALM 33:1–5

ALL CREATURES GREAT AND SMALL

MANY YEARS AGO, I walked forty-three miles of the Appalachian Trail in central Pennsylvania. I have many reasons for returning to the roots and rocks of the trail, but perhaps chief among them is the desire to break out of the artificial box I construct for myself as I maneuver through the concrete cityscape aspect of my life.

I suspect that I need to get closer to the earth itself to refresh my mind and revive memories of all the small marvels that move about with quiet intention all around my feet. Whole worlds of tiny beings seem to go about their important business, oblivious to my presence or even my existence.

The big things, like the mighty Susquehanna River or a powerful midnight storm or even the splendid beauty of the rolling hills of cultivated farmland do generally catch the eye and cause me to stop to enjoy the quiet wonder of it all. When viewed through the lens of the poetic imagination, though, it is the smaller things of the land, the insects and tiny creatures that suggest order and resolve and purpose rather than inscrutability and aimless disorder. For me the trail suggests coherence, but I need to slow down in order to see it at work, and that requires I put aside my singular drive to get from here to there. So give me the trail any day, for it provides me with bigger themes through the miracle of its smallest creatures.

Be sure of this: The wicked will not go unpunished,
but those who are righteous will go free. Like a gold ring in
a pig's snout is a beautiful woman who shows no discretion.
The desire of the righteous ends only in good, but the hope
of the wicked only in wrath.

—PROVERBS 11:21–23

SQUANDERED BEAUTY

ANCIENT SCRIPTURE TELLS us that swine were considered unclean creatures, unfit for eating or handling (Leviticus 11:7–8). So it would have been an appalling waste to place "a gold ring in a pig's snout."

When men and women choose to disregard God, when they thoughtlessly give into "the sinful desires of their hearts . . . for the degrading of their bodies with one another" (Romans 1:24), then they have wasted the gift just as surely as the gold ring has been wasted on the swine.

Instead, in everything we say and do, we should want to reflect the glory of God: "One thing I ask of the LORD . . . that I may dwell in the house of the LORD all the days of my life, to gaze upon the beauty of the LORD and seek him in his temple" (Psalm 27:4).

Hear me, O God, as I voice my complaint;
protect my life from the threat of the enemy.
Hide me from the conspiracy of the wicked,
from that noisy crowd of evildoers.

—PSALM 64:1–2

THE TIDE OF DARKNESS

WE HAVE TO avert our eyes not to see that "the mind and heart of man is cunning" (Psalm 64:6). Jesus saw clearly, describing the unredeemed world as an "adulterous and sinful generation," as well as an "unbelieving and perverse generation."

When men free themselves from God, the tide of darkness rolls in, covering the landscape with the evils of malice, conspiracy, and conflict. "There is no one righteous, not even one; there is no one who understands, no one who seeks God. All have turned away, they have together become worthless; there is no one who does good, not even one" (Romans 3:10–12).

Paul describes the condition of the world as he saw it. How little the main contours of the ageless conflict between the forces of good and evil have changed since then. At times, the world seems to hover on the razor's edge between the forces that would brutally destroy and the forces of life. It is important to understand the nature of the conflict and do our small or large part in making a difference for that which is true, noble, right, and admirable (Philippians 4:8). We should do nothing less.

When the righteous triumph, there is great elation;

but when the wicked rise to power, men go into hiding . . .

Like a roaring lion or a charging bear is a wicked man ruling

over a helpless people. A tyrannical ruler lacks judgment,

but he who hates ill-gotten gain will enjoy a long life.

—PROVERBS 28:12, 15–16

THEY CALL FOR A KING

IN THE DAYS of Samuel, the prophet Israel did not have a king. Eventually the people demanded that a king be appointed to rule over them: "You are old, and your sons do not walk in your ways; now appoint a king to lead us, such as all the other nations have" (1 Samuel 8:5).

Samuel asks God what he should do, and he receives this reply: "It is not you they have rejected, but they have rejected me as their king" (1 Samuel 8:7). And then God tells Samuel to warn the people of the terrible dangers that will come with an earthly king: "Warn them solemnly and let them know what the king who will reign over them will do" (1 Samuel 8:9).

To this day, people argue over the question of what makes a good ruler. It is clear from this verse that great suffering will come when we turn to wicked men to rule over us, which is why we should always say, "In God we trust." Or as David states it: "It is better to take refuge in the LORD than to trust in man. It is better to take refuge in the LORD than to trust in princes" (Psalm 118:8–9).

And David's son and heir to his crown King Solomon asks God for "a discerning heart to govern your people and to distinguish between right and wrong." (1Kings 3:9) "The Lord was pleased that Solomon had asked for this." (v 10)

Go and humble yourself; press your plea with your neighbor!
Allow no sleep to your eyes, no slumber to your eyelids. Free
yourself, like a gazelle from the hand of the hunter, like a bird
from the snare of the fowler.

—PROVERBS 6:3–5

BE FREE

THE FATHER IS admonishing his son to do everything in his power to stay free, but what does he mean by freedom?

Today freedom is a very loosely defined word that has come to mean many different things. Politicians behave as though freedom means license to do whatever it takes to augment their own power. Business people promote the idea that freedom is all about choosing consumer products, particularly their own. Others push sexual freedom or the freedom to use illegal drugs. And there are those who push the idea that we should be free of all societal constraints, period.

But none of this is consistent with the biblical idea of freedom. Peter says, "Live as free men, but do not use your freedom as a cover-up for evil" (1 Peter 2:16). And Jesus, quoting Isaiah, says, "He has sent me to proclaim freedom for the prisoners . . ." (Luke 4:18), by which he means prisoners to the sinful nature.

The freedom of Christ is the freedom to be free of the burdens of sin that separate us from God. This is the freedom that opens the door to the life God intended us to live.

In his arrogance the wicked man hunts down the weak,

who are caught in the schemes he devises. He boasts of the

cravings of his heart; he blesses the greedy and reviles the LORD.

In his pride the wicked does not seek him; in all his

thoughts there is no room for God.

—PSALM 10:2–4

GOD WILL NEVER QUIT

How can we successfully satisfy the cravings of our hearts? If we fasely assume that all our impulses are godly, then every desire translates into only virtuous actions. But notice what this psalm actually says: in order to follow the impulses of the unredeemed heart, we must leave "no room for God." Is that possible?

The truth is that every human heart is a hidden battlefield with eternal life hanging in the balance. Even the arrogant and wicked man has not fully given himself over to his own wicked schemes. He has not fully expelled God from the field of his plotting as he goes about his business. But when the rebellious desires of the heart are dominant, God is pushed aside. God will never quit on anyone, but if we insist on pursuing the path of our own passions, we will join the legion who "blesses the greedy and reviles the Lord."

Do not make friends with a hot-tempered man,
do not associate with one easily angered,
or you may learn his ways and get yourself ensnared.

—PROVERBS 22:24–25

THE COST OF ANGER

ANGER IS A fire that consumes many things in its path . . . and it is contagious. It may start in the heart of one man, but it soon spreads, causing confusion and conflict. "A fool gives full vent to his anger, but a wise man keeps himself under control" (Proverbs 29:11). An angry man is a fool because he may harm others, but he probably harms himself first. When circumstances shift against us and we are tempted to lash out in anger, we should remember to follow the example given to us by God Himself who is "slow to anger and abounding in love and forgiving sin and rebellion" (Numbers 14:18).

Anger is possible for anyone; the impulse of anger should be avoided by everyone. Instead, "Do not let the sun go down while you are still angry, and do not give the devil a foothold" (Ephesians 4:26–27).

To have a fool for a son brings grief;
there is no joy for the father of a fool . . .
A foolish son brings grief to his father and
bitterness to the one who bore him.

—PROVERBS 17:21, 25

A LOST SON

A GOOD AND righteous father can raise a rebellious and wicked son. Isaac's son Esau sold his birthright for a pot of stew. Eli, the chief priest of the Temple and the man who raised Samuel, the prophet, had two sons who "were wicked men; they had no regard for the LORD" (1 Samuel 2:12).

Samuel's own sons "did not walk in his ways. They turned aside after dishonest gain and accepted bribes and perverted justice" (1 Samuel 8:3). King David's son, Absalom, rebelled against his father and almost killed him, but even so, when Absalom was killed in battle, David was inconsolable (2 Samuel 18:33).

We pray that our sons will hear the voice of God and follow the right path, but we also must be aware that they are being pulled in many directions. Pray, therefore, that your own children will have a discerning heart that will keep "wisdom in view."

I cry out to you, O God, but you do not answer;

I stand up, but you merely look at me. You turn on me

ruthlessly; with the might of your hand you attack me.

You snatch me up and drive me before the wind; you toss me

about in the storm. I know you will bring me down to death,

to the place appointed for all the living.

—JOB 30:20–23

THE COST OF DISCIPLESHIP

JOB'S SUFFERING CAUSES him to cry out to God. He is experiencing pain and misery and he cannot fathom why this is happening.

We, on the other hand, see a fuller picture. We are witnesses to the beginning, when "the angels came to present themselves before the LORD, and Satan also came with them" (Job 1:6). We see Satan challenge God's claim that Job is "blameless and upright, a man who fears God and shuns evil" (Job 1:8). And we see how Satan lays one catastrophe after another on Job to show God that even a man as righteous as Job will turn on God in the end.

To Job, it seems that God has abandoned him. For us, there is an echo of the cry of despair that will be heard throughout the world: "My God, My God, why have you forsaken me?" (Psalm 22:1). It is the cry of another righteous man, Jesus of Nazareth, who has been nailed to a cross on a small hill called Calvary, outside of the gates of Jerusalem.

God's purpose behind this terrible event is redemption and restoration, but it can only begin when His one and only Son takes all the sin of the world upon Himself: "You see, at just the right time, when we were still powerless, Christ died for the ungodly. . . . But God demonstrates his own love for us in this: While we were still sinners, Christ died for us" (Romans 5:6, 8). When we consider Job's suffering and all that it suggests, we see a foreshadowing of the cross of the suffering servant, Christ, for the redemption of a world separated from God.

Praise the Lord, O my soul, and forget not all his benefits—
who forgives all your sins and heals all your diseases, who
redeems your life from the pit and crowns you with love and
compassion, who satisfies your desires with good things so that
your youth is renewed like the eagle's.

—PSALM 103:2–5

HE WILL SHARE ALL HIS BENEFITS

IN OUR TIME, health and youthfulness trump practically every other virtue. It is considered a liability to appear old, and we will go to great lengths to delay the onrush of physical decline that we are destined to experience.

So we invent new remedies to erase the ravages of time: new vitamins, new diets, and new forms of cosmetic surgery. We turn to a new solution a day, but we keep coming up empty and become anxiety ridden because delaying the inevitable has never been a cure.

In this passage, David reveals an answer that is a gift for the asking. God can open the way to eternal life ("your youth is renewed like the eagle's"). He can do this because only God can forgive sins and thereby heal you and redeem you from the penalty of death. He can do this because He is a God of love and compassion. If we turn to Him, we can partake of all of His benefits and find enduring peace even during our fleeting time in this world.

I know that everything God does will endure forever;
nothing can be added to it and nothing taken from it.
God does it so that men will revere him. Whatever is has
already been, and what will be has been before;
and God will call the past to account.

—ECCLESIASTES 3:14–15

REGAINING OUR LIGHTNESS OF BEING

HAVE YOU EVER noticed that as people age, some lose the lightness in their step? They begin to walk around slightly stooped over with their faces down, as if they were burdened with an enormous weight resting awkwardly on their shoulders.

Could it be possible that the accumulated weight of the past actually can catch up with us? Could it be that if we let the untreated poison of sin remain, we will slowly become weighed down and lose the lightness of our being.

The way of the world is to medicate, but does this reach the source of the problem? Here is the truth: "All of us also lived among them at one time, gratifying the cravings of the sinful nature and following its desires and thoughts. Like the rest, we were by nature objects of wrath" (Ephesians 2:3). Yet it need not remain this way: "But because of his great love for us, God, who is rich in mercy, made us alive with Christ even when we were dead in transgressions— it is by grace you have been saved" (Ephesians 2:4–5).

The LORD is righteous,
yet I rebelled against his command.

—LAMENTATIONS 1:18

INVITED TO STAY

THE LORD IS righteous. I am not righteous, but by rebelling, I claim righteousness as my own. As with Satan, in my defiance, I claim equality with God, and I begin to construct my own counterfeit kingdom. "'Let us break their chains,' they say 'and throw off their fetters'" (Psalm 2:3).

As rebels against God, we live to satisfy the unbridled desires of our nature, but we prefer not to do this in the open light of day. Our rebellion is built on lies, deception, and stealth. We make up our justifications as we go, little knowing that our denial of God is drawing us ever closer to the disastrous end.

"Then the king told the attendants, 'Tie him hand and foot, and throw him outside, into the darkness, where there will be weeping and gnashing of teeth'" (Matthew 22:13). These are the words of Jesus as He tells the parable of the wedding banquet. Will we be invited to stay? Or will we be cast out into the darkness? The choice is always ours to make.

I lift up my eyes to the hills—where does my help come from?
My help comes from the LORD, the Maker of heaven and earth.

—PSALM 121:1–2

A FELLOW PASSENGER

I WAS ON an airplane heading for Nashville and, like almost everyone else, I was quietly minding my own business. But I did notice the lady sitting by the window on my aisle; she was looking out at the world beyond our cabin, and in her hands was a Bible. She was an older black woman, and she had a quiet strength and dignity about her.

Well into the two-hour flight, we began to talk about the usual superficial things, but I really wanted to talk to her about her Bible as I had begun reading Scripture myself a few years earlier. I don't remember many of the details of that conversation, but I was startled when she told me that she was a missionary from Africa who had come to the mission fields of the United States. Moreover, she told me that she often traveled from city to city without knowing where she would stay or whom she would help. Then she told me that the verse that she loved the most was Psalm 121:1: "I lift my eyes to the mountains—where does my help come from? My help comes from the LORD, the Maker of heaven and earth." As it turned out, that verse was one of my own favorites.

I treasure that simple encounter on an otherwise unremarkable airplane ride to Nashville. My preconceptions were knocked off balance when I was forced to realize that we need missionaries here in America just as much as Africa might need them. But it was not the mission that impressed me. It was the person sitting in that seat by the window, so meek and unassuming, so gentle and faithful. She clearly was one of God's children doing God's business in a way that would not attract much notice, but still, she had that unique concentrated power that has been changing the world quietly and effectively one person at a time for over two thousand years.

What is man that you make so much of him,
that you give him so much attention, that you examine
him every morning and test him every moment?

—JOB 7:17–18

HERE IS THE MAN!

WHAT IS MAN, indeed? Job seems to be saying that man is no more than a plaything of God, but later he repents and says, "Surely I spoke of things I did not understand, things too wonderful for me to know" (Job 42:3).

Ages later, another man, wearing a crown of thorns and a purple robe, is the complete answer to Job's question. This man stands before an angry mob that does not recognize him for who He truly is, for instead of worshipping Him, they mock and insult Him and call for Him to be put to death on a cross.

Pilate, the human figure of authority, stands by His side and says to the frenzied crowd: "Here is the man!" (John 19:5). Yes, here is the man who "took up our infirmities and carried our sorrows. . . . He was pierced for our transgressions, he was crushed for our iniquities; the punishment that brought us peace was upon him, and by his wounds we are healed. We all, like sheep, have gone astray, each of us has turned to his own way; and the LORD has laid on him the iniquity of us all" (Isaiah 53:4–6).

Indeed, behold the man.

O LORD, you have searched me and you know me.

You know when I sit and when I rise; you perceive my

thoughts from afar. You discern my going out and my lying down;

you are familiar with all my ways. Before a word is on my

tongue you know it completely, O Lord.

—PSALM 139:1–4

DARKNESS IS AS LIGHT TO YOU

WE CAN DECEIVE our friends; we can even deceive ourselves, but can we really hide from the presence of God?

If we say that God cannot know everything about us, then we are diminishing His power and elevating our own. We put ourselves first, making God an afterthought in the conduct of our lives. David gives us a fuller picture: "When I was woven together in the depths of the earth, your eyes saw my unformed body. All the days ordained for me were written in your book before one of them came to be" (Psalm 139:15–16).

Acknowledging God only when it is convenient diminishes the reality of His presence in our lives from the moment we are conceived to the time of our death. This includes even the most secret and hidden parts of our life: "If I say, 'Surely the darkness will hide me and the light become night around me,' even the darkness will not be dark to you; the night will shine like the day, for the darkness is as light to you" (Psalm 139:11–12).

*. . . Bind them [my words] on your fingers; write them on the
tablet of your heart. Say to wisdom, "You are my sister," and call
understanding your kinsman; they will keep you from the
adulteress, from the wayward wife with her seductive words.*

—PROVERBS 7:3–5

THE BEGINNING OF WISDOM

IF WISDOM ORIGINATES with God, then our drive to engage in foolish and self-destructive behavior may be born of our own disbelief. The Bible explicitly says that "the fool says in his heart, 'There is no God'" (Psalm 14:1). Once a man pushes God aside, sin gains free rein to grow and prosper within a vulnerable heart. Boundaries and self-justication begin to reign and soon enough lies and deception become the coin of the realm.

The Bible reveals the only true and trustworthy place where wisdom is found: "The fear of the LORD is the beginning of wisdom" (Psalm 111:10). The well-lived life begins with the Lord; we are told to store up His commands, guard His teachings, and "write them on the tablet of your heart."

Without God's strong and steady hand, men are blown back and forth by every temptation, and the inevitable descent follows: "Then, after desire has conceived, it gives birth to sin, and sin, when it is full-grown, gives birth to death" (James 1:15).

Can a corrupt throne be allied with you——one that brings
on misery by its decrees? They band together against the
righteous and condemn the innocent to death.

—PSALM 94:20–21

A CORRUPT RULER POLLUTES THE LAND

THE FRAMERS OF the American Constitution knew that kings matter. They knew biblical history, and they understood that tyranny, corruption, and misery were more often the historical norm, the exception. A corrupt king matters because everything he does and says is magnified and therefore his or her influence ripples down to every corner of the land: "A king's wrath is like the roar of a lion; he who angers him forfeits his life" (Proverbs 20:2).

From the beginning, Israel has been warned about the dangers a king will bring to the people: "This is what the king who will reign over you will do: He will take your sons and make them serve with his chariots and horses . . . he will take your daughters to be perfumers and cooks and bakers. He will take the best of your fields and vineyards and olive groves and give them to his attendants. . . . He will take a tenth of your flocks, and you yourselves will become his slaves" (1 Samuel 8:11–17).

The abuse of power and privilege at the top infects the body of the kingdom, and all the people suffer. Why are we surprised when we find out that leaders have fallen into venial and corrupt behavior? The historical norm would suggest an inverse relationship between power and virtue. It is a rare man, indeed, who will not be tempted to turn to tyranny when the opportunity arises. If it could happen in ancient Israel, it can happen anywhere. "The wicked freely strut about when what is vile is honored among men" (Psalm 12:8).

*May the peoples praise you, O God; may all the peoples praise
you. May the nations be glad and sing for joy, for you rule the
peoples justly and guide the nations of the earth. May the
peoples praise you, O God; may all the peoples praise you. Then
the land will yield its harvest, and God, our God, will bless us.
God will bless us, and all the ends of the earth will fear him.*

—PSALM 67:3–7

MY HEART WILL SING TO YOU

WHAT HAPPENS WHEN the people stop praising God? What
happens when the people scorn God's abundant grace and they
break free to do whatever they want?

Whenever this happens, in recent or ancient times, such as in
Nazi Germany or Soviet Russia, a spiritual famine spreads
throughout the land, leaving poverty, sickness, death in its wake.
Without God's grace, we remain riveted to the fallen side of our
nature where "every intention of the thoughts of (our hearts) was
only evil continually." (Genesis 6:5).

But despite our inclination to reject God, he remains the source
of our salvation and our good, and so we should praise the Lord
mightily because His grace is life. It is by God's grace that we are
saved from our wandering into dangerous places. "O LORD my God
[we say with all sincerity of heart], I called to you for help and you
healed me" (Psalm 30:2). Therefore, we should say, I will praise
your holy name because "you turned my wailing into dancing; you
removed my sackcloth and clothed me with joy, that my heart may
sing to you and not be silent. O LORD my God, I will give you
thanks forever" (Psalm 30:11–12).

Who can say, "I have kept my heart pure; I am clean and without sin?

—PROVERBS 20:9

A WORLD OF INTENTIONAL INDIFFERENCE

MANY MAY NOT admit it, but people do believe that, despite evidence to the contrary,, they are free of sin and are pure in the eyes of God. We usually hear them say, "I am really a good person," which is a way of raising the bar high enough for them to walk right under it.

We all do it, but we should pause to be honest. By saying we are blameless, we are engaging in self-deception. To truly "know thyself," we need to acknowledge that we do not have a pure heart, that we are not clean, and that we sin against God and neighbor every day. Jesus tells the rich ruler, "No one is good—except God alone" (Luke 18:19).

If we are blind to the nature of what is afflicting us, how can we know that we even need a cure? Jesus tells the parable of the Good Samaritan to a self-righteous expert in the law. It is important to understand that the man stripped, beaten, and left for dead is each one of us.

I am that man, and so are you. We need someone to come and lift us out of the dust and to love us and heal us. Sin is what got us there. It is Jesus who crosses the road to bring us the help we so desperately need. While the world passes by with intentional indifference, God stops to care for us because that is God's nature. When we recognize who we actually are and who is willing to help us, we are on the road to recovery.

I am under vows to you, O God; I will present my
thank offerings to you. For you have delivered me from
death and my feet from stumbling, that I may walk
before God in the light of life.

—PSALM 56:12–13

LOVE, LIGHT, LIFE

WHAT DOES DAVID mean when he says that he will "walk in the light of life"? In one sense, he is prefiguring the very nature of Jesus: "One of your descendants [who] I will place on your throne" (Psalm 132:11). The gospel tells us that Jesus is the promised descendant who has come to restore access to eternal life for all who will accept Him. In Jesus, the love of God, the light of the world, and eternal life come together in one person.

Jesus says, "I am the light of the world. Whoever follows me will never walk in darkness, but will have the light of life" (John 8:12). Elsewhere Jesus says, "I am the resurrection and the life. He who believes in me will live, even though he dies; and whoever lives and believes in me will never die" (John 11:25–26). And John the apostle proclaims, "God is love. Whoever lives in love lives in God, and God in him" (1 John 4:16). Indeed, to believe in Jesus Christ is to open the door to God's love, to His light, and to eternal life.

The sluggard says, "There is a lion in the road, a fierce lion
roaming the streets!" As a door turns on its hinges, so a sluggard
turns on his bed. The sluggard buries his hand in the dish;
he is too lazy to bring it back to his mouth. The sluggard is
wiser in his own eyes than seven men who answer discreetly.

—PROVERBS 26:13–16

BE STRONG AND COURAGEOUS

BEING A "SLUGGARD" is not what you might think it is. Notice that the sluggard cries out that there is an obstacle in his path. The implication is that nothing but a fearful imagination stands in his way. The truth is that unreasonable fear holds him back. He is free to move forward, but something inside, some fear, stops him cold. Immobility, therefore, may be just another name for fear.

If we live in fear, taking the next step, any step, will become increasingly difficult until the day arrives when we are so paralyzed that we cannot even emerge from our own beds or lift a spoon to our own mouths. Baseless fear is sinful because we are too afraid to answer God's call to action. God says this to Joshua and to all men: "Be strong and courageous. Do not be terrified; do not be discouraged, for the Lord your God will be with you wherever you go" (Joshua 1:9). Fear can stop us from responding to God's call, but "not to decide is to decide." (Dietrich Bonhoeffer)

O Lord, the God who saves me, day and night I cry out before
you. May my prayer come before you; turn your ear to my cry.
For my soul is full of trouble and my life draws near the grave.

—PSALM 88:1–3

I AM IN CONTROL!

How do we react when we find that we are in a dangerous situation, particularly one where we are clearly not in control? Many of us, for example, have gone through the terrible experience of sitting comfortably in an airplane when a violent storm strikes, sending the plane into convulsions. In the midst of such moments, do we say, "I'm okay. Nothing can harm me because I am in control," or do we say a silent prayer, asking for God's help because we know that we are vulnerable to forces far greater than our ability to control them? And when the plane finally lands without incident, we very quickly forget our feeling of powerlessness, and return to the illusionary sense of invulnerability that normally informs our behavior?

The truth is we are always traveling through life in need of God's protective hand. To believe that we do not need God at all times is to believe that we are more than mere mortals, that we, in fact, have superhuman powers that can overcome all the forces of evil that may invade our fenced in world at any given time.

King David understood that all his blessings and all his favor came from God and from nowhere else: "O Lord, the God who saves me, day and night I cry out before you. May my prayer come before you; turn your ear to my cry."

He chose David his servant and took him from the sheep pens;

from tending the sheep he brought him to be the shepherd of his

people Jacob, of Israel his inheritance. And David shepherded

them with integrity of heart; with skillful hands he led them.

—PSALM 78:70–72

THE LEAST OF HIS SONS

MORE THAN A thousand years before the birth of Christ, the prophet Samuel was sent to Bethlehem to anoint a new king for Israel: God says, "I am sending you to Jesse of Bethlehem. I have chosen one of his sons to be king" (1 Samuel 16:1). The problem was that Jesse had eight sons and the first seven appeared to be qualified. But God tells Samuel not to be fooled by appearances: "The LORD does not look at the things man looks at. Man looks at the outward appearance, but the LORD looks at the heart" (1 Samuel 16:7).

David was the eighth son, and he was considered least important by his father, Jesse, so that he was not presented to Samuel. Instead, he was left in the pastures to tend the sheep.

In the eyes of men, David was the least likely to be a king. He was the youngest with very dim prospects before him. Yet in God's eyes, he is the qualified one because God can see what is in his heart.

God loves paradoxes. He loves to upset our narrow expectations of how things should be ordered. More than a thousand years after the youngest of Jesse's sons was anointed king, another unlikely King was born in David's city. Jesus was born in the humblest of circumstances, and yet the world would be forever altered by the magnificent insignificance of the birth of an infant. At that brief moment in history, the kings of the earth were blindly going about their usual business, but in a tiny town near Jerusalem, a child was born who one day would be called "KING OF KINGS AND LORD OF LORDS" (Revelation 19:16).

Like cutting off one's feet or drinking violence is the sending of a message by the hand of a fool. Like a lame man's legs that hang limp is a proverb in the mouth of a fool. Like tying a stone in a sling is the giving of honor to a fool.

—PROVERBS 26:6–8

THE FOOL

THE "FOOL" OF Proverbs lacks spiritual intelligence. He is an aimless talker (10:10), a slanderer (10:18) who is hotheaded and reckless (14:16). He spurns discipline (15:5), misuses money (17:16), and brings grief to his parents (17:21). In this passage, the fool shows himself to be ineffective, powerless, and undependable. He has no character, and he is a danger to everyone in his company.

On the other hand, the saint may have started out as a fool, but rather than remain in a state of spiritual stupor, he becomes a character builder following God's own model. The saint is a striver, not for self but for service on behalf of the God he loves. His solid foundation for everything is Jesus Christ. To him, Christ's "divine power has given him everything he needs for life and godliness through his knowledge of him who called us by his own glory and goodness" (2 Peter 1:3).

Test me, O LORD, and try me, examine my heart and
my mind; for your love is ever before me, and I walk
continually in your truth. I do not sit with deceitful men,
nor do I consort with hypocrites; I abhor the assembly
of evildoers and refuse to sit with the wicked.

—PSALM 26:2–5

A PERIODIC HEART EXAM

BECAUSE THE "HEART is deceitful above all things" (Jeremiah 17:9), it is important to undergo a thorough and frequent heart checkup. But this is hard and often inconvenient, so we spend valuable time finding excuses for avoiding what might be unpleasant news. If we refuse to undergo a daily "heart exam," we might consider wearing a sign around our neck similar to the one found on the side of cigarette packs: "Caution: This heart may kill you!"

Left untreated by God, the human heart is the center of great turmoil and conflict. Our affections shift like an altimeter in a storm; one moment we yearn to follow the right way, then the next we turn our back on the Lord just as Peter did three times immediately after claiming eternal allegiance to Him. The battle we face every day is over the constancy of our wavering heart.

In the end, the question for each of us is about one thing: whom do I love with all my heart? We can deceive ourselves into believing that we have been exempted from this conflict, but when we do, we are submitting to loves and desires that have nothing to do with the need to place God above all other desires of the heart.

Do not wear yourself out to get rich; have the wisdom to show
restraint. Cast but a glance at riches, and they are gone, for they
will surely sprout wings and fly off to the sky like an eagle.

—PROVERBS 23:4–5

THE LAST MOURNFUL NOTE

WHY ARE SO many obsessed with wealth? On one level, gold does glitter, giving the appearance of prominence and power for those who possess it. Money can create the illusion that the good times will roll on forever; that the lavish parties of the rich are the only worthwhile reality, and that the music will play on and on as the spectral guests dance into the early hours of the morning.

In this setting of extravagance, everything appears to be perfect, but soon enough, time ripples over the scene, and all that remains in the end is a wrecked vestige of what was before. The band is now playing its last mournful note, the guests are departing, and the despoiled tables have lost their ordered elegance.

Wisdom says, "Though your riches increase, do not set your heart on them" (Psalm 62:10). Money has the power to hold back the ravages of time for a period, but before long, the clock will exact its sweet revenge. If we stake everything on the deceptive power of money, and what it buys, we will always fear that the cold breath of mortality will find a way back into the innermost chambers of the guilded places. For despite our futile efforts, we sense in our hearts that our "days are like a fleeting shadow" (Psalm 144:4) that "vanish like smoke" (Psalm 102:3).

My companion attacks his friends; he violates his covenant.

His speech is smooth as butter, yet war is in his heart.

—PSALM 55:20–21

A WORLD ABSENT OF GOD

IF YOU ARE looking for a dose of reality, then immerse yourself in the 55th Psalm. David is in anguish, confronted with the "terrors of death" (v. 4) and filled with "fear and trembling . . . for [he] see[s] violence and strife in the city. Day and night they prowl about on its walls; malice and abuse are within it. Destructive forces are at work in the city; threats and lies never leave its streets" (vv. 5, 9–11). It is in such a world that even friends betray their companions. Here is the bad news: David is describing a world that has abandoned God, and so men have reverted to their natural state of godless corruption.

This is the very same world that Jesus entered on a cold night in the small town of Bethlehem. Soon the kings of the earth and their agents would set out to destroy this child, and eventually they would crucify Him outside the walls of Jerusalem.

But little did any of them know that this one death would set a multitude free. We cannot understand this saving act until we come to understand what we have been saved from. David paints a vivid picture of what the world looks like absent of God. It is a world in desperate need of God's saving grace.

Wisdom has built her house;

she has hewn out its seven pillars . . .

Leave your simple ways and you will live;

walk in the way of understanding.

—PROVERBS 9:1,6

A HOUSE BUILT ON ROCK

GOD'S WISDOM IS the adhesive that binds the holy structure built *with* stone and *on* stone and supported by seven pillars. This is the house that Jesus describes at the end of His Sermon on the Mount. It is a house that can withstand the worst storm: "The rain came down, the streams rose, and the winds blow and beat against that house; yet it did not fall, because it had its foundation on the rock" (Matthew 7:24–25).

But the foolish person often chooses not to seek the house built on a solid foundation. Instead they seek out a house that ensnares and destroys. "At the window of my house I looked out through the lattice. I saw among the simple, I noticed among the young men, a youth who lacked judgment. He was going down the street near her corner, walking along in the direction of her house. . . . All at once he followed her . . . little knowing it will cost him his life" (Proverbs 7:6–8, 22–23).

God invites each of us to enter His house of seven pillars. Other houses, of which there are many, are like prisons filled with sorrow and regret. Will we have the wisdom to take God's way or will we choose the other path?

Listen, my son, accept what I say,
and the years of your life will be many.

—PROVERBS 4:10

HIS BOUNDLESS LOVE

"LISTEN MY SON, accept what I say. . . ." Here we have every good father speaking words of wisdom and advice to his son out of natural love. Every good father, we would say, wants only the best for his own child. It is so natural that we do not much think about it.

In one of his parables, Jesus uses this natural relationship between father and son to make a deeper point: "Which of you fathers, if your son asks for a fish, will give him a snake instead? Or if he asks for an egg, will give him a scorpion? If you then, though you are evil, know how to give good gifts to your children, how much more will your Father in heaven give the Holy Spirit to those who ask?" (Luke 11:11–13).

Jesus is telling us a truth that we often find hard to believe. Just as it is natural that a father will give good things to his son because he loves him, so it is true that God the Father will give good things to His children out of His love for them. As children of God, when we pray to our Father in heaven, we can expect Him to respond in love, though not always in a way we might expect.

Under three things the earth trembles,
under four it cannot bear up: a servant who becomes king,
a fool who is full of food, an unloved woman who is married,
and a maidservant who displaces her mistress.

—PROVERBS 30:21–23

GOD'S ORIGINAL DESIGN

MARRIAGE ABSENT LOVE can be a shipwreck. God's original design did not contemplate an unloved wife. The first man and the first woman were made to complement one another, reflecting the harmony built into everything God created: "This is now bone of my bone and flesh of my flesh" [said Adam] . . . "For this reason a man will leave his father and mother and be united to his wife, and they will become one flesh. The man and his wife were both naked, and they felt no shame" (Genesis 2:21–25).

But with the Fall came self-consciousness, sin, and death, fracturing the original order and turning marriage into a vestige of the relationship of love God intended. Instead of the ideals of patience, kindness, protection, trust, hope, and perseverance, we often find envy, pride, rudeness, selfishness, and anger (1 Corinthians 13:4–7). Paul reminds men that they need to live within God's original purpose: "Husbands, love your wives, just as Christ loved the church . . ." (Ephesians 5:25).

When my heart was grieved and my spirit embittered,
I was senseless and ignorant; I was a brute beast before you.

—PSALM 73:21–22

DO NOT BE GRIEVED

THE PSALMIST'S HEART is grieved and his spirit embittered, not by external afflictions but by a corrosive envy of others, which is a source of alienation and frustration. He says that his own heart had become impure because "I envied the arrogant when I saw the prosperity of the wicked" (Psalm 73:3).

The psalmist also says that the wicked seem to be rewarded in this life, raising the question of justice. "They have no struggles; their bodies are healthy and strong. They are free from the burdens common to man; they are not plagued by human ills" (vv. 4–5). Who has not wondered about the purpose of life when they see the wicked prospering? But then the psalmist has a revelation from God that reminds him that, while his ways may seem inscrutable at times, God holds those who are faithful by their "right hand" and will not abandon his children. "When I tried to understand all this, it was oppressive to me till I entered the sanctuary of God; then I understood their final destiny" (vv. 16–17).

When the Holy Spirit enters our hearts, we begin to see with our own eyes God's wisdom in the words of Christ: "Pray for those who persecute you, that you may be sons of your Father in heaven. He causes his sun to rise on the evil and the good and sends rain on the righteous and the unrighteous. If you love those who love you, what reward will you get? Are not even the tax collectors doing that?" (Matthew 5:44–46).

We are called to live in the power of God's love. When we do, envy and frustration evaporate, and our lives become characterized by abundance.

Who is this that appears like the dawn, fair as the moon,

bright as the sun, majestic as the stars in procession?

—SONG OF SONGS 6:10

THE BRIGHT MORNING STAR

WHAT IS AN extended love poem doing in the middle of the Bible? Some consider the sensuality of the verses to be scandalous; others celebrate the beauty of the lyrical language and compare Song of Songs, for example, to Shakespeare's sonnets. But is Solomon limiting himself to a man and woman's passionate love for one another, or is there more going on here?

Solomon was the son of Bathsheba and David. He was blessed by God and was known throughout the world for his godly wisdom. He knew intimately about God's love for His children, even though those very same children often wandered away from Him. When we read: "How beautiful you are, my darling! Oh, how beautiful!" (Song of Songs 4:1), we should understand that Solomon is writing about human love, certainly, but he is also using poetic language to compare our own understanding of love to God's incomparable love for each one of us.

Four things on earth are small, yet they are extremely wise:
Ants are creatures of little strength, yet they store up their food
in the summer; coneys are creatures of little power, yet they make
their home in the crags; locusts have no king, yet they advance
together in ranks; a lizard can be caught with the hand,
yet it is found in kings' palaces.

—PROVERBS 30:24–28

NOTHING IS IMPOSSIBLE WITH GOD

As with the ant or locusts or a little lizard, we too are small when compared to the unimaginable size of the universe. When seen from the perspective of infinite time and space, we can become frozen by a sense of hopelessness because we ask how God could care for someone as small and insignificant as I am?

This is a mystery, but it is a mystery that the Bible confronts time and again. We read stories in almost every book of Scripture telling how God uses seemingly insignificant people to accomplish his own purpose. Here is Moses, exiled from his people, being called back to lead them out of slavery in Egypt. Here is Sarah, old and without children, being told that she would bear a child who would be the child of God's promise. Here is Esther, who summons all the courage she has to stand in the way of the total destruction of her people. And here is Mary, a young virgin, who is visited by an angel of God and who is told she will give birth to a child to be named Jesus who "will be great and will be called the son of the Most High" (Luke 1:31–32).

When Mary questions the visitor, she is told a truth that should lift our hearts: No matter how impossible, difficult, and terrible our situation might be, "Nothing is impossible with God" (Luke 1:37). When God calls us to His purpose, our answer should be the same as Mary's: "My soul glorifies the Lord and my spirit rejoices in God my Savior, for he has been mindful of the humble state of his servant" (Luke 1:46–48).

Who may ascend the hill of the LORD? Who may stand in his
holy place? He who has clean hands and a pure heart, who does
not lift up his soul to an idol or swear by what is false.

—PSALM 24:3–4

THE SERVANT OF THE VALLEY

MOSES RECEIVED THE Ten Commandments on Mount Sinai, Jesus gave His sermon on a hill, and His disciples witnessed the transfiguration on a mountaintop.

Yet while Moses was with God, the people of Israel abandoned him to worship a man-made golden calf. They were living in the valley of the shadow of death. When Jesus completed his sermon, he returned to the valley where He was immediately confronted by a man suffering with leprosy who begged that he would be cured. When Jesus, Peter, James, and John descended the mountain after the transfiguration, they encountered another man whose son was possessed with epilepsy.

The valley is the place where Jesus needed to be. Jesus did not stay on the mountaintop, nor did Moses. Their ministry was where the greatest need existed. Both had ascended the mountain of God, but both were servants of the valley.

Though Jesus was "in very nature God, [He] did not consider equality with God something to be grasped, but made himself nothing, taking on the very nature of a servant" (Philippians 2:6–7). God may call His servants to the mountaintop, but He always sends them back to the valley to accomplish the plan He has for them and for us.

Where can I go from your Spirit? Where can I flee from your
presence? If I go up to the heavens, you are there; if I make my
bed in the depths, you are there. If I rise on the wings of the
dawn, if I settle on the far side of the sea, even there your hand
will guide me, your right hand will hold me fast.

—PSALM 139:7–10

HE WILL NOT ABANDON

HAVE YOU BEEN hunting for God lately? Many claim to be searching high and low, proclaiming all the while that God just can't be found anywhere. But what if this claim is bogus and the opposite is true? What if, instead of seeking God, we have been steadfastly avoiding Him? What if we actually fear coming face to face with Him because that would hamper our strong inclination to live free of Him? The psalm tells us that the quest for independence is delusional and futile. "Where can I go from your Spirit? Where can I flee from your presence?"

The truth is we cannot flee from the presence of God. We can deny God, but our denial does not cause God to turn away. Peter proclaimed that he would defend Jesus unto death, and then he fled in the face of danger. In one way or another, Peter is all of us, but God did not abandon Peter, and He does not abandon us just because we may seek to abandon Him. "Let us celebrate. For this my son was dead, and is alive again; he was lost, and is found." (Luke 15:24)

And I saw something else under the sun: In the place of
judgment—wickedness was there, in the place of justice—
wickedness was there. I thought in my heart, "God will bring
to judgment both the righteous and the wicked, for there will
be a time for every activity, a time for every deed."

—ECCLESIASTES 3:16–17

SETTLING OUR ACCOUNT

SOLOMON SCANNED THE world and described what he found: "In the place of judgment—wickedness was there, in the place of justice—wickedness was there." To imagine a world without justice and judgment is contrary to our deepest convictions of how the world needs to work. But too often it does not work this way at all.

Jesus also speaks of justice and judgment, but with a panoramic lens. He knows that if we confine our understanding to what we experience in this world alone, as many people do, we will never comprehend God's overarching plan. Here is the way Jesus describes justice and judgment from God's perspective: "The good man brings good things out of the good stored up in him, and the evil man brings evil things out of the evil stored up in him. But I tell you that men will have to give account on the day of judgment for every careless word they have spoken. For by your words you will be acquitted, and by your words you will be condemned" (Matthew 12:35–37).

As for God, his way is perfect; the word of the LORD is flawless.
He is a shield for all who take refuge in him. For who is God
besides the LORD? And who is the Rock except our God? It is
God who arms me with strength and makes my way perfect.

—PSALM 18:30–32

THE SOURCE OF MY STRENGTH

IF WE DEPEND only on our own human resources, we will fail. While God's way is perfect, our way is not: "It is God who arms me with strength and makes my way perfect." Our strength and our success all come from the Lord. When we forget this and attribute success to our own abilities, we inevitably turn away from God to fight our own battles and travel on our own path based on our own standards.

But Jesus tells us it is fatal to fight alone. Every battle will weaken us a little more, preparing the way for our ultimate collapse. Paul understood through experience that we do not stand a chance unless we are fully armed through the Holy Spirit against all the weapons of the devil. (Ephesians 6:10–20). It is through the power of the Holy Spirit that we are equipped to do the Lord's work; only then will the odds turn in favor of salvation, and what seemed impossible before now is possible.

Go to the ant, you sluggard; consider its ways and
be wise! It has no commander, no overseer or ruler, yet it
stores its provisions in summer and gathers its food at
harvest. . . . A little sleep, a little slumber, a little folding
of the hands to rest—and poverty will come on you
like a bandit and scarcity like an armed man.

—PROVERBS 6:6–8, 10–11

A SPIRITUAL PENALTY BOX

HERE WE HAVE the contrast between the small but industrious ant, who seems to have the inborn wisdom to gather while time allows, and an indolent man who will not lift a hand to stave off scarcity and poverty.

The irony is clear. While the ant is merely an insect, man was made "a little lower than the heavenly beings and crowned . . . with glory and honor" (Psalm 8:5). When our behavior is below that of an ant, we dishonor the God who made us, and therefore, we end up living in a kind of spiritual penalty box until we choose to live up to the nature that God blessed us with.

Does the hawk take flight by your wisdom and spread his
wings toward the south? Does the eagle soar at your
command and build his nest on high?

—JOB 39:26–27

THE RIGHT PERSPECTIVE

MEN COMMAND ARMIES; they build corporations. They amass fortunes. Men design supersonic jets and engineer bridges and tunnels. They send rockets into the heavens and attempt to own everything great and small. But does the wisdom of man tell the hawk how to fly? And can we command the eagle? God asks Job dozens of questions, and to each question Job has no answer.

When men applaud their own ingenuity for building cities and civilizations, they might stop to consider the unanswerable questions addressed to Job (v. 38), for perhaps we are not the genuine architects after all. And this might help us put all human accomplishments in a better perspective.

Be merciful to me, O LORD, for I am in distress; my eyes grow
weak with sorrow, my soul and my body with grief. My life is
consumed by anguish and my years by groaning; my strength
fails because of my affliction, and my bones grow weak.

—PSALM 31:9–10

RELY ON GOD'S MERCY ALWAYS

DAVID IS IN distress: "Because of all my enemies . . . there is terror on every side; they conspire against me and plot to take my life" (Psalm 31:11–13). These words could just as well have been the words of Jesus as his tormentors pursued him with "hatred beyond reason."

This psalm is a prayer for every righteous man because this pitiless world desires to attack and punish him. Even the saint is not exempt from the terrible reality of opposition from those who pervert love in their quest to kill and destroy.

One of the seven words Jesus spoke from the cross is uttered here by David: "Since you are my rock and my fortress, for the sake of your name lead and guide me. . . . Into your hands I commit my spirit; redeem me, O LORD, the God of truth" (Psalm 31:3, 5).

Do you feel that God is calling you into his service? Do you feel overwhelmed by the challenges? The truth is Jesus suffered and died that you and I might live and not live for its own sake but live for the purposes God had for us from the beginning.

I said, "O LORD, have mercy on me; heal me, for I
have sinned against you."

—PSALM 41:4

GENUINE HEALTH

MOST OF US go through life in a semi-conscious state of spiritual blindness. If we prosper, we attribute success to our own abilities and think no more about it. Or if we are troubled with difficulties and problems, we attribute it to bad luck or bad circumstances or to someone else.

But the Psalmist says something fundamentally different. He says, "I have sinned against God." As a result, he is sick and cannot cure himself. His conscience is stricken, and he can only plead for mercy.

In *Biblical Psychology*, Oswald Chambers writes, "Conscience is the innate law in nature whereby man knows he is known." When we come to that place where we know that we are known by God, then the true state of our unhealthiness is placed in stark contrast to the holiness of God. We recognize, perhaps for the first time, that we are not as good as we think we are. In fact, this realization can come as an awful shock, but God is truly merciful and He provides, through Jesus Christ and the Holy Spirit, a way for us not only to ask for mercy but to receive it: "Ask and it will be given to you; seek and you will find; knock and the door will be opened to you. For everyone who asks receives; he who seeks finds; and to him who knocks, the door will be opened" (Matthew 7:7–8).

A wife of noble character who can find? She is worth far more than rubies. . . . She makes linen garments and sells them, and supplies the merchants with sashes. She is clothed with strength and dignity; she can laugh at the days to come. She speaks with wisdom, and faithful instruction is on her tongue. She watches over the affairs of her household and does not eat the bread of idleness. Her children arise and call her blessed; her husband also, and he praises her: "Many women do noble things, but you surpass them all." Charm is deceptive, and beauty is fleeting; but a woman who fears the LORD is to be praised. Give her the reward she has earned, and let her works bring her praise at the city gate.

—PROVERBS 31:10, 24–31

BEAUTY THAT TRANSCENDS YOUTH

SO MUCH IS asked of women, and so much is given by them. Women of noble character provide strength, dignity, and wisdom. They are teachers, and they manage their households with expert and strong hands. They are generous providers and exemplary citizens, upholding the family and supporting their husbands in their mutual goals. On almost every level, women are the link between the generation passing with the generation to come. Beauty may be fleeting, but a woman of noble character has a beauty that transcends youth, mirroring a soul right with God.

A despairing man should have the devotion of his friends,
even though he forsakes the fear of the Almighty. But my
brothers are as undependable as intermittent streams, as
the streams that overflow when darkened by thawing ice and
swollen with melting snow, but that cease to flow in the dry
season, and in the heat vanish from their channels.

—JOB 6:14–17

THE TIES THAT BIND

FRIENDSHIP, AS THE world defines it, is never enough to withstand the temptation of betrayal. The world with its passions and pressures will wear down the ties that bind people together, inevitably leading to conflict, sorrow, and separation. David addresses this in one of his psalms: "My companion attacks his friends; he violates his covenant. His speech is smooth as butter, yet war is in his heart; his words are more soothing than oil, yet they are drawn swords" (Psalm 55:20–22).

Friendships cannot survive unless they are bound together by the principle of the love that originates with God. "God is love," says John. "Whoever lives in love lives in God and God in him" (1 John 4:16). Jesus is even more precise: "As the Father has loved me, so have I loved you. Now remain in my love. . . . Love each other as I have loved you. Greater love has no one than this, that he lay down his life for his friends. You are my friends if you do as I command" (John 15:9, 12–14).

Genuine love is triangular. Love starts with God. To be strong and true, love must include God in every way. Without God, love between a man and a woman or between two friends is a thin string easily frayed and easily broken.

Who will rise up for me against the wicked? Who will take a
stand for me against evildoers? Unless the Lord had given me help, I
would soon have dwelt in the silence of death. When I said,
"My foot is slipping," your love, O LORD, supported me. When anxiety
was great within me, your consolation brought joy to my soul.

—PSALM 94:16–19

LIKE SODOM, LIKE GOMORRAH

THE PSALMIST ASKS, "Who will rise up for me against the wicked?"
The spiritual battle is fierce; the outcome seems to be uncertain.
Often it seems the whole world itself has risen up against the Lord
and all believers: "The kings of the earth take their stand and the
rulers gather together against the Lord and against his Anointed
One" (Psalm 2:2). The shining city on a hill is under siege and the
fate of the world hangs in the balance.

Without the strong but gentle hand of God, our footing will be
unsure, and the anxiety of war, near and far, will always threaten us.
It is the Holy Spirit that supports us in this fierce conflict. Otherwise,
it is inevitable that the world we live in will "become like Sodom and
like Gomorrah" (Romans 9:29)

Jesus prophesized that there would be "wars and rumors of
wars" and that "nation will rise against nation, and kingdom against
kingdom" and there will be deception, confusion, and suffering
(Matthew 24:4–8). How perfectly this describes the world we live
in today. But Jesus also said that, despite appearances, the battle
will be won and that "he who stands firm to the end will be saved"
(Mathew 24:13). And then He says this to encourage those who
are weary and discouraged: "And this gospel of the kingdom will
be preached in the whole world as a testimony to all nations, and
then the end will come" (Matthew 24:14).

I find more bitter than death the woman who is a snare,
whose heart is a trap and whose hands are chains. The man who
pleases God will escape her, but the sinner she will ensnare.

—ECCLESIASTES 7:26

SEDUCTION

SEDUCTION IS NOT a word that finds its way into polite conversation, but just because we pretend that all relationships are motivated by understandable and controllable emotions does not mean that seduction has been eradicated like some dreaded virus.

The truth is that all people suffer from faulty judgment, and when men fall in love with a beautiful woman, our vision may easily be clouded by what the apostle John calls "the cravings of sinful man, the lust of his eyes and the boasting of what he has and does [which] comes not from the Father but from the world" (1 John 2:16).

So when teaching our sons about the ways of the world, we need to be wise and realistic. It is easier than ever to enter into relationships that end up binding people in destructive ways. Women and men are meant to complement and bless one another, not trap, discard, and destroy.

Give ear to my words, O LORD, consider my sighing.

Listen to my cry for help, my King and my God, for to you I pray.

In the morning, O LORD, you hear my voice; in the morning I

lay my requests before you and wait in expectation.

—PSALM 5:1–3

NEW EVERY MORNING

DARKNESS GIVING WAY to gentle light is the hint of warmth and hope that is the dawning of a new day. We awake as the rising sun paints the earth in vibrant colors, and we rise to expectations of new opportunities and chances. But we should never attack the new day; rather, we should embrace it because God wants us to begin by acknowledging and appreciating Him and all the benefits He provides us with. (Psalm 103:1-13)

For me the new day is built on the foundation of the Word of God. At this point in my life, I will accept no substitutes. I must spend part of my morning setting aside part of an hour reading in the Bible as well as other related books. On some days, I seem to get very little out of these readings while on others, several thoughts will enter my mind as I read from a psalm or one of the Gospels. Whatever the case might be, I know that I have gained a great deal of cumulative knowledge over time. And with every new day, I gain a greater appreciation and love of the book that shifted the focus of my heart and mind in an unexpected new direction.

Like a thornbush in a drunkard's hand is a proverb in the
mouth of a fool. Like an archer who wounds at random is he
who hires a fool or any passer-by. As a dog returns to its vomit,
so a fool repeats his folly. Do you see a man wise in his own
eyes? There is more hope for a fool than for him.

—PROVERBS 26:9–12

PUT CHILDISH WAYS ASIDE

HAVE YOU EVER wished to be something you clearly are not? Children are constantly dreaming of being something they cannot possibly be during their youth, but when they grow older, these dreams, when unrealistic, become fantasies and quickly lose their charm.

A fool chases childhood dreams when he should have arrived at a realistic assessment of his abilities and his life. A fool looks in the mirror and sees the reflection of a king; he wishes to be greater than he is, and thus his folly is his pride. "When I was a child, I talked like a child, I thought like a child, I reasoned like a child. When I became a man, I put childish ways behind me" (1 Corinthians 13:11). To remain in a childish state soon enough will become inappropriate awkwardness. A time comes when we are called to make choices, and one of the most important choices is to leave behind childish ways.

My heart is in anguish within me; the terrors of death assail me.
Fear and trembling have beset me; horror has overwhelmed me. I
said, "Oh, that I had the wings of a dove! I would fly away and
be at rest—I would flee far away and stay in the desert; I would
hurry to my place of shelter, far from the tempest and storm."

—PSALM 55:4–8

CARRYING THE LIGHT

IT WOULD BE wonderful to "fly away" to be at rest "far from the tempest and storm," for there are times when the conditions of life seem to close in, leaving little apparent room for escape.

This was the situation that King David found himself in. His friends had betrayed him, and Jerusalem was under attack on all sides. But David was favored by God, and God said to him: "Call upon me in the day of trouble; I will deliver you, and you will honor me" (Psalm 50:15).

In our own day of trouble, we should never forget that God wants us to reach out to Him. He has promised that we will be delivered, but we must not forget Him once we have landed in a safe place. For no matter what the circumstance, whether in chains or free, we are called to carry His light in our hearts and in our lives. We are called to honor God with our lives by being "blameless and pure, children of God without fault in a crooked and depraved generation, in which you shine like stars in the universe as you hold out the word of life . . ." (Philippians 2:15–16).

Trust in the LORD with all your heart and lean not on your
own understanding; in all your ways acknowledge him,
and he will make your paths straight.

—PROVERBS 3:5–6

SEEK GUIDANCE

IT IS EASIER said than done to "lean not on our own understanding." We seem to want to believe we have a self-appointed board of directors bouncing around in our heads, always permitting us to do whatever we might want to do.

Rehoboam was the son of Solomon and upon Solomon's death, he succeeded his father to the throne of Israel. But immediately after becoming king, the people of Israel asked the King for relief from the heavy burden of taxes imposed by Solomon.

Rehoboam took counsel with the elders who had advised his father and then he turned to the young men who he surrounded himself with and listened to them; he "leaned on his own understanding" and made a foolish decision to reject the wisdom of the elders. What followed was civil war and the eventual division of the nation. Unlike Solomon, Rehoboam was not discerning and he and his nation would soon enough pay a great price.

Let all the earth fear the LORD; let all the people of the world
revere him. For he spoke, and it came to be; he commanded,
and it stood firm . . . But the plans of the LORD stand firm
forever, the purposes of his heart through all generations.

—PSALM 33:8–9, 11

THE DEVIL'S QUESTION

WHAT MAKES THE naturalistic understanding of the origin of the universe more reliable than the biblical account from Genesis? Actually, the motives behind much of scientific thinking may be more biblical than many might suspect.

Biblical history reveals that men have been trying to cancel out God from the very beginning; we have been in a state of continuous rebellion against God since a certain tragic question was asked of our first ancestors: "Did God really say, 'You must not eat from any tree in the garden?'" (Genesis 3:1). The answer was as false as the promise that followed: "You will be like God, knowing good and evil" (Genesis 3:5).

To become like God is not to make mankind greater but to make God less. The serpent in the Garden would like each one of us to believe that we can be gods by knowing what God knows. However, we should consider the nature of the one behind the original question. Here is how Jesus described him: "He was a murderer from the beginning, and does not stand in the truth, because there is no truth in him. When he lies, he speaks out of his own character, for he is a liar and the father of lies." (John 8:44)

Do not boast about tomorrow,
for you do not know what a day may bring forth.

—PROVERBS 27:1

ENGAGING THE MOMENT

ALL OF US stand precariously between past and future, and so, many respond to this unsteady state by seeking false stability. We may try to protect ourselves with wealth or excessive activity or living in denial, but all of this, no matter what the form, is defensive in nature. We look to the future with a fear-filled heart, seeking a false security when, in fact, we do not know if the next minute will be our last: "For you do not know what a day may bring forth."

The man who puts his faith in God does not need to address the future with anything but hope. Jesus summarizes this attitude in the Sermon on the Mount: "So do not worry, saying 'What shall we eat?' or 'What shall we drink?' or 'What shall we wear?' For the pagans run after all these things, and your heavenly Father knows that you need them. But seek first his kingdom and his righteousness, and all these things will be given to you as well" (Matthew 6:31–33).

The way we deal with the present moment should tell us everything we need to know about the condition of our faith. Are we fear-driven, thus missing the opportunities before us, or do we engage in the moment, letting the hand of God lead us forward to the next day and all the days beyond?

I will sing of your love and justice; to you, O LORD, I will sing

praise. I will be careful to lead a blameless life— when will you

come to me? I will walk in my house with blameless heart.

I will set before my eyes no vile thing.

—PSALM 101:1–3

FIGHT THE GOOD FIGHT

DAVID IS SPEAKING about a man who has a heart for God. The "blameless heart" loves God first above everything else, even before self. But the blameless man is warned to live thoughtfully. Virtue can be attacked and compromised. "I will have nothing to do with evil." We are cautioned to do even more because the threat to our integrity is real and dangerous: "Flee from sexual immorality" (1 Corinthians 6:18), "Flee from idolatry" (1 Corinthians 10:14), "But you, man of God, flee from all this, and pursue righteousness, godliness, faith, love, endurance and gentleness. Fight the good fight of the faith" (1 Timothy 6:11–12).

Flee from those things that will weaken or harm you. Flee from everything that will separate you from God. Instead, be strong in the Lord (Ephesians 6:20) because you need to be. Be prepared and armed because the world will do its best to weaken and disarm you, destroying your capacity to "fearlessly make known the mystery of the gospel" (Ephesians 6:19).

The heavens declare the glory of God; the skies proclaim
the work of his hands. Day after day they pour forth speech;
night after night they display knowledge.

—PSALM 19:1–2

GOD'S INVISIBLE QUALITIES

JESUS ASKS, "WHY is my language not clear to you?" (John 8:43). To another He asks, "But what about you? . . . Who do you say I am?" (Mark 8:29). And to another: "You do not know me or my Father . . . If you knew me, you would know my Father also" (John 8:20).

We are like foolish men wandering through a beautiful garden complaining about the insects. God stands before our very eyes, and we see merely our own reflection as if the world itself was our mirror. Ever since we departed that first garden, we have been afflicted by a spiritual blindness that passes down from one generation to the next.

God keeps calling out to us to open the eyes of our hearts (Ephesians 1:18) just as Elisha prayed that God would open the eyes of His servant so that he could see the power of God all around him (2 Kings 6:17). If we insist on remaining blind, we do it through our own choice. For God makes Himself evident throughout all of creation: "For since the creation of the world God's invisible qualities—his eternal power and divine nature—have been clearly seen, being understood from what has been made . . ." (Romans 1:20).

The poor are shunned even by their neighbors, but the
rich have many friends. He who despises his neighbor sins,
but blessed is he who is kind to the needy. He who oppresses
the poor shows contempt for their Maker, but whoever is
kind to the needy honors God.

—PROVERBS 14:20–21, 31

THE WEIGHT OF OUR COINS

JESUS WALKED AMONG the rich and poor alike, but his teaching never praised or judged people by their station in this life. He always looked beyond the normal lines that seemed to pit men against men and men against God.

The rich young ruler in the gospel account, for example, is a good man by human standards, but he rejects Jesus in sadness because he cannot discard the treasure he has for the treasure Jesus promises.

The rich young ruler rejects the true, eternal treasure for the "treasures on earth, where moth and rust destroy" (Matthew 6:19). In a parable recounted by Luke, Jesus reinforces the idea of the tragic divide between the treasures of this world and the treasure of eternal life: "But Abraham replied, 'Son, remember that in your lifetime you received your good things, while Lazarus received bad things, but now he is comforted here and you are in agony'" (Luke 16:25).

Jesus is saying that God will not judge us by the weight of the coins in our pocket. It may be hard to believe that another standard might exist, but Jesus is telling us that, indeed, there is another standard.

You answer us with awesome deeds of righteousness, O God

our Savior, the hope of all the ends of the earth and of the

farthest seas, who formed the mountains by your power, having

armed yourself with strength, who stilled the roaring of the seas,

the roaring of their waves, and the turmoil of the nations. Those

living far away fear your wonders; where morning dawns and

evening fades you call forth songs of joy.

—PSALM 65:5–8

EVER PRESENT, NEVER ABSENT

GOD IS EVER present, never absent. He formed the mountains, stilled the roaring sea, and quieted the turmoil of the nations. Without God's presence, the sun rises on hopelessness and despair. Wars and rumors of wars are commonplace, and the lament of Job is on every person's lips: "If only there were someone to arbitrate between us . . ." (Job 9:33).

But God heard our cry of distress, and in his own good time he sent his Son into the world to offer reconciliation to all men and women to himself. The joy of the morning and the evening is the resurrected Christ: "I am the Alpha and the Omega, the First and the Last, the Beginning and the End. Blessed are those who wash their robes, that they may have the right to the tree of life and may go through the gates into the city. . . . I am the Root and the Offspring of David, and the bright Morning Star" (Revelation 22:13–14, 16).

He who works his land will have abundant food,

but he who chases fantasies lacks judgment.

—PROVERBS 12:11

A FACT OF LIFE

WHOM ARE WE working for when we subscribe to the fantasy that we don't have to work? Work is a fact of life and has been part of the human condition since the earliest days of existence: "By the sweat of your brow you will eat your food until you return to the ground . . ." (Genesis 3:19). In nature we need food to survive; even if we cannot work ourselves, we depend on the work of others for sustenance; this applies to even the tiny ant who "stores its provisions in summer and gathers its food at harvest" (Proverbs 6:8).

On the other hand, "a sluggard does not plow in season; so at harvest time he looks but finds nothing" (Proverbs 20:4). No, to shun work is to buy into a lie that comes as a subtle whisper from the original purveyor of lies, Satan.

Oh, how I love your law! I meditate on it all day long . . .
I have more insight than all my teachers, for I meditate on
your statutes. How sweet are your words to my taste, sweeter
than honey to my mouth! I gain understanding from your
precepts; therefore, I hate every wrong path.

—PSALM 119:97, 99, 103-104

OBEYING GOD'S LAW

THE PSALMIST BEGINS with a description of those who are blessed: "Blessed are they whose ways are blameless, who walk according to the law of the LORD" (Psalm 119:1). But what about those who hate the Lord's law, who never meditate on it, who disregard teachers and obey no one?

God cannot be mocked. Either we love his way and desire to obey him, or we turn away from him even while we put on an extraordinary show to advertise our own goodness and virtue.

The Psalmist is speaking from his heart: I love the Lord and everything about him. When you love the Lord obedience is not a chore; it is a strong desire to do the right thing for the one you love. If you choose to live outside of the commands of the Lord, for whatever reason, you are saying with your own life that you love someone or something more than God himself.

*But I call to God, and the L*ORD *saves me.*

Evening, morning and noon I cry out in distress,

and he hears my voice. He ransoms me unharmed from

the battle waged against me, even though many oppose me.

—PSALM 55:16–18

⸺ ∞ ⸺

THE GOD OF THE RIGHTEOUS

COMPARE THE DEEP faith of David to the self-serving claims of some of our modern leaders who stake everything on the belief that man can save man. These contemporary leaders give lip service to God, but their genuine faith seems to be built on the premise that mankind has progressed to a point in history where we are better off acting as if the God of David did not exist at all. For many of our leaders, God represents a stumbling block to their own use of intellect, technology, and political power to erect monuments to their own self-defined heroic stature.

But is the enlightened leader really modern, or does he represent nothing more than mankind's ancient and ongoing rebellion against God? "Son of man, say to the ruler of Tyre, 'This is what the Sovereign LORD says: "In the pride of your heart, you say, I am a god; I sit on the throne of a god in the heart of the seas." But you are not a god, though you think you are as wise as a god'" (Ezekiel 28:2).

Have the leaders of our time fallen for the same old promise offered to our ancestors that we "will be like God, knowing good and evil"? If so, then like so many before them, their monuments to their own pride will, in the end, crumble into so many particles of dust. "Vanity of vanities, says the Preacher, vanity of vanities!" (Ecclesiastes 1:2)

My eyes are dim with grief. I call to you, O LORD, every day;
I spread out my hands to you . . . But I cry to you for help,
O LORD; in the morning my prayer comes before you.

—PSALM 88:9, 13

AN ANSWERED PRAYER

ARTHUR, MY SIXTEEN-YEAR-OLD son, and I were fifteen miles into an eighteen-mile day on the Appalachian Trail in Pennsylvania. We started early that morning in the small river town of Duncannon. We crossed the Susquehanna on a well-travelled bridge, ascended a moderate ridge, and then began the long, rocky trek north. The temperature was mild for August, but the long miles began to wear us down.

A few days before we started out on this journey, I had arranged to have a "trail angel" pick us up at an isolated road crossing in an isolated section of state forestland, as we would need a ride back to Duncannon when we finished. But as the miles passed by and it became time to call to connect with our ride, the phone failed. The day was drawing to a close, and my heart began to sink as we descended toward the road crossing.

Would we have to spend an uncomfortable night in the woods, or worse, would we be forced to walk back? It is in moments like this that we realize the extent of our own vulnerability. We were completely dependent on the good will of strangers. But as we approached the road, I began to hear voices. Like a guardian angel, the stranger and his wife had kept their appointment. Just as the cloud of anxiety had dominated my mood for a number of miles, now with the knowledge that we were saved from a variety of unpleasant outcomes, a wave of gratitude and joy flooded into my heart. At that moment, I felt a small touch of God's goodness, and I could say with all my heart that Arthur and I were blessed by the goodness of two "Trail Angels."

Remember your word to your servant, for you have given
me hope. My comfort in my suffering is this: Your promise
preserves my life. The arrogant mock me without restraint,
but I do not turn from your law. I remember your
ancient laws, O LORD, and I find comfort in them.

—PSALM 119:49–52

YOU STEADY US

GOD'S "ANCIENT LAWS" were a reminder to a wayward people that there are boundaries and that we wander away at our own risk. "Do not move an ancient boundary stone" (Proverbs 23:10) means that the spiritual path has been laid out and marked by God, and it leads as much away from trouble as towards good.

But we cannot embrace the law and disregard the creator of that law. The Psalmist can say he has hope and feels comfort and obeys because he has it fixed in his heart that God is the goodness and power behind everything. Without the Holy Spirit, the law would be empty and without power. In *Imitation of Christ*, Thomas à Kempis writes, "There is no holiness, O Lord, if you withdraw your comforting hand. . . . When you are not with us, we sink and perish, but when you visit us we rise up and live again. Of ourselves we are unstable, but you steady us; we are lukewarm, but you set us on fire."

Surely no one lays a hand on a broken man when he cries for help in his distress. Have I not wept for those in trouble? Has not my soul grieved for the poor? Yet when I hoped for good, evil came; when I looked for light, then came darkness.

—JOB 30:24–26

INTEGRITY UNDER PRESSURE

THE MODERN MIND has a problem with the story of Job. Job was a good man; he feared God and was a good husband, father, and neighbor. He did not misuse his wealth, and so he prospered. Job had it all, but then catastrophe struck. Even Job's closest friends are troubled by this apparent injustice and with them we say, "This is not right: Good things happen to good people. Why should a good man suffer?"

The interesting thing about the Job story is that we, as readers, are given the bigger picture. We know that God has permitted Satan to test Job's integrity: Will Job turn against God because of his sufferings, or will he remain steadfast in his faithfulness?

One of the keys to understanding the larger purpose of the story is to put ourselves in Job's place. How would we respond if we were suddenly confronted with a great loss or reversal? Would we blame God? Would we despair of everything? Would we let our friends and family convince us that it was really our fault? We can only speculate about what would happen if we were suddenly put to the test. We should pray that we will keep our integrity intact even under the most difficult of circumstances.

Lowborn men are but a breath, the highborn are but a lie;

if weighed on a balance, they are nothing;

together they are only a breath.

—PSALM 62:9

VICTORY OVER DEATH

OUR RELATIONSHIP WITH God determines our relationship with time. When we attempt to live without God, we begin to battle time as we grow older, and we become conscious that, for each of us, time is a finite commodity. We begin to be fearful of every little thing, because time is slipping through our fingers like so much dust: "Man is a mere phantom as he goes to and fro: he bustles about, but only in vain; he heaps up wealth, not knowing who will get it" (Psalm 39:6).

Whether rich or poor, all men are propelled toward death, unless . . . unless we accept the promise of a strong and loving God. We have heard the promise: "For God so loved the world that he gave his one and only Son that whoever believes in him shall not perish but have eternal life" (John 3:16). Acknowledging the love of God through the gift of His Son opens the way to the gift that defeats time and death: "When the perishable has been clothed with the imperishable, and the mortal with immortality, then the saying that is written will come true: 'Death has been swallowed up in victory'" (1 Corinthians 15:54). But we must seek to open the door: "Ask, and it will be given to you; seek and you will find; knock, and it will be opened to you." (Matthew 7:7)

The law of the LORD is perfect, reviving the soul.
The statutes of the LORD are trustworthy, making wise the simple.
The precepts of the LORD are right, giving joy to the heart.
The commands of the LORD are radiant, giving light to the eyes.
The fear of the LORD is pure, enduring forever. The ordinances
of the LORD are sure and altogether righteous.

—PSALM 19:7–9

HIS INCREDIBLE GIFT

JESUS TELLS US, "Be perfect, therefore, as your heavenly Father is perfect" (Matthew 5:48). But how can we be perfect if we struggle with sin? We are let to wonder how we can ever get anywhere near the ideal when Paul says in writing about the power sin has over us, "for I do not do what I want, but the evil I do not want is what I keep on doing." (Romans 7:19). Without grace, we are stuck and depressed.

Listen, though, to the Psalmist. He is pointing to the way that is perfect, trustworthy, wise, and simple. He is speaking of a heart filled with joy. He is praising someone who has infinitely more value than gold. He is speaking of the one who will come after him to recover a people lost wandering in life's barren regions.

He is speaking of Jesus, the healer of all wounds, the giver of hope, the way to life eternal, the Son of God. Jesus asks only one thing in return for the incredible gift He wants to bestow: "Do you love me?" (John 21:17). If we have it in our hearts to say yes to his question, then we will also want to love the laws, commands, and precepts of God. And then we can say with true joy, "thanks be to God through Jesus Christ our Lord!" (Romans 7:25)

The visions of your prophets were false and worthless;

they did not expose your sin to ward off your captivity.

The oracles they gave you were false and misleading.

—LAMENTATIONS 2:14

FALSE PROPHETS?

WE LIVE IN dangerous times. False prophets are preaching everywhere. Whether radical clerics in the Middle East or the notorious Jim Jones in Guyana in the 1970s, false prophets are declaring death to infidels or claiming the world has entered end times.

The phenomenon is not new. False prophets are found throughout the Bible. Jesus warns, "Watch out for false prophets. They come to you in sheep's clothing, but inwardly they are ferocious wolves" (Matthew 7:15).

Over six hundred years before Jesus, Jeremiah spoke about how the false prophets and priests have brought corruption and trouble to the land: "'The prophets follow an evil course and use their power unjustly. Both prophet and priest are godless; even in my temple I find their wickedness,' declares the Lord" (Jeremiah 23:10–11).

In times such as these, it is especially difficult to filter the false from the true. We hear so many claims, many sounding legitimate, but John in his first letter does tell us how to test the spirit of truth. "This is how you can recognize the Spirit of God: Every spirit that acknowledges that Jesus Christ has come in the flesh is from God, but every spirit that does not acknowledge Jesus is not from God. This is the spirit of the antichrist, which you have heard is coming and even now is already in the world" (1 John 4:2–3).

Blessed is the man who finds wisdom, the man who gains
understanding, for she is more profitable than silver and yields
better returns than gold. She is more precious than rubies;
nothing you desire can compare with her.

—PROVERBS 3:13–15

THE POWER OF GOD

THOSE WHO CLAIM to possess special "insider" knowledge of the mind of God are in danger of placing themselves in opposition to the will of God. Instead of walking in step with God, they jump out in front of Him in an attempt to get God to walk behind them. But this raises a question: Is it possible to build a life in step with God's purpose? If we are to find the good ways that lead to peace and if we desire to gain access to the tree of life, then our wisdom will come through reconciliation, not rebellion.

Christians believe that this reconciliation comes only through the cross of Christ: "For God was pleased to have all his fullness dwell in him, and through him to reconcile to himself all things, whether things on earth or things in heaven, by making peace through his blood shed on the cross" (Colossians 1:19–20).

To the world, the cross of Christ is foolishness, but to those who believe, it is the wisdom of God: "For the message of the cross is foolishness to those who are perishing, but to those of us who are being saved it is the power of God" (1 Corinthians 1:18).

Men do not despise a thief if he steals to satisfy his hunger when he is starving. Yet if he is caught, he must pay sevenfold, though it costs him all the wealth of his house. But a man who commits adultery lacks judgment; whoever does so destroys himself. Blows and disgrace are his lot, and his shame will never be wiped away; for jealousy arouses a husband's fury, and he will show no mercy when he takes revenge. He will not accept any compensation; he will refuse the bribe, however great it is.

—PROVERBS 6:30–35

THE ONLY GENUINE FRUIT OF LOVE

STEALING AND ADULTERY are both forms of theft, but the degrees of seriousness of the two crimes are worlds apart. If caught, the thief will face punishment. But the writer says that "men will not despise (him) if he steals to satisfy his hunger when he is starving."

According to the writer, though, no such quarter is given the one who steals a wife. The adulterer may offer excuses, but he "lacks judgment," and his crime will often lead to lies, dissension, and sometimes even murder. Adultery fractures; it does not unite.

How often do we hear the sad lament of the adulterer who, amidst the ruins of his life, claims that he did it all for love? But if this is true, why does "the eye of the adulterer [watch] for dusk?" Why does he think, "No eye will see me?" And why does he keep "his face concealed?" (Job 24:15).

Love is never about betrayal or stealing. The fruit of love is patience, kindness, protection, trust, hope, and perseverance. Adultery is about theft; the only genuine fruit it is bound to produce is the sorrow of strife.

Unless the LORD builds the house, its builders labor in vain.

Unless the LORD watches over the city, the watchmen stand

guard in vain. In vain you rise early and stay up late, toiling for

food to eat—for he grants sleep to those he loves.

—PSALM 127:1–2

WHAT ABOUT YOU? WHAT ABOUT ME?

SAUL IS A righteous Jew, a Pharisee, instructed in the letter of the law. He has determined that he must destroy the troublesome Christian sect that is causing turmoil in Jerusalem and beyond. He has gained the permission of the high priests to go to Damascus to find and arrest the agitators and bring them back to Jerusalem in chains.

Saul has the authority of the high priests behind him. He has the force of the Hebrew law supporting him, but he is fruitlessly laboring against the will of God. On the way to Damascus, he is stopped by a blinding light and he hears a voice: "Saul, Saul, why do you persecute me?" (Acts 9:4). From that time on, Saul (who would become known as Paul) begins to labor mightily as an apostle of Christ. Until that flash of light near Damascus, Saul was a builder laboring in vain. He was the watchman standing guard over Judaism in vain.

God had a purpose for Paul as He has a purpose for each one of us. But to work within that purpose, we need to stop working against the will of God. Paul was transformed into an apostle by his encounter with Jesus.

What about you? What about me? Are we, like Saul, builders laboring in vain? Or are we fulfilling God's purpose by working within His will rather than against it?

The elders are gone from the city gate; the young men have
stopped their music. Joy is gone from our hearts; our dancing
has turned to mourning. The crown has fallen from our
head. Woe to us, for we have sinned! Because of this our hearts
are faint, because of these things our eyes grow dim for Mount
Zion, which lies desolate, with jackals prowling over it.

—LAMENTATIONS 5:14–18

THE DAY OF RECKONING

WHY HAS JERUSALEM, David's city, fallen into the hands of its enemies? The answer: "We have sinned!" This great city, so favored by God, has turned away in favor of corruption, violence, and strife. "Destructive forces are at work in the city; threats and lies never leave its streets" (Psalm 55:11).

Isaiah had warned what would come: "Woe to those who make unjust laws, to those who issue oppressive decrees, to deprive the poor of their rights and withhold justice from the oppressed of my people, making widows their prey and robbing the fatherless" (Isaiah 10:1–2). To those who pervert justice he says, "What will you do on the day of reckoning, when disaster comes from afar? To whom will you run for help? Where will you leave your riches?" (Isaiah 10:3).

The leaders of Jerusalem had abandoned their God given heritage. Through Moses, God provided a promise and a warning: "See, I set before you today life and prosperity, death and destruction. . . . This day I call heaven and earth as witnesses against you that I have set before you life and death, blessings and curses. Now choose life, so that you and your children may live and that you may love the Lord your God, listen to his voice and hold fast to him. For the LORD is your life." (Deuteronomy 30:15, 19–20).

When the Lord is cast aside, the city of God will become a city of man. When this happens, desolation, death, and exile cannot be far off.

No king is saved by the size of his army; no warrior escapes
by his great strength . . . But the eyes of the LORD are on those
who fear him, on those whose hope is in his unfailing love, to
deliver them from death and keep them alive in famine.

—PSALM 33:16, 18–19

THE LORD IS MY STRENGTH

IT IS HARD not to be impressed by the stature of a prince or king or president. He is surrounded by his armies and protected by his staff. When he speaks, the people listen; when he is angered, people tremble. And yet the strongest leader in the greatest nation is nothing compared to the strength of God: "For the foolishness of God is wiser than man's wisdom, and the weakness of God is stronger than man's strength" (1 Corinthians 1:25). David says, "It is God who arms me with strength and makes my way perfect" (2 Samuel 22:33).

We can easily confuse the strength God confers on men with a human strength. Stalin, at the height of his power in the Soviet Union, reportedly asked with an air of sarcasm, "Where are the Pope's armies?" We might ask the same question today, but only in reverse: "Where is Stalin? Where is the Soviet Union? Where are the statues? Where are the adoring crowds?"

In the end, Stalin and others like him proved by their own mortality to be merely human. It is clear Stalin did not lean on the Lord for his strength and his salvation and that all the monuments and statues built to commemorate his greatness and grandeur sat as ironic silent sentinels on the day of his death. When a leader shows genuine humility and displays, through his actions, wisdom, and temperance, then it is highly probable that this leader knows where his strength comes from.

Two are better than one, because they have a good return
for their work: If one falls down, his friend can help him up.
But pity the man who falls and has no one to help him up! . . .
A cord of three strands is not quickly broken.

—ECCLESIASTES 4:9–10, 12

A WALK IN THE WOODS

I ENJOY HIKING in the woods alone. On one particular trip, the trail took me up to a ridge on a low-lying mountain range in central Pennsylvania. On such trips, the familiar noises of civilization can often be heard: the distant rumble of a passing freight train or the subtle hum of an interstate or just the low-grade sounds of distant activity filtering up to the trail.

But on this particular day everything was different, for as I moved further along the rocky path, I began to notice the absence of sound. The feeling of isolation became palpable, and the sense of sudden vulnerability crept into my thoughts.

It is at times like this that one can feel a deep appreciation for the power of two. If I had fallen while alone, I would have been in trouble, but if a companion had been with me, I would have been helped. If I had become lost, my friend would have assisted in finding the way back to the trail. Alone, my chances of success would have been greatly diminished.

This noiseless world, beautiful and intriguing as it was, left me with a feeling of aloneness and mild foreboding. Quite suddenly, a bunch of "what ifs" flooded into my thinking and it seemed like I had stumbled into a world outside of God's design. I strongly felt the need for a companion. So while the walk was memorable, I was relieved, in the end, to hear all the familiar sounds of human activity once again. For to me these noises were the sound of friendship and safety. It even occurred to me that the noises from below were the sounds of love. It felt good to be back.

My eyes will be on the faithful in the land, that they may
dwell with me; he whose walk is blameless will minister to me.
No one who practices deceit will dwell in my house;
no one who speaks falsely will stand in my presence.

—PSALM 101:6–7

KNOWING GOD

WHAT DOES GENUINE faith look like? Can it be associated with advanced degrees in theology? Perhaps. Can faith be perceived through moving oratory? Maybe. Or can faith be found in someone who does good works day in and day out? I think that is very possible.

But all of these things—theology, oratory, and works—are not the source but are rather the out-workings from the source. The source for Christians is belief in the truthfulness of the evidence contained in the New Testament. Christ's words and the word of his witnesses serve as a window through which we can answer Jesus' question to his disciples: "But who do you say that I am?" (Matthew 16:15).

Faith for Christians is faith in the Lordship of Jesus Christ. In His own time and in ours, the world seems to believe in almost anything but Jesus Christ. So faith in Christ asks us to be strong and courageous, for we can anticipate being disregarded, confronted, and scorned, but that should never be a surprise. Even many of Jesus' own disciples became discouraged and abandoned Him (John 6:66).

The world provides many things for us to believe in, but God provided His Son, Jesus Christ, only once. He did His part. Now it is up to us. Will we believe or shall we put our faith and our trust in something or someone else? The Gospels serve as the best way to answer Jesus' question to his own disciples: "But who do you say that I am?"

Speak up for those who cannot speak for themselves,
for the rights of all who are destitute. Speak up and judge
fairly; defend the rights of the poor and needy.

—PROVERBS 31:8–9

⊷

THE RIGHTEOUS KING'S EXAMPLE

POLITICIANS OFTEN QUOTE Scripture for self-serving purposes. How wonderful and rare it is when a political leader actually serves those who cannot speak for themselves or do not have the money or power to gain access to the corridors of power. More frequently, politicians claim allegiance to the poor and the needy while making deals to line their own corrupt pockets with the powerful groups who do have access.

But the bad behavior of some does not negate the importance of this proverb. The ideal should always be the aim. But anyone attempting to pursue a political career must be realistic. From the first day in office, endless "special" interests with money and influence will cascade down upon the politician with relentless consistency. To withstand the onslaught, a politician needs strong principals, a clear vision, and a steadfast heart. And the best foundation to reinforce the great virtues of good leadership would be daily Bible study and prayer. The good political leader needs to be equipped to deal with all the temptations coming his or her way. They need to put on what Paul calls "the full armor of God." (Ephesians 6:10-20)

The LORD is my shepherd; I shall not be in want. He makes me
lie down in green pastures, he leads me beside quiet waters, he
restores my soul. He guides me in paths of righteousness for his
name's sake. Even though I walk through the valley of the shadow
of death, I will fear no evil, for you are with me; your rod and
your staff, they comfort me. You prepare a table before me in the
presence of my enemies. You anoint my head with oil; my cup
overflows. Surely goodness and love will follow me all the days
of my life, and I will dwell in the house of the LORD forever.

—PSALM 23:1–6

THE VALLEY OF THE SHADOW OF DEATH

UNTIL ONE CLEAR, bright September morning in 2001, it would be fair to say that America had taken a short vacation from history. The smaller matters of everyday life were paramount, with the nature of evil receding to an irrelevance, as chasing wealth seemed to become the only worthwhile obsession. America seemed to float in a sea of distractions until nineteen men exploded our national revelry in an instant.

By the end of that day, people were lighting candles all over America. People were praying in groups and individually. They were shocked out of their everyday lives and pursuits into a realization that something unexpected and terrible had happened. While television covered the unfolding events minute by minute, people understood that this time it was different. They could imagine the horror of being trapped in the World Trade Center or being a passenger on one of the four planes that had been used as weapons. At the same time, they could identify with Todd Beamer and the other heroes of Flight 93 out of Newark or the policemen and firefighters who risked everything to save some.

At a certain moment that day, millions of people were shocked out of the reveries of everyday life into a realization that something had changed and changed utterly. No one could say what that change might mean or be, but it is possible to imagine that millions called out to God that day from the valley of the shadow of death and for some, maybe for the first time in a long time.

My eyes fail from weeping, I am in torment within, my heart
is poured out on the ground because my people are destroyed,
because children and infants faint in the streets of the city.

—LAMENTATIONS 2:11

THE PEOPLE WOULD NOT LISTEN

IN 586 B.C., the fierce and powerful armies of Nebuchadnezzar finally overwhelmed the defenders of the city of David. Those who were not slaughtered immediately were led away in chains to live in exile in Babylon. A small and poor remnant was left behind, but the magnificent temple build by King Solomon was reduced to rubble.

The tragedy was not inevitable, however. The leaders and people of Jerusalem had heard the prophetic messages of Jeremiah and others, but they stubbornly disregarded God's warnings and continued to adhere to their own misguided and treacherous ways. Speaking through Jeremiah, the Lord says, "There is a conspiracy among the people of Judah and those who live in Jerusalem. They have returned to the sins of their forefathers, who refused to listen to my words. They have followed other gods to serve them. Both the house of Israel and the house of Judah have broken the covenant I made with their forefathers" (Jeremiah 11:9–10).

Tragically, the people of Jerusalem rejected the warning of their prophets who warned them against abandoning the God of their forefathers. They threatened Jeremiah with death if he continued to prophesy in the name of the Lord (Jeremiah 11:21).

If Jerusalem, or any other city or nation, abandons God, what are we to expect? God provided many clear warnings leading up to the final disaster, including this warning to Moses right before he died: "These people will soon prostitute themselves to the foreign gods of the land they are entering. They will forsake me and break the covenant I made with them. . . . I will certainly hide my face on that day because of all their wickedness in turning to other gods" (Deuteronomy 31:16, 18).

For men are not cast off by the Lord forever. Though he brings

grief, he will show compassion, so great is his unfailing love. For

he does not willingly bring affliction or grief to the children of men.

—LAMENTATIONS 3:31–33

SEIZE THE MOMENT

No grief equals the grief of being separated from God. After murdering his brother Abel, Cain is condemned and becomes "a restless wanderer on the earth" (Genesis 4:12). Cain cries out that this punishment of exile is more than he can bear: "I will be hidden from your presence" (Genesis 4:14).

Time and again, we hear the cry of despair of those who believe that they have lost their relationship with God forever. Peter breaks down in tears after denying the Lord the third time. Judas hangs himself after attempting to give back the thirty silver coins to the chief priests: "'I have sinned,' he said, 'for I have betrayed innocent blood'" (Matthew 27:4). Of the three, Peter, in his remorse, seeks the Lord's forgiveness and is forgiven. While all men sin, God is gracious to those who genuinely seek him.

David prays, "Have mercy on me, O God, according to your unfailing love, according to your great compassion blot out my transgressions. . . . Against you, you only, have I sinned and done what is evil in your sight . . ." (Psalm 51:1, 4). This prayer should be our prayer every day. God hears our plea, and His compassions are new every morning (Lamentations 3:22–23). Every morning we have a chance to renew our relationship with God. Every morning we should seize the moment.

Whoever loves money never has money enough; whoever loves
wealth is never satisfied with his income. This too is meaningless.
As goods increase, so do those who consume them.

—ECCLESIASTES 5:10–11

COME NEAR TO GOD

IT MIGHT BE said that whoever lusts after anything will never have enough. What begins as an inclination soon becomes a passion and finally ends as a consuming fire.

C. S. Lewis has spoken of hell as an act or desire that begins as something very small but, with time, expands into something that overwhelms the whole person to the point where there is no other reality. Once Satan has gained a foothold in our hearts, it is exceedingly difficult to shake him off. It is not wealth or money that corrupts and destroys; it is the lust for money that squeezes out the capacity to love anything else, especially God. Our sin becomes our sole obsession.

While we were created to enjoy fellowship with God, sinning will block that relationship. When we turn away from God to gain the treasures offered by this world, whatever they may be, we flee into the arms of the adversary. "Resist the devil, and he will flee from you. Come near to God and he will come near to you" (James 4:7–8).

Listen to your father, who gave you life, and do not despise
your mother when she is old . . . The father of a righteous man
has great joy; he who has a wise son delights in him.

—PROVERBS 23:22, 24

WHAT GOD WANTS FOR YOUR CHILDREN

WHAT DO PARENTS want for their children? Is it enough to desire that your child be obedient or successful in school or a star on the athletic fields? A better question might be: What does God want your child to be? A clue to the answer might be found in the following verse: "The father of a righteous man has great joy; he who has a wise son delights in him."

God does not ask parents to produce persuasive lawyers or great scholars or star athletes; this is what the *culture* may want. Paul instructs Timothy as a father would a son: "Pursue righteousness, godliness, faith, love, endurance and gentleness. Fight the good fight of the faith. Take hold of the eternal life to which you were called when you made your good confession in the presence of many witnesses" (1 Timothy 6:11–12).

Precious in the sight of the LORD is the death of his saints.

O LORD, truly I am your servant;

I am your servant, the son of your maidservant;

you have freed me from my chains.

—PSALM 116:15–16

A DANGEROUS MISSION

EVEN BEFORE WE face physical death, as children of God, we have been called to die to the cravings and passions that grow out of our desires for many of the things of this world. "If anyone would come after me, he must deny himself and take up his cross daily and follow me. For whoever wants to save his life will lose it, but whoever loses his life for me will save it" (Luke 9:23–24).

If we do not allow transformation of the passions that grow out of the yearnings of the sinful nature, then a very real conflict will continue to create turmoil in our hearts, especially when God calls us to His purpose. As Christians, we are called out of fear for our life to be "strong and courageous" (Joshua 1:6); and to "stand [our] ground, and after [we] have done everything, to stand" (Ephesians 6:14). When we become disciples, we are embarking on difficult missions in a hostile world, but we should remember that we are not alone: In God we place our trust. And it gives us comfort to know that our "brothers throughout the world are undergoing the same kind of sufferings" (1 Peter 5:9).

If I have denied justice to my menservants and maidservants
when they had a grievance against me, what will I do when God
confronts me? What will I answer when called to account?

—JOB 31:13–14

CONFRONTED BY GOD

"DO NOT BE deceived: God cannot be mocked" (Galatians 6:7). Yet we live as if God is not close. We would like to believe we can cover up our petty crimes in the darkness of night, where eyes cannot see nor ears hear the work of our folly. But while we can deceive ourselves into believing that we are independent of God, we cannot deceive the one who made us: "From heaven the LORD looks down and sees all mankind; from his dwelling place he watches all who live on earth—he who forms the heart of all, who considers everything they do" (Psalm 33:13–15).

So much of anxiety, stress, and sorrow comes from the misapprehension that we are free to perpetrate our favorite indulgences. We say in our hearts, "Who will see us, who will hear us, who will know?" Instead, we might ask Job's question: "What will I do when God confronts me?"

The woman Folly is loud; she is undisciplined and without knowledge . . . "Stolen water is sweet; food eaten in secret is delicious!" But little do they know that the dead are there, that her guests are in the depths of the grave.

—PROVERBS 9:13, 17–18

BEING STALKED

THE FOOL DOES not seek a woman of noble character; rather, he would prefer to keep the company of prostitutes. He does not hear the call of wisdom that cries out: "To you, O men, I call out; I raise my voice to all mankind. You who are simple, gain prudence; you who are foolish, gain understanding. . . . My mouth speaks what is true, for my lips detest wickedness" (Proverbs 8:4–5, 7).

The fool abandons God for the sweetness of "stolen water" and the delicious taste of "food eaten in secret." And in abandoning God (who forever is calling out to every hidden corner of the earth), the fool turns away to embrace that which will only bring him trouble. The folly of the fool is to discount the dangers lurking all around him. He stalks his prey unarmed, not realizing that it is he who is being stalked. Recognizing the danger is the first step of those who are prudent. "I love those who love me, and those who seek me find me" (Proverbs 8:17).

Listen to my prayer, O God, do not ignore my plea; hear me and
answer me. My thoughts trouble me and I am distraught at the
voice of the enemy, at the stares of the wicked; for they bring
down suffering upon me and revile me in their anger.

—PSALM 55:1–3

ELIJAH

THE MAN OF God lives under a constant threat of danger and strife. Elijah is one of the great prophets, a true man of God, but King Ahab calls him a "troubler of Israel" (1 Kings 18:17).

The king has married Jezebel, who worships Baal, and she has set out to kill all the prophets of the Lord. When Elijah confronts her and exposes her four hundred and fifty corrupt prophets for who they are, Jezebel swears an oath on his life: "May the gods deal with me, be it ever so severely, if by this time tomorrow I do not make your life like that of one of them" (1 Kings 19:2).

Elijah escapes into the wastelands, but soon he despairs and prays to God to take his life. It is then that a miracle happens. At his lowest moment, an angel appears and tells him to eat and gain strength and then go to Horeb, the mountain of God. Shortly after this, he hears the voice of God as a gentle whisper in the wind. And it is then that he is told to go and find Elisha so that together they can continue to do God's work of restoring the Lord's place in Israel.

In fulfilling the purpose of God as children of God, we are promised difficulties, and even persecution: "Blessed are those who are persecuted because of righteousness, for theirs is the kingdom of heaven. Blessed are you when people insult you, persecute you and falsely say all kinds of evil against you because of me" (Matthew 5:10–11). No matter what the circumstance may be, we are called to persevere.

There are three things that are stately in their stride,
four that move with stately bearing: a lion, mighty among beasts,
who retreats before nothing; a strutting rooster, a he-goat,
and a king with his army around him.

—PROVERBS 30:29–31

KING OF KINGS

HERE IS THE king with his powerful army, clad in his armor, surrounded by his generals and lieutenants, and ready for war. The king is powerful, and he impresses with his stately bearing. Any other image of the king would seem to be inappropriate, unless, of course, the king reversed our preconception of what it means to be a genuine king.

In fact, another king does appear who does not have "a stately bearing." He may be "KING OF KINGS AND LORD OF LORDS" (Revelation 19:16), but "he had no beauty or majesty to attract us to him, nothing in his appearance that we should desire him. He was despised and rejected by men, a man of sorrows, and familiar with suffering. Like one from whom men hide their faces he was despised, and we esteemed him not" (Isaiah 53:2–3).

He is the King who says, "If anyone wants to be first, he must be the very last, and the servant of all" (Mark 9:35). He is the King who "made himself nothing," and who "humbled himself and became obedient to death—even death on a cross" (Philippians 2:7–8).

It is Jesus who gives us something that no earthly king can give—eternal life. Here is a king who has descended into an "unbelieving and perverse generation" (Matthew 17:17), not to condemn the world but to save it.

How many are your works, O LORD! In wisdom you made
them all; the earth is full of your creatures. There is the sea,
vast and spacious, teeming with creatures beyond number—
living things both large and small. There the ships go to and fro,
and the leviathan, which you formed to frolic there.

—PSALM 104:24–26

THINGS TOO WONDERFUL FOR ME

How EASY IT is to peer at the world and see only as far as the narrowness of our own imaginations will allow! Rather than the stress and strain of mystery, we choose the safety of simplicity, transforming a brilliant full color picture into a plain black and white two-dimensional image.

In this passage, intimations of the complexities of the canvas are suggested: "There is the sea, vast and spacious, teeming with creatures beyond number—living things both large and small." When the element of mystery is removed, we are reduced to "explanations" that elucidate very little. Our current approach to understanding the world would suggest that the human mind can formulate a theory of everything, whereas the truth can only be approached if we abide in the mystery of creation and the mystery of the Creator.

"The Lord answered Job out of the storm. He said, 'Who is this that darkens my counsel with words without knowledge. Brace yourself like a man; I will question you, and you shall answer me. Where were you when I laid the earth's foundation? Tell me, if you understand'" (Job 38:2–4). After being presented with countless unanswerable questions, Job submits to the Lord: "Surely I spoke of things I did not understand, things too wonderful for me to know" (Job 42:3).

Wisdom begins by acknowledging the mystery that exists at the center of life and of our lives: "It is the glory of God to conceal a matter . . ." (Proverbs 25:2).

There is not a righteous man on earth who does
what is right and never sins.

—ECCLESIASTES 7:20

THE SELF-RIGHTEOUS HOLY MAN

SOLOMON STATES A hard truth: all men sin, including the best and brightest among us. No one is exempt, and to argue otherwise is to deny the reality of biblical revelation. Yet we persist in the blindness of our own pride by proclaiming our own righteousness to anyone who is foolish enough to listen.

Jesus tells the parable of the holy man and the tax collector. Whereas the tax collector simply prays, "God, have mercy on me a sinner," the holy man looks down his imperious nose and declares: "God, I thank you that I am not like other men—robbers, evildoers, adulterers—or even like this tax collector. I fast twice a week and give a tenth of all I get" (Luke 18:10–13).

The holy man is not righteous in the eyes of God, but self-righteous. He is denying the reality of sin in his own life yet sees sin in others. Jesus always sees the difference and says so to His disciples: "I tell you that this man [the tax collector] went home justified before God. For everyone who exalts himself will be humbled, and he who humbles himself will be exalted" (Luke 18:14).

He who robs his father and drives out his mother is a son who brings shame and disgrace. Stop listening to instruction, my son, and you will stray from the words of knowledge.

—PROVERBS 19:26–27

HONOR YOUR FATHER AND MOTHER

PARENTS KNOW THAT obedience is a choice a child may or may not exercise. Also, most of us realize that disobedience is characteristic of behavior that many carry well into adult life.

The command to honor your father and your mother was given to Moses by God, but even while Moses was receiving the Ten Commandments, disobedience reigned among the Jewish people at the base of Mount Sinai. And as the people of Israel would soon learn, choosing to break God's natural law is an invitation to chaos, not peace.

When we disobey, whether as children or as adults, we disrupt the natural order and harmony that flows from obedience. Hatred and discord replace love and trust, and the most intimate familial relationships are torn asunder. When a son dishonors his father and mother, that son is establishing shame and disgrace as the central condition of the relationship, with only sorrow and suffering binding together parent and child. We see it everywhere, but the great commandment of love reminds us that disobedience is not from God, but from us.

The fear of the LORD is the beginning of wisdom;
all who follow his precepts have good understanding.
To him belongs eternal praise.

—PSALM 111:10

THE TRUTH IS A PERSON

TO THE PSALMIST, "fear" means that we acknowledge and submit to the reality of God as the author of all creation. If we live a life built on this firm belief in God, then we open our eyes to the reality that everything comes from God.

We also bridle our own inclination to place ourselves at the center of all things by seeing the reality of our own existence in relationship to the utter immensity of God. The very nature of God cannot be circumscribed by time or space. God's nature is eternal, and genuine human wisdom perceives, even if dimly, that truth.

John begins his gospel by declaring the Word was before all time and has now come to earth in the person of Jesus Christ: "In the beginning was the Word, and the Word was with God, and the Word was God. He was with God in the beginning" (John 1:1). This passage builds on the Genesis account of creation: "In the beginning God created the heavens and the earth" (Genesis 1:1). God pre-existed the heavens and the earth, as did the Word, and as did His Son, Jesus Christ, who says, "And now, Father, glorify me in your presence with the glory I had with you before the world began" (John 17:5).

For the LORD will vindicate his people and have compassion

on his servants. The idols of the nations are silver and gold,

made by the hands of men. They have mouths, but cannot speak,

eyes, but they cannot see; they have ears, but cannot hear,

nor is there breath in their mouths.

—PSALM 135:14–17

MADE TO WORSHIP

IN HIS BOOK, *The Purpose Driven Life*, Rick Warren tells us that man is made for worship. Even if we were isolated on a desert island, cut off from all the world, we would still feel an ache in our hearts to worship something.

But who or what do we choose to worship? It can be just as dangerous to worship something other than God as it is to attempt to worship nothing at all. This psalm warns against the worship of man-made idols.

Idols are merely "gods" built by human hands. They satisfy our need to worship, but only on the most superficial level. God wants us to worship Him and nothing else. He warns us away from the inclination to worship something just because we find comfort in it. God gave Moses Ten Commandments, but the first four deal exclusively with our relationship with Him: *You shall have no other gods but me; you shall not make idols to worship; you shall not misuse my name; and you shall set aside one day to rest and to worship me.*

In America today, the Ten Commandments are controversial. Groups bring lawsuits to have the Commandments removed from public buildings, schools, and courthouses. It is hard to imagine people objecting to "Do not steal" and "Do not murder," but in all probability the last six Commandments are not what gives offense. Clearly it is the mention of God, a supernatural God, that causes so many people to object. They want God out of the public view, which is neither new nor surprising. But one has to wonder what the replacement will be. Surely these deniers have a substitute in mind. Or on second thought, perhaps they do not.

Though my father and mother forsake me,
the LORD will receive me . . . I am still confident of this:
I will see the goodness of the LORD in the land of the living.
Wait for the LORD; be strong and take heart and wait for the LORD.

—PSALM 27:10, 13–14

BE STRONG, BE PATIENT

WHY DO YOU need to be strong in order to wait for the Lord? Here is one reason: God is not the God of instant gratification. In another context, He says through Isaiah, "Neither are your ways my ways" (Isaiah 55:8). He will use us and deliver us when it is His will to do so and not before.

Thus, Joseph languishes in prison accused of a crime he never committed until the time was right for his release. Moses escapes into the desert for forty years before being called by God to return to deliver his people from bondage. And even though at the age of twelve, Jesus amazed the teachers and scribes with his depth of knowledge, he was not ready for another eighteen years to begin his ministry. In fact, even during his short three-year ministry, his true purpose kept being delayed for "his time had not yet come" (John 7:30).

So we should take heart: the Bible says that God will work His purpose in our lives. We need to call upon Him in prayer while exercising patience, even if our circumstances are difficult and no clear path is seen. This is why, in waiting for the Lord, we should be strong and steadfast.

It is not good to have zeal without knowledge,
nor to be hasty and miss the way.

—PROVERBS 19:2

THE FRUIT OF THEIR ZEAL

THE LAST CENTURY was the century of the political zealot; it was a time of enormous upheaval, savage wars, and fanatical beliefs. The political leaders who brought civilization to a boil were zealous to establish a new political order and were willing to sacrifice millions of citizens to see their bloody vision to its logical end.

Whether it was Stalin, starving whole populations in Ukraine; or Hitler, massacring defenseless men, women, and children in prison camps; or Pol Pot, destroying a large percentage of the population of Cambodia, the fruit of their zeal was terror, torture, and death. They were zealous, but they lacked wisdom. They substituted their own heretical beliefs for God's eternal truth, so they were bound to fail.

Zeal delinked from God is a deadly weapon. The fruit harvested by the twentieth-century political zealot is there for all to see. Tens of millions of people were essentially murdered to make way for a cruel new world order. The fruit of all their labor was war, murder, starvation, and torture.

When the believer in Jesus loses his or her passion for the Lord, he or she creates a vacuum that will be inevitably be filled by something else. "Then (the evil spirit) goes and brings with it seven other spirits more evil than itself, and they enter and dwell there, and the last state of that person is worse than the first." (Matthew 12:45)

Who is like the wise man? Who knows the explanation of things?
Wisdom brightens a man's face and changes its hard appearance.

—ECCLESIASTES 8:1

HE OPENED THE SCRIPTURES TO US

THE ASSOCIATION OF wisdom, light, and God is never more evident than when the two travelers, despondent over the terrible events in Jerusalem, suddenly discover that the Lord has been walking with them to Emmaus. Their reaction confirms that the wisdom of God indeed brightens a man's face through his awakened heart: "Were not our hearts burning within us while he talked with us on the road and opened the Scriptures to us?" (Luke 24:32).

Wisdom and light are both essential attributes of God. John says, "God is light; in him there is no darkness at all" (1 John 1:5). The very first words of God in the creation story are, "Let there be light" (Genesis 1:3), and Jesus says, "This is the verdict: Light has come into the world, but men loved darkness instead of light because their deeds were evil" (John 3:19).

He who rejects can be said to reject God's eternal wisdom and so he lives in darkness. But he who embraces God embraces wisdom and light: "The path of the righteous is like the first gleam of dawn, shining ever brighter till the full light of day" (Proverbs 4:18).

Like a coating of glaze over earthenware are fervent lips with an
evil heart. A malicious man disguises himself with his lips, but
in his heart he harbors deceit. Though his speech is charming,
do not believe him, for seven abominations fill his heart.

—PROVERBS 26:23–25

MALICIOUS INTENT

MALICE IS MOST effective when it wears a friendly mask. The heart of the malicious man may be boiling with hatred, but revealing the truth of his corruption would take the edge off the sweetness of his dark intent. On the surface, he appears to be a close friend: "My companion attacks his friends; he violates his covenant. His speech is smooth as butter, yet war is in his heart; his words are more soothing than oil, yet they are drawn swords" (Psalm 55:20–21).

The man who gives his life over to serving God is especially susceptible to the malice of the wicked. David prays for deliverance from his enemies: "Those who seek my life set their traps, those who would harm me talk of my ruin; all day long they plot deception. . . . Many are those who are my vigorous enemies; those who hate me without reason are numerous" (Psalm 38:12, 19).

From the earliest days of his ministry, Jesus is under attack from Satan and from his acolytes, the religious leaders of Israel, and even from members of his own family.

The world will often go to great lengths to cover up its own darker designs. We are warned to be alert, to be fully armed, and to know God's Word, for we will often find ourselves operating behind enemy lines where we are in danger of the forces of subversion at any time.

A man who loves wisdom brings joy to his father,

but a companion of prostitutes squanders his wealth.

—PROVERBS 29:3

ONCE LOST, NOW FOUND

IT IS HARD to read this verse and not imagine that Jesus had it in mind when He told the parable of the lost son. On one level, the parable is about a young man who receives an inheritance from his father but lacks wisdom and goes far away from home and "squandered his wealth in wild living" (Luke 15:13).

You might think that the story would end here with the good son inheriting the father's estate, while the bad son receives the severe punishment he deserves. But Jesus turns the tables on our expectations. Instead, the disobedient son repents of his profligate life and returns home, completely humiliated and expecting nothing from his father: "The son said to him, 'Father, I have sinned against heaven and against you. I am no longer worthy to be called your son'" (Luke 15:21).

With that, the father immediately accepts this son back into the household, just as God the Father accepts His own lost children when they genuinely turn back and say, "I have sinned against you." The father expresses emphatic joy at having his son back: "For this son of mine was dead and is alive again; he was lost and is found" (Luke 15:24). The Father wants all of His lost children back. And He is ready to celebrate when He sees we have turned back to Him.

There is a way that seems right to a man,
but in the end it leads to death.

—PROVERBS 14:12

WHITE BLAZES

DON AND I had a late start the night before. Touches of winter were in the air even though we were only in the first week of October. By the time we reached Baldpate Shelter, it was night. Others were there preparing for bed, and soon, we too were in our sleeping bags.

The trail in Maine is rough; it is often wet, steep, and rocky. And the hiker also needs to stay alert for moose who occasionally use the trail as a pathway as they forage for food. Around noon, Don and I reached the summit of Baldpate; we spent about an hour there appreciating the fall landscape far below.

From there we descended sharply into Frye Notch. We stopped at a lean-to for a quick lunch and water refill. Don went to fill up his water bottle first; then, as I started to walk down to the stream, he pushed off to ascend Surplus Mountain. I was more concerned about water and paid no attention to Don leaving. But after I packed up, I noticed that two trails departed north from the shelter and neither had any markings. I looked at my map, but it gave no indication that two trails existed.

The Appalachian Trail is well known for its white blazes. Usually these markers are painted on trees every few hundred feet. They are essential for the hiker because often several trails can converge. Without a blaze or some kind of marker, the hiker would be reduced to guessing what way was the right way.

I had no idea which way Don had gone. If I chose the wrong way, I would be heading away from him. Or perhaps he chose the wrong path. If I was wrong, would he continue ahead or come back? Phones did not work, so it was possible that we would end up spending many frustrating hours trying to find each other.

I became troubled because I had to make a choice, which could easily be wrong. I started up the trail to the right, as it seemed more worn. As I ascended, I cried out several times only to be answered by the still silence of the Maine woods. Where are the blazes? Where is Don? Is he up ahead or back at the shelter? Suddenly, I doubted the rightness of every step. I felt lost, and I was angry that I had briefly let my guard down back at the shelter.

Jeremiah 6:16 says, "Stand at the crossroads and look. . ." Almost every day brings us to one or more crossroads. I was careless that October day in the woods of Maine, and I almost took the wrong way. As it turned out, I had made the right decision. Don was at the summit of Surplus Mountain. My worries dissipated, and we moved on to the next challenge.

Blessed is he whose transgressions are forgiven,
whose sins are covered. Blessed is the man whose sin the LORD
does not count against him and in whose spirit is no
deceit. When I kept silent, my bones wasted away through my
groaning all day long. For day and night your hand was heavy
upon me; my strength was sapped as in the heat of summer.
Then I acknowledged my sin to you and did not cover up my
iniquity. I said, "I will confess my transgressions to the LORD"—
and you forgave the guilt of my sin.

—PSALM 32:1–5

A HEAVY BURDEN

SIN IS AN affliction that is powerful enough to bring on physical pain and suffering. "When I kept silent, my bones wasted away. . ."

When a paralytic is lowered on a mat through a roof, Jesus does not play the ordinary doctor by checking the physical source of the disease; rather He simply says, "Son, your sins are forgiven" (Mark 2:5). All we know of this afflicted man is what we are told in the Gospel account. Jesus pronounced him forgiven and he immediately recovered. Are we living like the paralyzed man on a mat, debilitated by a life of unacknowledged sin? Are we carrying around a burden that we cannot possibly bear alone? The Psalmist tells us exactly what we must do to become well: "Then I acknowledged my sin to you and did not cover up my iniquity . . . and you forgave the guilt of my sin."

Many of us deceive ourselves by claiming we have not sinned, and consequently, the symptoms of our afflictions appear to be untreatable. There is a "doctor" who can cure the spiritual source of our paralysis. Jesus is that "doctor." "Those who are well have no need for a physician, but those who are sick. I have not come to call the righteous but sinners to repentance." (Luke 5:31-32)

May God be gracious to us and bless us and make his face
shine upon us, that your ways may be known on earth,
your salvation among all nations.

—PSALM 67:1–2

THE WORK OF AN EVANGELIST

OFTEN WE PRAY for our own well-being: "O, Lord, deliver me from this disease," or "Lord, save me from financial ruin." Of course, it is perfectly right to pray for safety in a dangerous world or for financial or physical deliverance when our well-being is threatened. However, it is a far greater act to pray for what this sorrowful and "crooked and twisted generation" (Philippians 2:15) really needs by asking that God's "ways may be known on earth, [his] salvation among all nations."

The heart of God is love, and when we come to know this through God's grace, we are called out to share his love with the rest of the world, particularly with those who have not yet heard of God's goodness and graciousness. Jesus calls His disciples to "go and make disciples of all nations . . ." (Matthew 28:19). He commands us to make His ways known to all nations near and far. As Paul tells Timothy: "Endure hardship, do the work of an evangelist, discharge all the duties of your ministry" (2 Timothy 4:5).

The righteous will flourish like a palm tree, they will grow
like a cedar of Lebanon; planted in the house of the LORD,
they will flourish in the courts of our God.

—PSALM 92:12–13

SPIRITUAL WARFARE

THE SPIRITUAL BATTLE was finally won on the cross on Calvary, but at times it seems as though the wicked are in ascendance—for the enemy is a guerilla fighter, cunning and vicious and capable of appearing to be counted among the upright. He often adapts the guise of being the holiest of men, though hidden from view is a heart full of malice. And he has troops willingly working under his command: "These people come near to me with their mouth and honor me with their lips, but their hearts are far from me. Their worship of me is made up only of rules taught by men. . . . Woe to those who go to great depths to hide their plans from the LORD, who do their work in darkness and think, 'Who sees us? Who will know?'" (Isaiah 29:13, 15).

On the other side are those who have been transformed through God's grace and over whom darkness does not prevail. No matter the circumstance, the righteous will flourish even when the situation appears to be hopeless. "He is like a tree planted by streams of water, which yields its fruit in season and whose leaf does not wither" (Psalm 1:3).

While the righteous might prefer a tranquil and sequestered life, God is calling them into his service. If you count yourself as one of the righteous doing your part in advancing the kingdom, ask yourself this: Are we ready? Are we willing? You have heard God's call; are you prepared to join?

Two things I ask of you, O LORD; do not refuse me before I die:
Keep falsehood and lies far from me; give me neither poverty nor
riches, but give me only my daily bread. Otherwise, I may have
too much and disown you and say, "Who is the LORD?" Or I may
become poor and steal, and so dishonor the name of my God.

—PROVERBS 30:7–9

APPETITES

WE IN THE west live in a time of extravagant prosperity, and many of us have forgotten what it means to pray for our daily bread. Abundance can be a good thing, but when we forget the source of our good fortune, we are tempted to satisfy our own appetites by wanting more and more of whatever it is we desire. Here the writer recognizes the temptation to attribute our abundance to our own success, which inevitably causes us to begin to drift away from God. Our appetite for things begins to drive out our appetite for God.

To be human is to have appetites; the question is: will we fill our hearts, minds, and bodies with an unquenchable appetite for God? "But if we have food and clothing, we will be content with that. People who want to get rich fall into temptation and a trap and into many foolish and harmful desires that plunge men into ruin and destruction. For the love of money is the root of all kinds of evil. Some people, eager for money, have wandered from the faith and pierced themselves with many griefs" (1 Timothy 6:8–10). There is danger in indulging our appetites for money and the things money will buy, for then we find it increasingly difficult to seek the spiritual food we need that is a life-giving source of health for our souls.

He will defend the afflicted among the people and save the
children of the needy; he will crush the oppressor. He will endure
as long as the sun, as long as the moon, through all generations.

—PSALM 72:4–5

FAITH IS OUR JOB

THE AUTHOR OF Hebrews says, "Now faith is being sure of what we hope for and certain of what we do not see" (Hebrews 11:1). When faith is absent, darkness, despair, and depression flood in, cutting us off from the future by incapacitating us in the present with foreboding.

Read this passage from Psalms as a statement of truth and faith. The truth is God exists and existed before time and "he will endure . . . through all generations." Faith is our job. We need to live with the belief that God will care for us, day in and day out. He will defend the afflicted and crush the oppressor. Even if our backs are against the wall and the enemies are at the gate and the city has been given over to unrighteousness, we are to put all our trust in God, knowing, with Job, that our "Redeemer lives, and that in the end he will stand upon the earth" (Job 19:25).

Now then, my sons, listen to me; blessed are those who keep my

ways. Listen to my instruction and be wise; do not ignore it.

Blessed is the man who listens to me, watching daily at my

doors, waiting at my doorway. For whoever finds me finds life

and receives favor from the Lord. But whoever fails to find

me harms himself; all who hate me love death.

—PROVERBS 8:32–36

THROUGH ALL AND IN ALL

SCRIPTURE TELLS US that the Wisdom of God, the Word of God, and the Spirit of God are different aspects of the same God. In Proverbs 8, Wisdom, speaking through the words of Solomon, says, "I was there when he set the heavens in place, when he marked out the horizon on the face of the deep, when he established the clouds above and fixed securely the fountains of the deep . . . and when he marked out the foundations of the earth" (Proverbs 8:27–29).

The gospel of John begins with the Word: "In the beginning was the Word, and the Word was with God, and the Word was God. He was with God in the beginning" (John 1:1–2). And the second verse of Genesis introduces the Holy Spirit as the central agent in the creation of the world: "Now the earth was formless and empty, darkness was over the surface of the deep, and the Spirit of God was hovering over the waters" (Genesis 1:2).

All three, the Wisdom of God, the Word of God, and the Spirit of God, come together in the person of Jesus Christ. We are told that the young Jesus "grew in wisdom and stature, and in favor with God and men" (Luke 2:52). The Gospel of John opens by stating, "The Word became flesh and made his dwelling among us" (John 1:14). And Mark tells us the Spirit of God descended on him like a dove (Mark 1:10). We are told that when we proclaim the Lordship of Jesus, we affirm the oneness of God. We affirm that He has in Himself the wisdom, Word, and Spirit of God. Jesus is our Lord and our Savior.

Then I said, "Here I am, I have come—it is written about
me in the scroll. I desire to do your will, O my God; your law is
within my heart." I proclaim righteousness in the great assembly;
I do not seal my lips, as you know, O LORD.

—PSALM 40:7–9

YOUR LAW IS WITHIN MY HEART

CHANGE IS AN iron law of the natural world, but it is a law that applies to spiritual reality as well as natural. God calls us to change; He asks us to depart from the rutted path we are treading and depart for places that might be new and unfamiliar. He calls us to service as He called Moses in the desert or David from the sheep pens or Paul before the gates of Damascus from his zeal to persecute followers of Christ.

We are called out of a passive into a dynamic life, but we must be willing to answer that call and David was. When we give our lives to Christ, we drop our reservations, discard our objections, pick up our walking stick, and begin to follow him, wherever that may lead. As we begin to walk in faith with Jesus, His path we walk becomes the preferred and only way.

*By wisdom the L*ORD *laid the earth's foundations,*
by understanding he set the heavens in place; by his knowledge
the deeps were divided, and the clouds let drop the dew.

—PROVERBS 3:19–20

THE FOUNDATION OF THE WORLD

THE POPULAR VIEW is that the universe, and later the earth, just "happened." No God, no creator, no wisdom. Living with this view raises serious questions about the underlying purpose of life. If the life we are living is seen as accidental and meaningless, it is not clear what would cause us to do anything beyond satisfying own needs and desires. Few will overtly admit that they have chosen to adhere to the view that the universe is a random accident, but it does seem to be a philosophy of life that has taken hold in certain circles in many countries around the world, particularly in the West.

The Christian view is built on the Genesis story of creation, where God intentionally creates the heavens and the earth. Furthermore, it says that He found the act of creation to be good: "And God said, 'Let there be light,' and there was light. God saw that the light was good, and he separated the light from the darkness" (Genesis 1:3–4).

One account of the creation of the world speaks to a huge, mysterious cosmic accident. The other, also filled with mystery, tells of a world created by God as an intentional act. Of course, the Genesis story is only the beginning, but it is the only story that includes each one of us. Whether or not we choose to live within the framework of God's story is another story.

At the end of your life you will groan, when your flesh
and body are spent. You will say, "How I hated discipline!
How my heart spurned correction! I would not obey my
teachers or listen to my instructors. I have come to the
brink of utter ruin in the midst of the whole assembly."

—PROVERBS 5:11–14

REGRETS

IS IT POSSIBLE to experience regret if we are right with the Lord? The short answer is yes because even the greatest saint has fallen short and must seek God's forgiveness.

But what of those who would deny the Lord? If we knew such people well enough, we might be surprised at how often they bounce from crisis to crisis, feeling as the Psalmist does that they have come to the brink of utter ruin. You might find that such a life is marked by a parade of regrets and lost opportunities.

There is a difference between the person who seeks forgiveness for offending the Lord or a neighbor and the person who regrets a mistake that has upset his own well-being. If you place your life in the hands of the Lord, your only regret might be that you squandered so much time before accepting Jesus' call on your life.

Let the redeemed of the LORD say this—those he redeemed from
the hand of the foe, those he gathered from the lands, from east
and west, from north and south. Some wandered in desert
wastelands, finding no way to a city where they could settle.
They were hungry and thirsty, and their lives ebbed away.
Then they cried out to the LORD in their trouble, and he
delivered them from their distress. He led them by a straight way
to a city where they could settle. Let them give thanks to the
LORD for his unfailing love and his wonderful deeds for men, for
he satisfies the thirsty and fills the hungry with good things.

—PSALM 107:2–9

HE SATISFIES THE THIRSTY

AFTER THE MIRACULOUS escape through the Red Sea, the Jewish people found themselves in a desert with little to sustain them. They wandered there for forty years before Joshua led them across the Jordan River into the land that Abraham had been promised generations before.

On another level, this psalm applies to everyday experience because it reveals the universal pattern of human suffering and deliverance. All wander in a spiritual desert as long as they live apart from God. In this condition, men and women lack the spiritual provisions that would sustain them; it does not take long for thirst and hunger to drain us of hope and bring us to a point where our strength begins to ebb away. Often it is when we face extreme circumstances that we turn to God for help. Elsewhere it says, "Though I walk in the midst of trouble, you preserve my life" (Psalm 138:7) and "call upon me in the day of trouble; I will deliver you and you will honor me" (Psalm 50:15).

The recurring pattern is one of danger, of hopelessness, of a desperate call for help, and of divine deliverance. It is when we are spared that we realize that we could not have survived on our own. Yet at the same time we often forget God's amazing grace and return to our wanton ways by not giving thanks "to the Lord for his unfailing love and his wonderful deeds for men…"

For the LORD gives wisdom, and from his mouth come knowledge
and understanding. He holds victory in store for the upright,
he is a shield to those whose walk is blameless, for he guards the
course of the just and protects the way of his faithful ones.
Then you will understand what is right and just and fair—every
good path. For wisdom will enter your heart,
and knowledge will be pleasant to your soul. Discretion
will protect you, and understanding will guard you.

—PROVERBS 2:6–11

BE ALERT AND ARMED

IF SATAN WERE to revise this proverb for his own purposes, he would only need to make small changes of emphasis in order to shift the focus away from God. He would offer the benefits while obscuring the source of those benefits. He would imply that knowledge and understanding could be won through our own efforts and abilities. He would entice us into believing that it is just a matter of putting in the time and hard work to become a "Master of the Universe."

For those who listen to the subtle whispers of Satan, wisdom becomes little more than practical knowledge of everyday things, and self-reliance becomes the altar where they will ultimately worship Satan encourages us to take credit for the good things of life that actually are gifts of God. The devil would have us believe that wisdom, knowledge, and understanding are products of our good education or our own good works. Once we fall into this deception, the Evil One gains a foothold, which is enough to divert us from the path God intended for us. Therefore, we need to be alert; otherwise, we can easily fall prey to the one who would devour us (1 Peter 5:8).

Your word is a lamp to my feet and a light for my path.
I have taken an oath and confirmed it, that I will follow
your righteous laws. I have suffered much; preserve my life,
O LORD, according to your word. Accept, O LORD, the willing
praise of my mouth, and teach me your laws.

—PSALM 119:105–108

A WILLFUL OR WILLING SPIRIT?

HOW DO WE reach a point in our lives when we can offer a "willing" spirit to the Lord? Typically we display the spirit of a stubborn mule, unwilling to move forward or back. Sometimes we describe a child as "willful," but rarely do we see this willful spirit in ourselves.

But the more brittle we become as we ossify into monuments of willfulness, the greater the crisis when we hear the call of the Lord. This is what happened to Paul as he approached Damascus to stamp out the followers of Jesus. Though he was highly regarded by the chief priests and Pharisees, he had become a religious monster. Then, unexpectedly, as he approached the city "a light from heaven flashed around him. He fell to the ground and heard a voice say to him, 'Saul, Saul why do you persecute me?" (Acts 9:3–4).

Paul was blinded by the heavenly light; he faced a crisis of conflicting purposes. He must either disregard the light from heaven or submit to the voice that tells him, "Now get up and go into the city, and you will be told what you must do" (Acts 9:6). From that moment on, Paul chose to follow the commands of the Lord. This is what is meant by conversion. Paul is Paul, but he changed at that moment from being an opponent of God to being an ambassador of Jesus Christ. Paul experienced an extraordinary change of heart and a complete change in the direction in his life. Paul was on a mission to destroy the followers of Christ, but God had other plans for him. At that moment, Paul had a choice. He could have remained willfully disobedient to the call because God did not force him to change the direction of his life. The same is true for each one of us; God is not forcing us to change directions. We have a choice, but as with many things, our choice does have consequences. Choosing to follow Jesus will often make things harder, not easier which is why many follow the path of the "Rich Young Leader." (Matthew 19:16-26)

I will exalt you, O LORD, for you lifted me out of the depths and did not let my enemies gloat over me. O LORD my God, I called to you for help and you healed me. O LORD, you brought me up from the grave; you spared me from going down into the pit.

—PSALM 30:1–3

A DANGEROUS FANTASY

DAVID WAS BLESSED with many gifts, but he still faced many trials throughout his long life. Yet, while his circumstances may have varied wildly, David seldom wavered in his absolute allegiance to his Lord and his Creator. At various times in his psalms, David calls the Lord his rock, his strong tower, his fortress, his refuge, and his salvation. No wonder David begins this psalm with "I will exalt you, O Lord." David knows that God is his strength and the protector of his soul.

By contrast, today it seems quite normal to praise our own strengths and talents. Or we might seek the praise of others as if our good accomplishments deserve praise comparable to the self-adulation lavished on our cultural icons. But from David's point of view, self-praise is nothing more than seeing things through the wrong end of the lens. God is great, strong, and powerful. We are not; our genuine strength comes through acknowledging God in all aspects of our lives. According to Scripture, to see it otherwise is to indulge in fearful and dangerous fantasies.

For all can see that wise men die; the foolish and the senseless
alike perish and leave their wealth to others. Their tombs will
remain their houses forever, their dwellings for endless generations,
though they had named lands after themselves. But man, despite
his riches, does not endure; he is like the beasts that perish.

—PSALM 49:10–12

THE GIFT OF GOD IS ETERNAL LIFE

DAVID REPEATEDLY REMINDS us that life is short even for those who have lived a great many years: "Man is but a breath; his days are like a fleeting shadow" (Psalm 144:4). Therefore, he says, "Teach us to number our days aright, that we may gain a heart of wisdom" (Psalm 90:12).

Elsewhere, Paul tells us that what we experience in this life is temporary (2 Corinthians 4:18), and Jesus tells us: "Do not store up for yourselves treasures on earth, where moth and rust destroy, and where thieves break in and steal" (Matthew 6:19).

The common denominator to all of these passages is the transitory nature of life on earth. But behind the appearance of the finality of death is the promise of eternal life for those who believe. "For our light and momentary troubles are achieving for us an eternal glory that far outweighs them all. So we fix our eyes not on what is seen, but on what is unseen. For what is seen is temporary, but what is unseen is eternal" (2 Corinthians 4:17–18).

Sow your seed in the morning, and at evening let not your
hands be idle, for you do not know which will succeed,
whether this or that, or whether both will do equally well.

—ECCLESIASTES 11:6

BE WILLING TO RISK

THE MODERN PARADIGM for living the good life is based on an almost obsessive need to predict outcomes. Now it is a normal preoccupation to know what the future will bring before the future actually arrives. Any business worth its salt will try to minimize risk and will use all kinds of metrics and analysis to do just that. But just to be clear, there is no chance that chance can be eliminated.

Risk is part of living; the future will arrive whether we are brave or fear driven. Hanging onto the present for dear life is to abandon the role that faith plays in living life well.

When Jesus is confronted with a question by a rich young ruler, He does not tell the young man to acquire more things or even to become more virtuous. Instead He tells him to risk everything (Luke 18:18–25) by stepping out of his safe existence. Jesus says leave your good life behind; sell everything because all the wealth in the world will never save you. Leave all that behind and come and follow me. Jesus is saying risk it all in order to gain what you can never gain through money, fame or power.

Jesus is not saying the choice is easy, but He is saying that choosing is necessary. He is asking the rick young ruler to follow Him; He is asking us as well.

*The seas have lifted up, O L*ORD*, the seas have lifted up*
their voice; the seas have lifted up their pounding waves.
Mightier than the thunder of the great waters, mightier than
*the breakers of the sea—the L*ORD *on high is mighty.*

—PSALM 93:3–4

WONDROUS GOD OF THE UNIVERSE

WHEN WE STAND on the edge of the sea, contemplating its awesome power and mystery, David wants to remind us that the One who created the seas also created the entire universe. This is the God who created us and while we may seem insignificant in comparison to oceans and planets and galaxies, this is a God who watches over our every thought and our every action.

In another psalm, David says, "Your works are wonderful, I know that full well. My frame was not hidden from you when I was made in the secret place. When I was woven together in the depths of the earth, your eyes saw my unformed body. . . . How precious to me are your thoughts, O God! How vast is the sum of them" (Psalm 139:14–17).

This is truly an amazing God who created the stars in the heavens, the earth, the seas, and all the creatures in it, and yet He is so close to us that He can know our every thought.

Even in darkness light dawns for the upright,
for the gracious and compassionate and righteous man.
Good will come to him who is generous and lends freely,
who conducts his affairs with justice.

—PSALM 112:4–5

GOD ARMS ME WITH STRENGTH

DAVID WAS ONCE a mere shepherd from a small town miles from Jerusalem. He was the youngest of many brothers and showed little promise of what he would become until God called him from tending sheep to become the future king of Israel. He was chosen because God could see what others could not see. David had all the qualities of righteousness that a good king must have. He was gracious, compassionate, generous, and just. He had a brave and steadfast heart. But beyond all that, he was "a man after [God's] own heart" (1 Samuel 13:14).

David had an opportunity to demonstrate these qualities even before he became king when he faced the Philistine giant Goliath, a warrior so powerful that no Israelite would dare do battle with him. When David stepped forward, he was told, "You are not able to go out against this Philistine and fight him; you are only a boy." (1 Samuel 17:33).

David defied the common sense of those around him and said, "The Lord who delivered me from the paw of the lion and the paw of the bear will deliver me from the hand of this Philistine" (v. 37). David had the confidence that flows from a heart that trusts in God. He knew "that it is not by sword or spear that the LORD saves, for the battle is the LORD's . . ." (v. 47). His courage came from the sure knowledge that "It is God who arms me with strength and makes my way perfect." (Psalm 18:32).

When I consider your heavens, the work of your fingers,
the moon and the stars, which you have set in place, what is
man that you are mindful of him, the son of man that you care
for him? You made him a little lower than the heavenly beings
and crowned him with glory and honor.

—PSALM 8:3–5

THE HOPELESSNESS OF MAN WITHOUT GOD

WHAT IS MAN apart from God? If we look at recent history, we see a creature that, through his behavior, more accurately reflects the frightening monsters of horror films than the being described here as "made a little lower than the heavenly beings and crowned . . . with glory and honor."

The long, sorry history of mankind wandering in the wilderness of godlessness is perfectly summarized in the first chapter of Paul's letter to the Romans. It is a tough minded picture, but it is hard to deny the truth of what Paul is saying: "Since they did not think it worthwhile to retain the knowledge of God, he gave them over to a depraved mind, to do what ought not to be done. They have become filled with every kind of wickedness, evil, greed and depravity. They are full of envy, murder, strife, deceit and malice. They are gossips, slanderers, God-haters, insolent, arrogant and boastful; they invent ways of doing evil; they disobey their parents; they are senseless, faithless, heartless, ruthless. Although they know God's righteous decree that those who do such things deserve death, they not only continue to do these very things but also approve of those who practice them" (Romans 1:28–32).

Man apart from God is profoundly prone to corruption. Paul paints an unvarnished picture of what men and women really look like when they choose to live without God. It is a choice, but the good news is that our story does not have to end that way. God has provided a way, through the cross of Jesus Christ, that can transform the condition of the worst of us into saints who are "crowned . . . with glory and honor."

My son, give me your heart and let your eyes keep to my ways,
for a prostitute is a deep pit and a wayward wife is a narrow well.
Like a bandit she lies in wait, and multiplies the
unfaithful among men.

—PROVERBS 23:26–28

A PATTERN OF UNFAITHFULNESS

THE COST OF falling into the pit of sexually loose living often is terrible, causing the break up of marriages, dislocation of children, and guilt and grief, but the unwary person rarely sees it this way. When we live a faithless life, we betray those we love on many levels, and before we fully see what is happening, a pattern of infection and conflict has taken over. No aspect of our life is exempt from harm, but especially our relationship with God.

Hosea, a later prophet, pronounces God's condemnation of a favored land gone astray: "There is no faithfulness, no love, no acknowledgment of God in the land. There is only cursing, lying and murder, stealing and adultery; they break all bounds and bloodshed follows bloodshed. . . . A spirit of prostitution leads them astray; they are unfaithful to their God" (Hosea 4:1–2, 12).

How we live, both publicly and privately, counts not only for today, but for tomorrow as well. Everything we do really does matter.

An unfriendly man pursues selfish ends;
he defies all sound judgment. A fool finds no pleasure in
understanding but delights in airing his own opinions.

—PROVERBS 18:1–2

WHO DO YOU SAY I AM?

WHEN PONTUS PILATE stood before Jesus in the hours before the crucifixion, he asked, "What is truth?" (John 18:38). Down through the centuries, those who have followed in the footsteps of Jesus Christ have based everything on the truth of His life, crucifixion, and resurrection. Foolishly today, many professed Christians have transformed the truth of Jesus Christ into their "opinion" about Jesus Christ.

Truth is universal, timeless, and always applicable. Opinions are individual, time-constricted, and sometimes applicable. Opinions can be informed or ignorant, tested or invented, but they do not rise to the level of truth. Opinions save us from certain kinds of confusion, but they do not save us.

We need to face Jesus and decide if He is the one who embodies the full truth of God. Pilate's political position blinded him to the truth of who Jesus is, but what about us? We need to answer, in our own time and place, the question Jesus asked His own disciples: "But who do you say that I am?" (Mark 8:29).

But it is the spirit in a man, the breath of the Almighty,
that gives him understanding. It is not only the old who are
wise, not only the aged who understand what is right.

—JOB 32:8–9

GOD IS SPIRIT

BY SPEAKING OF "the spirit in a man, the breath of the Almighty," Elihu, the fourth questioner of Job, places himself at the very center of biblical orthodoxy. In the second verse of Genesis, we are told that the "spirit of God was hovering over the waters" (Genesis 1:2). David, in his psalm of contrition, pleads with God to not "cast me from your presence or take your Holy Spirit from me" (Psalm 51:11). Jesus tells the Samaritan woman that "God is spirit, and his worshipers must worship in spirit and in truth" (John 4:24), and Paul writes that God is within those who love Him: "Your body is a temple of the Holy Spirit, who is in you, whom you have received from God" (1 Corinthians 6:19–20).

The Spirit of God is near, but if we have not asked Him into our heart with humility and contrition, we will find that the world seems empty of that very same Spirit.

Men cry out under a load of oppression; they plead for
relief from the arm of the powerful. But no one says,
"Where is God my Maker, who gives songs in the night,
who teaches more to us than to the beasts of the earth
and makes us wiser than the birds of the air?"

—JOB 35:9–11

A HARD TEACHING

WE OFTEN EXPRESS disappointment with God because our plea for help seems to go unanswered. They say, "Well, if God loves me, why won't he help me? Or, why did God let this happen to me?" But God is not a marionette dancing at the other end of our needs. When we pray, do we pray with humility and supplication, or do we make demands? And we might also ask, what is the condition of my own heart? Who do I really love?

Job continues: "He does not answer when men cry out because of the arrogance of the wicked. Indeed, God does not listen to their empty plea; the Almighty pays no attention to it" (Job 35:12–13). And Psalm 66 says, "If I had cherished sin in my heart, the Lord would not have listened" (v. 18).

This is difficult to hear, but we really do need to examine the condition of our hearts when we are entering the presence of God through prayer.

How deserted lies the city, once so full of people!
How like a widow is she, who once was great among
the nations! She who was queen among the provinces has
now become a slave. Bitterly she weeps at night, tears are upon
her cheeks. Among all her lovers there is none to comfort her.
All her friends have betrayed her; they have become her enemies.

—LAMENTATIONS 1:1–2

THE DOOMED CITY

IT WAS INCONCEIVABLE to the people of Jerusalem that their city
would fall. After all, this was the city of David, and it was the site
of the Holy Temple built by Solomon. The people, particularly the
leaders, could not believe that God would permit the barbarians at
the gate to prevail.

But the invasion should not have been a surprise because God
had sent messengers to warn of what would come if the leaders
and the people refused to turn away from their idols and corruption.
Both Isaiah and Jeremiah warned of the impending doom: "Disaster
will come upon you, and you will not know how to conjure it away.
A calamity will fall upon you that you cannot ward off with a
ransom; a catastrophe you cannot foresee will suddenly come
upon you" (Isaiah 47:11).

The decline and fall of Jerusalem did not happen all at once. It
had been "a shining city on a hill," but over time it drifted away
from God. When change is slow and incremental, it is hard for us
to see that we have veered off from the original way. And it is still
harder to hear that we need to stop doing what we are doing or we
might face disaster.

Have we drifted away in our own time and place? The signs
would suggest we have, and it appears that the way back will be
long and hard.

I waited patiently for the Lord; he turned to me and heard my

cry. He lifted me out of the slimy pit, out of the mud and mire;

he set my feet on a rock and gave me a firm place to stand.

He put a new song in my mouth, a hymn of praise to our God.

Many will see and fear and put their trust in the Lord.

—PSALM 40:1–3

GOD'S GRACIOUS PROTECTION

How does David do it? How can he be patient in the face of danger and death? How can any of us be courageous when we are surrounded by trouble on every side?

When it comes to faith in God's power to protect and lift up, David is one of the great pillars of the Bible who we look to for inspiration. But David is not the source of his own strength. In his confessional psalm he attributes all joy, goodness, and power to God through the presence of the Holy Spirit (Psalm 51:11).

David knows that without God he would be defenseless against wicked men who "rise up against me, breathing out violence" (Psalm 27:12). Elsewhere, he describes what life feels like without the presence of God: "My heart is blighted and withered like grass; I forget to eat my food. Because of my loud groaning I am reduced to skin and bones" (Psalm 102:4–5). With the presence of the Holy Spirit, David has the confidence and courage to transform the impossible into the possible.

The good news is that God has made His Holy Spirit available to each of us through the work of his son for all who accept this extraordinary gift of grace. "For it is by grace you have been saved, through faith—and this is not from yourselves, it is the gift of God—not by works, so that no one can boast. For we are God's workmanship, created in Christ Jesus to do good works, which God prepared in advance for us to do" (Ephesians 2:8–10). It is the Holy Spirit dwelling within that makes all the difference. In *Imitation of Christ*, Thomas à Kempis writes that God's "grace is the mistress of truth, the teacher of discipline, the enlightener of hearts, the comforter of the afflicted, and the refuge of the sorrowing. [God's] grace banishes sadness, expels fear, nurtures devotion, and breeds tears. Without [God's] grace, I am but a piece of dry wood—a useless log—fit only to be set aside."

No man has power over the wind to contain it;

so no one has power over the day of his death.

As no one is discharged in time of war,

so wickedness will not release those who practice it.

—ECCLESIASTES 8:8

MY LORD AND MY GOD!

SOLOMON MAKES TWO statements about what is possible for a mere man. First, Solomon says, "No man has the power over the wind to contain it," but we find Jesus doing just that when the boat he is in nearly capsizes in a furious squall. "He got up, rebuked the wind and said to the waves, 'Quiet! Be still!' Then the wind died down and it was completely calm. . . . [his disciples] were terrified and asked each other, 'Who is this? Even the wind and the waves obey him'" (Mark 4:39, 41).

Then, Solomon says, "No one has power over the day of his death." He is right when he says all men will die, even if they do not know when, but Jesus cannot be contained by the grave. All four accounts of His life and death on a cross tell in detail the account of his resurrection.

What are we to make of this? Even the wisdom of Solomon could not conceive of a man who could still the winds, perform countless miracles, and conquer death. But the angel Gabriel says otherwise when Mary responds to the news that she will give birth to the "Son of the Most High by asking, "How will this be?" Gabriel simply says, "nothing will be impossible with God." (Luke 1:26-38)

But you, O Sovereign LORD, deal well with me for your name's sake;
out of the goodness of your love, deliver me.
For I am poor and needy, and my heart is wounded within me.
I fade away like an evening shadow; I am shaken off like a locust.
My knees give way from fasting; my body is thin and gaunt.
I am an object of scorn to my accusers;
when they see me, they shake their heads.

—PSALM 109:21–25

NOT MY WILL BE DONE

HERE IN THE 109th Psalm, we hear echoes of Isaiah: "He was despised and rejected by men, a man of sorrows, and familiar with suffering. Like one from whom men hide their faces he was despised, and we esteemed him not" (Isaiah 53:3).

We also might think of the suffering experienced in another psalm that describes the punishment of crucifixion: "I am poured out like water, and all my bones are out of joint. My heart has turned to wax; it has melted within me" (Psalm 22:14).

Then we might fix our gaze on Gethsemane on the Mount of Olives where a lone figure is praying while His friends sleep nearby. We hear His voice as He prepares for the agony to come: "'Father, if you are willing, take this cup from me; yet not my will but yours be done. . . . ' And being in anguish, he prayed more earnestly, and his sweat was like drops of blood falling to the ground" (Luke 22:42–44).

Then we think of the implications of this scene. Jesus is preparing to go to the cross as a perfect sacrifice for all mankind so that we might not have to pay the terrible penalty ourselves. This may be difficult to fathom for those who have been blinded to their own sin and rebellion.

If we believe that we are good enough as we are, then the message of the cross will have no traction for us. But if we know in our hearts the truth about our condition, then the cross will represent the work of a merciful and loving God who loved us so much that He gave His one and only Son that we might live." For our sake he made him to be sin who knew no sin, so that in him we might become the righteousness of God." (2 Corinthians 5:21)

Do you have eyes of flesh? Do you see as a mortal sees?
Are your days like those of a mortal or your years like those of a
man, that you must search out my faults and probe after my sin—
though you know that I am not guilty and that no one can
rescue me from your hand?

—JOB 10:4–7

ARE WE PREPARED FOR THE TEMPEST?

JOB IS A good man; he has not turned against God by blaming God for the terrible suffering he has endured. Job's pain is all the greater because he knows that he is not guilty of any offense against God; he is not guilty of a crime or willful sin. This only heightens his perplexity because he has lost everything without apparent reason. This is why he asks God, "Do you see as a mortal sees?"

The temptation for Job, and for us, is to follow the admonition of Job's wife when she sees the depth of his suffering. When we experience personal loss, do we turn against God and accuse him of betraying us? The book of Job tells us that we should persevere through all circumstances because there are times when God's purposes cannot be understood by the usual norms. Faith is hard duty, for we will surely be tested in this life. Faith requires resolve, endurance, patience, and humility so that we will stand firm, like a rock, when the tempest strikes.

God is our refuge and strength, an ever-present help in trouble.
Therefore we will not fear, though the earth give way and the
mountains fall into the heart of the sea, though its waters roar
and foam and the mountains quake with their surging.

—PSALM 46:1–3

PURIFIED

THE SHENANDOAH NATIONAL Park is part of a thin strip of the
Blue Ridge Mountains located in central Virginia. This section of
the Appalachian Trail is a welcome change for hikers because the
ups and downs are moderate, and the trail is never very far from
the Blue Ridge Parkway.

I hiked this section in May 2005. The first few days were easy;
I kept the mileage to a tolerable ten miles or so, finishing well
before nightfall. But on the fourth day, I planned an eighteen-mile
day in order to reach a cabin that the guidebook said provided a
view east toward Old Rag Mountain and other lesser peaks. The
temperature that day was fine for hiking, and the trail provided
easy footing; but the climbs were more numerous than before,
and I began to wear out.

The last big climb of the day was Bald Face Mountain, which by
North Carolina and Tennessee standards was nothing special, but I
had run low on energy, so I merely slogged along. When I was
about halfway up the mountain, a bright idea dawned on me.
Rather than suffer every miserable step, why not march up the rest
of the way. I usually do not like to hike with music playing in my
ears because I feel I will be missing part of the nature experience,
but this time I put aside my concerns and began listening to Michael
W. Smith's album, *Worship*.

I like many of Michael's songs, particularly "Above All," but as I
neared the summit, his song "Purified" began to play. I don't know
if you have ever heard it before, but it was the perfect song, for as I
reached the summit, the amazing chorus reached a crescendo with

the words, "I will stand in cleansing fire, by you I'm purified . . . (for) you are Holy." Music and moment met together on that mountaintop, and for an instant, I felt as if I were walking on holy ground. I stopped to appreciate the view of the world all around me, and felt gratitude for the beauty and power of Michael W. Smith's song. Soon enough, though, the moment passed and I moved on in the twilight toward the cabin with a view.

*If clouds are full of water, they pour rain upon the
earth. Whether a tree falls to the south or to the north,
in the place where it falls, there will it lie.
Whoever watches the wind will not plant;
whoever looks at the clouds will not reap.*

—ECCLESIASTES 11:3–4

LITTLE DID SHE SUSPECT

THE SLUGGARD MAY dream of riches but if he never gets up and plants, he will never reap. God calls each one of us to purpose and action no matter how insignificant that action may seem at the time. When Ruth went to the fields of Boaz to glean the grain left behind by the harvesters, little did she suspect that her seemingly insignificant work would lead to marriage and later to the birth of Obed, the father of Jesse who was the father of David (Ruth 2). And it is through David that we received the promise of God that would lead to Bethlehem and the birth of the Savior for the whole world: "I will establish his line forever, his throne as long as the heavens endure" (Psalm 89:29). Out of the gleaning of one woman would grow the vine of Jesus Christ.

Do not be quick with your mouth,

do not be hasty in your heart to utter anything before God.

God is in heaven and you are on earth, so let your words be few.

As a dream comes when there are many cares,

so the speech of a fool when there are many words.

—ECCLESIASTES 5:2–3

―――∞∞∞―――

KEEPING GOD OUT

IN MY FIRST year in college, I took an anthropology class that attempted to provide a comprehensive definition of man as distinct from all the other species on the earth. I remember reading of several definitions such as "tool maker," but the one that seemed to work the best was the concept that man was a "word maker."

Since this was a science class, no one pointed out that the Bible supported this idea—except for causation. For in the Bible, the Word first comes from God: "In the beginning was the Word, and the Word was with God, and the Word was God" (John 1:1). So when God created man in His own image, He gave man the gift of the word as well as the responsibility to name the creatures of the earth (Genesis 2: 19–20).

My science class arrived at the right definition of man; they just left out the reason why the Word is central to our human nature. The mystery of the origin of the Word was beyond the scope of this science class because it was assumed that all causation could only rise out of the forces in the natural world. It would be considered scientific heresy to suggest that the Word originated before nature.

C.S. Lewis says, "Does the whole vast structure of modern naturalism depend not on positive evidence but simply on an *a priori* metaphysical prejudice? Was it devised not to get in facts but to keep out God?"

The path of the righteous is like the first gleam of dawn,
shining ever brighter till the full light of day.
But the way of the wicked is like deep darkness;
they do not know what makes them stumble.

—PROVERBS 4:18–19

THE SUMMIT AND THE VALLEY

MANY YEARS AGO, some friends and I decided to climb one of the "High Peaks" in the Adirondacks in upstate New York. It is a wild and beautiful place with rocky mountains rising above lakes and ponds whose waters reflect the majestic images of the surrounding region.

In the waning hours of a late autumn afternoon, we decided to cross the lake to climb to the summit of Haystack before night closed in on us. Confidently, we ascended quickly, and in a few hours, we reached the summit as the sun was declining toward the horizon.

Though we knew that we would have only a short time on top, the view of the surrounding mountains overcame our better judgment, and we stayed to enjoy the inspiring beauty of the world spreading out before us on every side. The air was so clear it felt as if we could reach across the divide and touch the rounded summit of Mt. Marcy.

But too soon the sun fell below the horizon, painting the languid clouds shades of orange and red. We held out until the last minute and then began the race down the trail to the lake and the cabin on the opposite shore.

There is no darkness equal to the darkness of the woods after night fall. And so as we descended from the grayness of twilight into the pitch black of night, we became so lost that we could not find the shore of the lake, not to mention the boat we had used in the afternoon. We wandered aimlessly for hours and eventually came upon the lake and later the boat that had been patiently waiting for our return.

Our mistake had been our desire to hold onto the passing glory of the sunset at the summit. The valley below does not hold the same sense of eternal promise as a sunset in the mountains or on the coast. Solomon says in Ecclesiastes that God "has made everything beautiful in its time. Also, he has put eternity into man's heart...." (Ecclesiastes 3:11)

For those brief moments on the summit of Haystack, the beauty of the surrounding world was visible to us. The valley could wait. "For (God's) invisible attributes, namely his eternal power and divine nature, have been clearly perceived, ever since the creation of the world, in the things that have been made." (Romans 1:20) Staying on the top cost us, but it was worth the price.

Better is one day in your courts than a thousand elsewhere;
I would rather be a doorkeeper in the house of my God than
dwell in the tents of the wicked. For the LORD God is
a sun and shield; the LORD bestows favor and honor;
no good thing does he withhold from those whose walk is blameless.
O LORD Almighty, blessed is the man who trusts in you.

—PSALM 84:10–12

BLESSED IS HE WHO TRUSTS

FAITH IS THE staff we hold in our hands when our "walk is blameless." For unlike the fence-sitter, the faithful sojourner has the perseverance that comes from commitment, courage, and self-sacrifice.

As Christians, we place our faith in the person of Jesus Christ; we acknowledge His claim on us and the truthfulness of His witnesses. And as we travel through this for Christ, we need to remain strong and courageous because the world resists His followers as it resisted Jesus Himself. And we accept sacrifice because Jesus calls us out of our self-indulgent nature into service in His name on behalf of others. "O Lord Almighty, blessed is the man who trusts in you."

You [God] said, "Listen now, and I will speak;
I will question you, and you shall answer me."
My ears had heard of you but now my eyes have seen you.
Therefore I despise myself and repent in dust and ashes.

—JOB 42:4–6

IN AN INSTANT, EVERYTHING CHANGED

TRY TO IMAGINE what it would be like to suddenly find yourself standing before God. You did not expect to be there at all; until a mere moment ago, you were content with your small successes, and you expected, in your heart, to live long past your retirement. You were looking forward to moving south to the house you bought near the ocean. Everything was going as planned, but now, in a split second, you are standing before the throne of God.

What would you say to the Lord? Would you try to justify your unspent life? Would you be defiant? Would you plead for mercy? After suffering mightily, Job faces God, and his reaction should tell us a lot about how we should live in relationship to the holiness of God before we actually must stand before the throne of judgment.

When Job recognizes the majesty of God, he can only say, "I despise myself and repent in dust and ashes." Paul, in his letter to the Romans, gently guides us toward the right attitude: "Do not think of yourself more highly than you ought." (Romans 12:3).

When we think highly of ourselves, we then turn the natural order of things upside down. We crowd God out with the smaller concerns of everyday life, losing sight of fact that we will stand for judgment before Creator of heaven and earth.

My son, pay attention to my wisdom,
listen well to my words of insight, that you may maintain
discretion and your lips may preserve knowledge.
For the lips of an adulteress drip honey, and her speech is
smoother than oil; but in the end she is bitter as gall, sharp as a
double-edged sword. Her feet go down to death; her steps lead
straight to the grave. She gives no thought to the way of life;
her paths are crooked, but she knows it not.

—PROVERBS 5:1–6

GENUINE FREEDOM

THE BIBLE NEVER claims that we do not have the freedom to engage in all kinds of liberties, including adultery and other forms of sexual license. But the Bible is a book that helps us keep our eyes on the eternal consequences flowing out of our freely chosen act.

The true path of freedom is the freedom from self-destructive impulses and appetites. Paul says, "You, my brothers, were called to be free. But do not use your freedom to indulge the sinful nature; rather, serve one another in love" (Galatians 5:13). And Peter says, "Live as free men, but do not use your freedom as a cover-up for evil; live as servants of God" (1 Peter 2:16).

We are free, but freedom to commit adultery and any other sin is no freedom at all; these things lead us away from God, not toward him.

The rod of correction imparts wisdom, but a child left to himself
disgraces his mother. . . . Discipline your son, and he will give
you peace; he will bring delight to your soul.

—PROVERBS 29:15, 17

SOFT-FOCUS PARENTING

THE BIBLE TELLS us that we are not born as a blank slate; rather, each baby has an inherent moral sense designed into the fabric of his or her DNA. If this is true, then, as parents, we are enabling bad behavior in the child when we withhold judgment and discipline in the name of compassion or sensitivity.

Today, too many parents seem to engage in soft-focus parenting, thinking that punishment harms when discipline is really an act of love. "He who spares the rod hates his son, but he who loves him is careful to discipline him" (Proverbs 13:24). The battleground for all of us, from the earliest age, is to avoid the grip of sin as we seek the wisdom of God. The struggle begins in early childhood; where there is no struggle; there is apt to be no relationship with a righteous God.

Do not be overawed when a man grows rich, when the
splendor of his house increases; for he will take nothing with
him when he dies, his splendor will not descend with him.
Though while he lived he counted himself blessed—and men
praise you when you prosper—he will join the generation of his
fathers, who will never see the light of life. A man who has riches
without understanding is like the beasts that perish.

—PSALM 49:16–20

ARE THE RICH EXCLUDED?

IT IS HARD to overcome the awe we often feel when we are in the presence of the rich and powerful, for it seems as if such people have almost superhuman virtues. And often those blessed with wealth often agree: "The wealth of the rich is their fortified city; they imagine it an unscalable wall" (Proverbs 18:11).

This is one reason why His disciples are so shocked when Jesus says, "How hard it is for the rich to enter the kingdom God!" (Mark 10:23). It was assumed that the rich had a fast track to heaven while the poor would be left behind to wallow in the dust.

More recently, this common assumption has been turned on its head; now the poor have the inside track while the rich remain outside, condemned as villians through and through. But when it comes to the final judgment, both assumptions are wrong. "Is [God] not the One . . . who shows no partiality to princes and does not favor the rich over the poor, for they are all the work of his hands?" (Job 34:18–19).

The central question for rich and poor alike is the one posed by the rich young man: "'Good teacher,' he asked, 'what must I do to inherit eternal life?'" (Mark 10:17). The young man turns away from Jesus because what he had was more valuable to him than what he might have. If he had accepted Jesus' offer to sell everything and follow Him, he would have been on the road to eternal life. He was not excluded because he was rich; he was accepted. He was the one who declined because the riches of this life outweighed for him the riches of the next.

For God does speak—now one way, now another—though man
may not perceive it. In a dream, in a vision of the night, when
deep sleep falls on men as they slumber in their beds, he may
speak in their ears and terrify them with warnings, to turn man
from wrongdoing and keep him from pride, to preserve his soul
from the pit, his life from perishing by the sword.

—JOB 33:14–18

THE SPIRIT OF TRUTH

GOD SPEAKS TO people through his Holy Spirit. He speaks through dreams and songs and answered and unanswered prayers. He shows signs, and he has provided His authoritative Word through His Holy Scriptures. God speaks through our gifts whether it is teaching, preaching, praying, singing, painting, or any one of the many other spiritual gifts.

But in order to be used by God, we need to relinquish our obsessive focus on self and open our hearts to the truth and power of the Holy Spirit. This is the promise that Jesus gave directly to His disciples and to all who believe: "All this I have spoken while still with you. But the Counselor, the Holy Spirit, whom the Father will send in my name, will teach you all things and will remind you of everything I have said to you" (John 14:25–26). "When the Counselor comes, whom I will send to you from the Father, the Spirit of truth who goes out from the Father, he will testify about me. And you also must testify, for you have been with me from the beginning" (John 15:26–27).

To many, the way the Holy Spirit speaks is a great mystery, but to those who believe, it is the truth that transforms life itself.

Listen, my sons, to a father's instruction;

pay attention and gain understanding . . .

"Lay hold of my words with all your heart;

keep my commands and you will live.

Get wisdom, get understanding;

do not forget my words or swerve from them."

—PROVERBS 4:1, 4–5

BLESSED ARE THE PURE IN HEART

WHEN THE FATHER says to his son, "Gain understanding by taking hold of my words with all your heart," he is making a distinction that is considered of little value in our information-soaked time. Today the experts generally think that learning is simply a matter of brainpower, so they measure IQ with standardized tests to determine a child's promise of success in life. But this approach places value on certain human gifts at the expense of others. In *Biblical Psychology*, Oswald Chambers writes, "In the Bible, the heart, and not the brain, is revealed to be the center of thinking. The Bible puts in the heart all the active factors we have been apt to place in the brain. The head is the exact outward expression of the heart. . . . as a tree is the outward expression of the root."

Jesus doesn't say blessed are the scholars and intellectuals and all those with extraordinary IQs; He says, "Blessed are the pure in heart, for they will see God" (Matthew 5:8).

Confuse the wicked, O Lord, confound their speech, for I see
violence and strife in the city. Day and night they prowl about
on its walls; malice and abuse are within it. Destructive forces
are at work in the city; threats and lies never leave its streets.

—PSALM 55:9–11

CITIZENS OF THE CITY

LONG BEFORE JERUSALEM fell to invaders, corruption had undermined the strength of its foundations. Jerusalem had been built as a place to honor and praise God; it was a citadel of peace, a place that protected the innocent and weak and promoted justice and godliness. Yet when the leaders of the city forgot God and began to honor only themselves, then "malice and abuse" began to roam within its walls; then the destructive forces of "violence and strife" came out of hiding, and "threats and lies" replaced truth and righteousness.

This persistent pattern of man betraying his Creator can be traced back to the biblical account of the cities of the plains: "The outcry against Sodom and Gomorrah is so great and their sin so grievous that I will go down and see if what they have done is as bad as the outcry that has reached me" (Genesis 18:20–21).

Sadly, what he found was worse, and even though he would have shown mercy if a few righteous men were found there, He found an utterly godless place where all "are corrupt and their ways are vile; there is no one who does good" (Psalm 53:1).

When men fall into full rebellion against God through sin, then the consequences are predictable; only the timing is not. As citizens of the city, we should always remember the pattern of drift and decline and turn back to God in all haste: "Put on sackcloth, O priests, and mourn; wail you who minister before the altar. . . . For the day of the LORD is near; it will come like destruction from the Almighty" (Joel 1:13, 15).

The eyes of the LORD are everywhere, keeping watch on
the wicked and the good. The tongue that brings healing is
a tree of life, but a deceitful tongue crushes the spirit. . . .
The house of the righteous contains great treasure,
but the income of the wicked brings them trouble.

—PROVERBS 15:3–4, 6

HIGH-TECH PROPHETS

IN THE EARLY days of the "Internet Revolution," many of the high-tech prophets sold the world on the transformative power of this new form of communication. Dot-com wizards, hardly out of their teens, became instant paper millionaires, and the world gazed in wonder on this new phenomenon. There was only one problem—the Internet was created by people.

Soon a common medical term became an ominous threat to all users of the Internet. Viruses started invading computers and computer networks. New businesses had to be built to fortify systems against alien invasions, and so the battle began.

We should not be surprised. The computer virus is really no different than a person becoming infected by sin. Everything is working according to plan when suddenly the system begins to demonstrate strange and uncharacteristic behaviors. A virus slips through the defenses, and our behavior begins to malfunction. We begin to lie or stir up dissension or stop working and start squandering our wealth and our gifts.

As Paul explains it, "I do not understand what I do. For what I want to do I do not do, but what I hate I do" (Romans 7:15). Once again, technology becomes the instrument of our human nature—including the darker side of it.

A foolish son is his father's ruin, and a quarrelsome wife is like
a constant dripping. Houses and wealth are inherited from
parents, but a prudent wife is from the LORD.

—PROVERBS 19:13–14

THE GOOD WIFE

WHEN IT COMES to choosing a wife as a lifelong companion to share all of the blessings of life and its woes, men are often foolish because their focus is so singular and shallow. For in the end, a wife's character counts higher than everything else. She will become a partner in every important decision. She will be a mother, an educator, a provider and as a strong partner, she will be steadfast and wise in times of stress and trouble.

A good wife will never divide a man from home and wealth but will help to build both. "She is worth far more than rubies. Her husband has full confidence in her and lacks nothing of value. She brings him good, not harm, all the days of her life" (Proverbs 31:10–12).

All this I tested by wisdom and I said, "I am determined to be wise"—but this was beyond me. Whatever wisdom may be, it is far off and most profound—who can discover it? So I turned my mind to understand, to investigate and to search out wisdom and the scheme of things and to understand the stupidity of wickedness and the madness of folly.

—ECCLESIASTES 7:23–25

A MERE PHANTOM

WISDOM IS UNOBTAINABLE without seeing the presence of God in the "scheme of things." Many modern thinkers do not look for the hand of God in the physical universe but, instead, seek to understand physical laws to explain the natural world. They would answer Solomon by saying, "We can understand; we can investigate and discover what is at the heart of everything!"

But in the end, all the theories of human progress through human knowledge come up short. The universe without God is devoid of meaning and purpose. It is a world of stone and dust with nothing but darkness lying ahead and with the conclusion being this: "Each man's life is but a breath. Man is a mere phantom as he goes to and fro: he bustles about, but only in vain; he heaps up wealth, not knowing who will get it" (Psalm 39:5–6).

Yet you brought me out of the womb; you made me trust in you
even at my mother's breast. From birth I was cast upon you;
from my mother's womb you have been my God. Do not be far
from me, for trouble is near and there is no one to help.

—PSALM 22:9–11

MY BURDEN IS LIGHT

IT IS EASY to fall into the trap of believing that God can betray us. Look at what is being said: "Trouble is near and there is no one to help." When you contrast this statement with "you brought me out of the womb; you made me trust in you," you see the dilemma that suffering mankind faces.

If God created us, then why does He allow us to suffer? This is the problem that confronts Job. Suffering showers down on him and he is asked both to defend himself and justify God. In the end, though, he places all his faith in God: "I have heard of you by the hearing of the ear, but now my eye sees you; therefore I despise myself and repent in dust and ashes." (Job 42:5-6)

Jesus experienced conflict from the earliest days of His ministry, and He warns us that, as followers, we can expect nothing less. "In this world you will have trouble," but He adds, "Take heart! I have overcome the world" (John 16:33).

In the end, the experiences of the everyday cannot be equated with the eternal. Jesus sees beyond the horizon of this life, and He asks us to do the same, but He also offers us comfort in our labors and in our suffering: "Come to me, all you who are weary and burdened, and I will give you rest. Take my yoke upon you and learn from me, for I am gentle and humble in heart, and you will find rest for your souls. For my yoke is easy and my burden is light" (Matthew 11:28–30).

If I sinned, you would be watching me and would not let
my offense go unpunished. If I am guilty—woe to me!
Even if I am innocent, I cannot lift my head,
for I am full of shame and drowned in my affliction.

—JOB 10:14–15

DESCENT INTO DARKNESS

PAUL, IN HIS letter to the Romans, expresses the deepest anguish over the conflicting desires within his heart, demonstrating that no one is exempt from the passions competing with the desire to love and follow the Lord. "When I want to do good, evil is right there with me . . . waging war against the law of my mind and making me a prisoner of the law of sin at work in my members" (Romans 7:21, 23).

When we turn our backs on God, the battle within our heart is over; standing alone and disarmed, we are defenseless against the power of the desire to sin. Without God's armor, we are stripped of all protection, including the will to resist. Our own wild nature takes full charge, and the course of our life begins to move further and further away from God: "They have become filled with every kind wickedness, evil, greed and depravity. They are full of envy, murder, strife, deceit and malice. . . . Although they know God's righteous decree that those who do such things deserve death, they not only continue to do these very things but also approve of those who practice them" (Romans 1:29, 32).

I will instruct you and teach you in the way you should go;
I will counsel you and watch over you. Do not be like the horse
or the mule, which have no understanding but must be
controlled by bit and bridle or they will not come to you.

—PSALM 32:8–9

STUBBORN LIKE A MULE

A MULE IS a sterile hybrid between a male donkey and a female horse—a strange and stubborn creature. It would be safe to say that most people would consider it an insult if someone were to compare them to such an animal. The trouble is that many people act like mules when it comes to being obedient to the call of God. Instead, as willful sinners (Psalm 19:13), they kick back in stubborn fury rather than acknowledge God's place in their lives. For them, it is nearly impossible to say with a sincere and contrite heart "your will be done . . ." (Matthew 6:10).

All of us face the same stark choice: Either we can choose to be like the mule, or we can become children of God. God wants us to return to Him, but He will never force us to come back. If we want to be fully human, fully children of God, then we have to say with Jesus: "My Father . . . not as I will, but as you will" (Matthew 26:39).

For a man's ways are in full view of the LORD, and he examines
all his paths. The evil deeds of a wicked man ensnare him;
the cords of his sin hold him fast. He will die for lack of
discipline, led astray by his own great folly.

—PROVERBS 5:21–23

GOD IS NEAR

IF WE PROCLAIM God loudly then we must be ready to accept the fact that this is a God who knows when we are playing the hypocrite. Solomon acknowledges God's closeness when he said that our ways are in full view of the Lord. Whereas it is difficult for us to know what might be behind another person's action, God has no problem piercing the veil. The author of Hebrews says, "Nothing in all creation is hidden from God's sight. Everything is uncovered and laid bare before the eyes of him to whom we must give account" (Hebrews 4:13).

God's nearness and intimate knowledge of our every thought may be uncomfortable for some, but for believers, this is a huge plus. God knows what I need before I need it; He hears me when I am in trouble. He helps me get back on the right path; He does not abandon me when I am lost.

God's nearness is a great encouragement because we will always face troubles as we move through life, to know that God is near makes all the difference.

For he remembered his holy promise given to his servant
Abraham. He brought out his people with rejoicing, his chosen
ones with shouts of joy; he gave them the lands of the nations,
and they fell heir to what others had toiled for—that they
might keep his precepts and observe his laws.

—PSALM 105:42–45

ABRAHAM

ABRAHAM'S FATHER, TERAH, had set out for Canaan long before Abraham responded to God's call. We do not know if God called Terah first, but we do know that he never got to his original destination. Instead, he came to Haran, settled there, and never left. He began a journey that he never finished, but Abram (as he was then called), the son, was different.

The Lord appeared to Abram and said: "Leave your country, your people and your father's household and go to the land I will show you. . . . So Abram left" (Genesis 12:1, 4).

Then God made a promise that must have seemed incredible because both Abram and his wife Sarai were very old and without children: "To your offspring I will give this land" (Genesis 12:7). And later God appears to Abram again and says, "A son coming from your own body will be your heir. . . . Look up at the heavens and count the stars—if indeed you can count them . . . So shall your offspring be" (Genesis 15:4–5). Finally comes one of the great turning points in the Bible: "Abram believed the LORD, and he credited to him as righteousness" (Genesis 15:6).

At the center of Judaism and Christianity is belief in the truthfulness and trustworthiness of God's Word. Abram cast doubt aside and followed the Lord. He believed; and by believing, he fulfilled God's purpose for his life, and he began the journey that would find its culmination in an empty tomb outside the walls of Jerusalem.

At this, Job got up and tore his robe and shaved his head. Then
he fell to the ground in worship and said: "Naked I came from
my mother's womb, and naked I will depart. The LORD gave and
the LORD has taken away; may the name of the LORD be praised."
In all this, Job did not sin by charging God with wrongdoing.

—JOB 1:20–22

BLESSINGS AND CURSES

ALMOST EVERY POSSIBLE catastrophe descended on Job. His herds
were stolen, his servants were slain, and his own sons and daughters
were killed suddenly.

How would you react upon experiencing these terrible events?
It is inconceivably tragic, yet Job does not raise his fist toward
heaven to accuse God of wrongdoing. He simply states a universal
truth about the nature of life: "Naked I came from my mother's
womb, and naked I will depart." Praising the Lord is more than an
utterance from the mouth; it is complete devotion to God who
"has brought down rulers from their thrones but lifted up the
humble" (Luke 1:52).

Job rightly says to his wife, "Shall we accept good from God, and
not trouble?" (Job 2:10) Job's integrity is based on his absolute faith
in a God of love and ultimate mercy. What about us? Will we fall
away in fear and doubt, or will we stand strong in our faith? This is
not an easy question to answer.

Say among the nations, "The LORD reigns."
The world is firmly established, it cannot be moved;
he will judge the peoples with equity.
Let the heavens rejoice, let the earth be glad;
let the sea resound, and all that is in it;
let the fields be jubilant, and everything in them.

—PSALM 96:10–12

HE CANNOT BE MOVED

To UNDERSTAND THE claims of the Psalmist, we have to read beyond the literal words to appreciate what we are being told. He says, "The world is firmly established, it cannot be moved . . ." but we know that the earth and the stars and the moon are moving constantly and at great speed. And every living creature is moving, even if that movement is only blood flowing through the heart.

Movement represents an observable fact, so we must infer that the Psalmist is speaking of a spiritual truth that underpins the natural facts. For this moving universe is knitted together by laws that cannot be moved. A tiny change in the laws propelling the earth around the sun would end all life on earth instantly.

The question is: Who created the laws that allowed life to flourish? The Psalmist says that everything in nature, the seas and the forests, the fields and the sky, all shout for joy to the one God who reigns over and cannot be moved. He is the God who reigns: "Your statutes stand firm; holiness adorns your house for endless days, O LORD" (Psalm 93:5).

My son, if sinners entice you, do not give in to them . . .

my son, do not go along with them, do not set foot on their paths.

—PROVERBS 1:10, 15

THE DEPTH OF HIS LOVE

IT IS POPULAR to believe that we have little power over the self-destructive impulses and behaviors emanating from within. According to this view, all are slaves to their chemical and biological makeup. If this is true, it follows that we are excused from any need to change our ways.

No wonder this quasi-scientific understanding of human nature is accepted by so many people. It opens a wide path for self-indulgent behavior and exempts virtually everyone from judgment, discipline, and shame. It further permits us to disregard the idea that life is deeply moral, that "sin is lawlessness" (1 John 3:4), and that God is a God of judgment as well as mercy. In the passage from Proverbs, the father warns the son that there is great danger in embracing the sinful life: "Do not set foot on their paths, for their feet rush into sin, they are swift to shed blood (vv. 15–16)."

Even though the son stands warned, he may choose to indulge his natural inclination to sin. But what seems natural to him is unnatural in the eyes of God. When we are permissive to our sinful nature, we pay the price of further alienation from God. Paul says, "'Everything is permissible for me'—but not everything is beneficial" (1 Corinthians 6:12).

God is always calling us to walk with Him. Can we hear? Will we listen? Will we choose well?

Blessed are they whose ways are blameless,
who walk according to the law of the LORD.
Blessed are they who keep his statutes
and seek him with all their heart.
They do nothing wrong; they walk in his ways.

—PSALM 119:1–3

THE EARLY CHURCH

OH, HOW WE love to organize in our church life. Not that there is anything wrong with strong organizational skills. It is important to have committees and groups and events. We need a schedule so that we can allocate our time and our energy. But organizational skills do not necessarily signify that a particular church is healthy and effective.

As a Christian, what does it mean to "walk in his ways"? As a church member, how do we live out seeking the Lord with all of our heart? Do the walls of the church close out the world rather than inviting the outside into meeting Jesus?

I can't help but think of the first-century church. They did not meet in fancy buildings. They did have music and they did meet regularly, but the place was not the focus. Rather it was about training up believers rather than building: Jesus' great commission to his followers was to "Go and make disciples of all nations" (Matthew 28:19). And they did. And the church spread throughout the Mediterranean world as the disciples and their followers spread the good news of Jesus Christ.

The kings of the earth did not believe, nor did any of the world's people, that enemies and foes could enter the gates of Jerusalem. But it happened because of the sins of her prophets and the iniquities of her priests, who shed within her the blood of the righteous.

—LAMENTATIONS 4:12–13

THE ENEMY WITHIN

THE LONG AND painful decline of Jerusalem began with the sin of its greatest king. God spared David, but conflict and rebellion would erupt and would infect the generations that followed.

By the time of the great prophets, Jerusalem had turned against God, and even her high priests had fallen into corrupt practices: "The idols speak deceit, diviners see visions that lie; they tell dreams that are false, they give comfort in vain. Therefore the peoples wander like sheep oppressed for lack of a shepherd" (Zechariah 10:2). A city that forsakes God and embraces corruption is a city that will decay and die long before the enemy arrives to tear down its walls.

When you make a vow to God, do not delay in fulfilling it.
He has no pleasure in fools; fulfill your vow.

—ECCLESIASTES 5:4

DO YOU BELIEVE THIS?

MAKING A VOW is serious business. We should never commit to something when we have no intention of keeping our word. Vows are promises that may be hard to keep, but when we make a promise, we pledge our word and stake our reputation on fulfilling our part of the bargain. Our word must be our bond.

Jesus' entire ministry is a promise made and a promise kept. God's Word rests on the shoulders of His Son. This promise means that, through what he did on the cross, He opened the way to an everlasting relationship with God the Father, through the work of the Son (2Corinthians 5:16-21).

Here's the promise from Jesus: "I am the resurrection and the life. He who believes in me will live, even though he dies, and whoever lives and believes in me will never die" (John 11:25–26). Then He turns to Martha, the sister of Lazarus, and asks: "Do you believe this?" (v. 26). Do you believe that I am the Son of God? Do you believe in this glorious promise?

Then He says to you and to me: What about you? Will you stake your life on the truth of my claim and my promise? Will you say with Peter that I am the "the Christ, the Son of the living God"? (Matthew 16:16). Or will you choose to believe something else?

My son, preserve sound judgment and discernment,
do not let them out of your sight; they will be life for you,
an ornament to grace your neck.

—PROVERBS 3:21–22

WHAT CAN MAN DO TO ME?

YOUR SLEEP WILL never be sweet when you choose to partner with the devil. Fear destroys sleep, and the author of fear is Satan. In your waking and sleeping hours, he accuses you, berates you, and spreads doubts where there should be none. This is what the father means when he says to his son, "Preserve sound judgment and discernment, do not let them out of your sight."

When Jesus is tempted by Satan in the wilderness, He uses the Word of God to combat the adversary and so prevails: "Then the devil left him, and angels came and attended him" (Matthew 4:11).

When we place our confidence in the Lord, then we have nothing to fear and we can say with David: "The LORD is with me; I will not be afraid. What can man do to me? The LORD is with me, he is my helper. I will look in triumph on my enemies" (Psalm 118:6–7).

Who has woe? Who has sorrow? Who has strife?

Who has complaints? Who has needless bruises?

Who has bloodshot eyes? Those who linger over wine,

who go to sample bowls of mixed wine.

Do not gaze at wine when it is red,

when it sparkles in the cup, when it goes down smoothly!

In the end it bites like a snake and poisons like a viper."

—PROVERBS 23:29–32

BE HOLY IN ALL YOU DO

THE DRUNKARD DRINKS from his cup of despair; he drowns his sorrows and adversities in the false comfort of the bottle, thinking that drink will dull the pain of broken relationships, failed ventures and disappointing expectations. But the pain will only become more unbearable over time until despair completely floods out hope. Drunkenness opens the floodgates of darkness, driving out the Holy Spirit rather than enabling it.

This is why Peter warns us not to do what the pagans do, "living in debauchery, lust, drunkenness, orgies, carousing and detestable idolatry" (1 Peter 4:3). Instead, we are to drink from the cup of the Holy Spirit, which is the desire of God for each one of us: "Just as he who called you is holy, so be holy in all you do; for it is written: 'Be holy because I am holy'" (1 Peter 1:15–16). Without the power of the Holy Spirit working within our hearts, we will remain susceptible to quick fixes that are not fixes at all.

Rise up, O LORD, confront them, bring them down;
rescue me from the wicked by your sword.
O LORD, by your hand save me from such men,
from men of this world whose reward is in this life.
You still the hunger of those you cherish;
their sons have plenty, and they store up wealth for their children.
And I—in righteousness I will see your face; when I awake,
I will be satisfied with seeing your likeness.

—PSALM 17:13–15

WE HAVE AN INHERITANCE

THE "LOST SON" spoken of in Jesus' parable takes his inheritance and heads off for a far country to enjoy his newfound wealth. But he quickly turns an apparent blessing into a very real curse. He squanders everything. In another story, Jesus is approached by a rich young ruler who wants to inherit eternal life but won't give up his riches to take possession of what he most desires. In another parable, a rich man "lived in luxury every day" but neglected the poor man begging at his gate. When the rich man dies, he finds himself ensnared in the horrors of hell and calls out to the poor man who has gone to heaven. Then he learns why there will be no help: "Son, remember that in your lifetime you received your good things, while Lazarus received bad things, but now he is comforted here and you are in agony" (Luke 16:25).

Jesus gives us three stories about wealth with three very different outcomes. The lost son does squander everything he has been given by his father, but before he reaches his rope's end, he turns back to seek his father's forgiveness, which he receives in abundance.

The second story is about a rich young ruler blessed with great wealth and power. But he wants more: he wants to earn "eternal life." Jesus shocks him by telling him to give up his money, power, and position to follow him and you "will have treasure in heaven."

The young man walks away from the most generous offer he will ever have.

Finally, we have the story of the man who indulges himself with the good things of this life while disregarding poor Lazarus who lies sick and hungry outside the rich man's gate. Here the rich man seeks neither forgiveness nor goodness but instead leads a self-indulgent life up until the bitter end.

In a sense, following Jesus is represented in each story through the grace of the father, the spiritual poverty in abiding in worldly wealth and the blessings of heaven even if we have suffered greatly on earth.

Rulers persecute me without cause, but my heart trembles at your
word. I rejoice in your promise like one who finds great spoil.
I hate and abhor falsehood but I love your law. Seven times a
day I praise you for your righteous laws. Great peace have they
who love your law, and nothing can make them stumble.
I wait for your salvation, O LORD, and I follow your commands.
I obey your statutes, for I love them greatly. I obey your precepts
and your statutes, for all my ways are known to you.

—PSALM 119:161–168

DANIEL

DANIEL WAS EXCEPTIONAL in every respect. King Nebuchadnezzar found Daniel and his three companions to be "ten times better than all the magicians and enchanters in his whole kingdom" (Daniel 1:20). If Daniel had only been a man of outstanding achievement, we would never have heard of him. Though he started out as a slave in exile and though he rose to the highest ranks of power in Babylon, he never forgot the God who guided and loved him. His enemies thought they could destroy him by issuing a decree that forced all to worship the king only.

But Daniel never wavered: "Now when Daniel learned that the decree had been published, he went home to his upstairs room where the window opened toward Jerusalem. Three times a day he got down on his knees and prayed, giving thanks to his God, just as he had done before" (Daniel 6:10). He prayed to the living God who saves, knowing the danger he faced.

His enemies seem to prevail—and Daniel is cast into a den of lions. It is at this moment that God intervenes miraculously. Daniel's prayer in his time of great peril could easily have been the words of this psalm: "Rulers persecute me without cause, but my heart trembles at your word. . . . Seven times a day I praise you for your righteous laws. Great peace have they who love your law, and nothing can make them stumble."

O Lord God Almighty, how long will your anger smolder
against the prayers of your people? You have fed them with the
bread of tears; you have made them drink tears by the bowlful . . .
Restore us, O God Almighty; make your face shine upon us,
that we may be saved.

—PSALM 80:4–5, 7

THE TRUE VINE

THE VINE STARTS with Abraham who believed the command of
the Lord, and it was credited to him as righteousness. God promised
that Abraham would be the father of many nations: "I will make
you very fruitful" (Genesis 17:6).

His descendant Joseph, son of Jacob, son of Isaac, is sold into
slavery in Egypt where his own descendants became slaves. Moses
brings the vine out of Egypt, and Joshua plants that vine in the land
promised. And David, anointed by God to be king of Israel, receives
a new promise: "I will establish his line forever, his throne as long
as the heavens endure" (Psalm 89:29). But the fruit of the promise
does not become manifest for one thousand years: "In the sixth
month, God sent the angel Gabriel to Nazareth, a town in Galilee,
to a virgin pledged to be married to a man named Joseph, a
descendant of David" (Luke 1:26–27).

So when Jesus says to His disciples on the eve of His crucifixion
that He is the "true vine," He is reaching all the way back to
Abraham, as well as all the way forward to us. He is the very
embodiment of the promise. He says, "I am the true vine; you are
the branches. If a man remains in me and I in him, he will bear
much fruit" (John 15:5).

Create in me a pure heart, O God, and renew a steadfast spirit within me. Do not cast me from your presence or take your Holy Spirit from me. Restore to me the joy of your salvation and grant me a willing spirit, to sustain me. Then I will teach transgressors your ways, and sinners will turn back to you.

—PSALM 51:10–13

WE MUST CALL OUT

DAVID IDENTIFIES THE seriousness of the human dilemma when he says, "Surely I was sinful at birth, sinful from the time my mother conceived me" (Psalm 51:5). Sin separates us from God. Therefore, sin must be washed out of the human heart, which is why Jesus tells us that we must be born again: "No one can see the kingdom of God unless he is born again" (John 3:3). Consequently, David confesses his sin to God and prays for mercy that his iniquity might be blotted out and his heart made clean. David yearns to praise God once again and "teach transgressors your ways. . ."

Without confession, contrition, and prayer, we keep the Holy Spirit hovering at a distance. We remain in our sinful state alienated from God and from His purpose for us. God wants us back; He is merciful and gracious, and He can purify a sinful nature, transforming a sinner into a saint through Jesus Christ. But we need to call out, "Create in me a pure heart, O God, and renew a steadfast spirit within me."

Show me, O LORD, my life's end and the number of my days;

let me know how fleeting is my life . . .

Man is a mere phantom as he goes to and fro:

he bustles about, but only in vain;

he heaps up wealth, not knowing who will get it.

—PSALM 39:4, 6

GOD'S WORD STANDS FOREVER

ISAIAH WRITES THAT "all men are like grass, and all their glory is like the flowers of the field. The grass withers and the flowers fall, because the breath of the LORD blows on them. Surely the people are grass. The grass withers and the flowers fall, but the word of our God stands forever" (Isaiah 40:6–8).

Jesus frequently talked about time. He often called us to the present moment. He said: Do not worry about tomorrow; let tomorrow worry about itself. He said: Do not store up riches for yourself, for in time those riches will prove to be worthless to you.

Jesus said at the very beginning of His ministry, "The time is fulfilled, and the kingdom of God is at hand; repent and believe in the gospel."(Mark 1:15) Jesus never wasted time; He spent it.

He is always bringing us back to the present moment and saying: spend your time now; spend it wisely; spend it with the perspective of eternity in mind; spend it not on yourself, but spend it lavishly as if you are the most generous gift giver in the world. Lastly, Jesus is saying: Spend your time with me, for then it is certain that you are spending your time very well indeed.

Praise the LORD. Praise the LORD from the heavens,
praise him in the heights above. Praise him, all his angels,
praise him, all his heavenly hosts. Praise him, sun and moon,
praise him, all you shining stars.

—PSALM 148:1–3

THE HEAVENS

HAVE YOU EVER ventured outside on a clear, cold, winter night and gazed into the heavens? Millions of tiny stars speckle the dark expanse, lighting up the world so that all can see the evidence of the glory, beauty, and majesty of the work of the Creator of all things.

Too many of us look up into the vast sparkling canvas of the universe and see only . . . nothingness. But when you look with the eyes of your heart on God, you see the handprint of the Divine. Thomas à Kempis sums this up in *Imitation of Christ*: "Therefore, I wish to offer and present to You the jubilant joy found in all devout hearts, their burning love, their ecstasies, their supernatural illuminations and heavenly visions, together with all the virtues and praises that have been or shall ever be given You by the creatures of heaven and earth, for myself and for all who have been recommended to my prayers and that You may receive fitting praise from men and be glorified without end."

Hear my words, you wise men; listen to me, you men of learning.

For the ear tests words as the tongue tastes food.

Let us discern for ourselves what is right;

let us learn together what is good.

—JOB 34:2–4

THE RIGHT RULE

IF CHRISTIANS WERE asked only to memorize and follow a set of rules, then their faith could be properly categorized as legalistic and sternly moralistic. Many Christians do define Christian living as a moral "to do" checklist, but the Bible tells us that wisdom grows from a "discerning heart" that will guide us "to distinguish between right and wrong" (1 Kings 3:9).

To walk the path of discernment requires attention to each step, understanding to the ways of the world, knowledge of the implements needed for the journey, and a steadfast heart to carry the sojourner over the difficult hills and through the dark valleys.

When I am afraid, I will trust in you.
In God, whose word I praise, in God I trust;
I will not be afraid. What can mortal man do to me?
All day long they twist my words; they are always
plotting to harm me. They conspire, they lurk,
they watch my steps, eager to take my life.

—PSALM 56:3–6

AUTHENTIC TRUST

HAVE YOU CHECKED your internal "trust meter" lately? We all have one, but we usually don't pay much attention to it as we usually operate on trust autopilot. Remove us from our familiar environments, however, and watch our "trust meters" go haywire. Suddenly, suspicious characters are seen to be lurking around every corner; business transactions that once were done on a handshake are now reviewed by a battery of lawyers; and tomorrow always seems to bring a new crisis. When trust evaporates, fear and doubt flood through the breach.

Jesus shows us what the authentic life of trust looks like. During much of His ministry, He was beset with threats and trouble on all sides, but He kept his composure with every circumstance. For He placed his trust in the one place where it should repose—God the Father.

While Jesus came to save sinful men, He never put his trust in mortals, "For he knew all men" (John 2:24). He did not need man's testimony about man, for he knew what was in a man. "In God I trust; I will not be afraid" should be the rock we stand on. Then in times of confusion and change, we can remain confident and secure: "Do not let your hearts be troubled. Trust in God, trust also in me" (John 14:1).

Who can speak and have it happen if the Lord has not decreed it?
Is it not from the mouth of the Most High that both calamities
and good things come? Why should any living man complain
when punished for his sins?

—LAMENTATIONS 3:37–39

EXCUSES DO NOT SAVE

IF WE BELIEVED in divine justice, we would neither complain about
our calamities nor brag about our successes. But most of us, when
caught in wrongdoing, immediately rummage around in our vast
bag of excuses to find the perfect "get out free" card.

When we hear someone say, "It wasn't my fault; she made me
do it," we should recognize that these are the same words that
Adam used when confronted by God in the garden: "The man said,
'The woman you put here with me—she gave me some fruit from
the tree, and I ate it'" (Genesis 3:12).

We marvel at Adam's ingenuity in blaming both God and Eve in
the same breath. If it is God's fault for creating Eve to be Adam's
companion, then God should let him off the hook. And if it is Eve's
fault, then she should be punished.

Clever, but God makes the rules, and the rule was "You will not
eat of the tree of knowledge of good and evil." By eating the fruit,
Adam broke God's one prohibition. No excuse would change that,
nor will any excuse help us if we were to choose to follow the
tragic course set by Adam.

When I applied my mind to know wisdom and to observe man's
labor on earth——his eyes not seeing sleep day or night——
then I saw all that God has done. No one can comprehend what
goes on under the sun. Despite all his efforts to search it out,
man cannot discover its meaning. Even if a wise man claims
he knows, he cannot really comprehend it.

—ECCLESIASTES 8:16–17

THE SECRET THINGS OF GOD

THE INTELLECTUAL AND scientific enterprise of the past several centuries has been to disprove the idea that "No one can comprehend what goes on under the sun." When we liberate ourselves from God the Creator, then we are free to begin to become substitute gods through the power of science and technology.

In Greek mythology, Prometheus stole fire from the gods of Olympus and gave it to the human race. In literature, Mary Shelley wrote a story about a Promethean doctor who used his science to create a perfect human being. Prometheus paid a terrible price for his crime, as did Victor Frankenstein, and we will, too, if we fail to acknowledge the limits of our own competence. The fire that lights the winter night can also become the flame of our ruin.

Believing we can know what the Creator knows is foolhardy, and for the temporary good it might produce, science does not bring salvation. "The secret things belong to the LORD our God, but the things revealed belong to us and to our children forever, that we may follow all the words of this law" (Deuteronomy 29:29).

Using science to better understand the beauty and complexity of God's universe is a noble enterprise; when we forget God in our scientific pursuits, we are at risk of attempting to play God when clearly we are only mortals composed of both dust and divinity.

Because of the LORD's great love we are not consumed,
for his compassions never fail. They are new every morning;
great is your faithfulness. I say to myself,
"The LORD is my portion; therefore I will wait for him."

—LAMENTATIONS 3:22–24

HIS COMPASSION NEVER FAILS

PITY PEOPLE WHO experience affliction and bitterness but choose not to call out to God. What hope do they have? What would be the reason for wanting to live another day?

We have learned from Job that even the righteous suffer, and we know that Jesus was the suffering servant who was the object of hatred without reason (John 15:25). But God suffers along with us when we suffer on behalf of Him. He will lift up the downcast soul and give comfort to those in need. Indeed, His compassion never fails those who believe: "Through glory and dishonor, bad report and good report; genuine, yet regarded as impostors; known, yet regarded as unknown; dying, and yet we live on; beaten, and yet not killed; sorrowful, yet always rejoicing; poor, yet making many rich; having nothing, and yet possessing everything" (2 Corinthians 6:8–10).

Indeed, these are the words of the man of faith. Our prayer, given the realities of life on earth, should be for courage and strength in times of trouble. We should pray that we will not abandon God even if we feel abandoned ourselves.

How can a young man keep his way pure?
By living according to your word. I seek you with all my heart;
do not let me stray from your commands. I have hidden your
word in my heart that I might not sin against you.

—PSALM 119:9–11

HIS OUTSTRETCHED HAND

"LORD, WHO MAY dwell in your sanctuary? Who may live on your holy hill?" (Psalm 15:1). Who, indeed? For many, the assumption is that all children are born innocent. With this in mind, the parent metaphorically believes that the child is born on the hill of human goodness and that their job, as parents, is simply to help the child stay there.

The Bible reverses this assumption. It tells us that life's journey is an ascent because we are born with an oppositional will. Left alone, we will not even bother to make the attempt to draw closer to God. There has been only One born without sin, and He came into this world to deal with the fact of sin, once and for all. When we call upon His name to guide us, we recognize that, without His outstretched hand, our condition is no different than Cain who cries out that he has become "a fugitive and a wanderer of the earth." (Genesis 4:14).

He sends his command to the earth; his word runs swiftly.

He spreads the snow like wool and scatters the

frost like ashes. He hurls down his hail like pebbles.

Who can withstand his icy blast? He sends his word and melts them;

he stirs up his breezes, and the waters flow.

—PSALM 147:15–18

GUYOT SHELTER

THE DAY WAS cold and the snow deep. We were attempting to get to West Bond, one of the four-thousand-footers located deep within the Pemigawasset Wilderness in New Hampshire. Our progress had slowed to a crawl as we broke trail through four feet of snow pack.

Eventually, we got to the summit of Guyot Mountain, but by then it was dark. The wind was blowing across the ridge, and snow was swirling all around us. Guyot Shelter was somewhere out there, but finding it presented a challenge. Because the mountain was so isolated, there was no discernable path, no footprints to follow. No one had been in these parts for weeks.

We couldn't stay on the ridge, and as I had been in those location in milder times, I decided to leave my companions behind to scout for Guyot Shelter. I knew enough about the terrain not to become hopelessly lost. After probing and hunting for an hour, I found a trail sign that pointed the way down to the elusive shelter. I found my companions where I had left them and together we returned to the path to the shelter. The trail down was steep and covered in deep snow. I was hoping the shelter would soon come into view but that never happened. It probably was buried under the snow and because it was late and the search seemed fruitless, we built a snow platform on the side of the mountain and bivouacked for the rest of the night. In the light of the next morning we were able to find the log shelter buried under a mountain of snow, except for the front. We ate breakfast there and then headed back toward the comforts of civilization. We were relieved to have escaped unscathed from our foolish adventure into isolation and danger. Yet all along I felt safe and protected. Despite the extreme environment, difficult terrain, and uncomfortable night, I never experienced fear. As the "guide" on this trip, I felt guided.

Before I was afflicted I went astray, but now I obey your word.
You are good, and what you do is good; teach me your decrees.
Though the arrogant have smeared me with lies, I keep your
precepts with all my heart. Their hearts are callous and
unfeeling, but I delight in your law. It was good for me to be
afflicted so that I might learn your decrees.

—PSALM 119:67–71

WHY DO WE SUFFER?

THE PSALMIST SAYS he "went astray" before he was afflicted and that it was through suffering that he turned away from his folly, realizing that only God is good. He now "delights in [God's] law." And by expressing joy in suffering, he pinpoints one of the central paradoxes for those who follow Christ.

Paul was not a stranger to suffering. At one point in his second letter to the Corinthians, he catalogues the sufferings he endured for the greater glory of Christ: "In great endurance; in troubles, hardships and distresses; in beatings, imprisonments and riots; in hard work, sleepless nights and hunger . . ." (2 Corinthians 6:4–5).

But rather than lament his bad fortune, he speaks triumphantly about the good fortune of being able to suffer for so great a purpose. "Rather as servants of God, we commend ourselves in every way . . . in truthful speech and in the power of God; with weapons of righteousness in the right hand and in the left; through glory and dishonor, bad report and good report; genuine, yet regarded as impostors; known, yet regarded as unknown; dying, and yet we live on; beaten, and yet not killed; sorrowful, yet always rejoicing; poor, yet making many rich, having nothing, and yet possessing everything" (2 Corinthians 6:4, 7–10).

In his first letter, Peter explains why we accept suffering with a humble but determined heart: "To this you were called, because Christ suffered for you, leaving you an example, that you should follow in his steps" (1 Peter 2:21).

As a father has compassion on his children, so the LORD has

compassion on those who fear him; for he knows how we are

formed, he remembers that we are dust . . . But from everlasting

to everlasting the LORD's love is with those who fear him, and

his righteousness with their children's children—with those

who keep his covenant and remember to obey his precepts.

—PSALM 103:13–14, 17–18

IN HIS OWN IMAGE

WHEN THE PSALMIST says that God remembers that we are dust, he is echoing the second of two creation stories in the book of Genesis: "The Lord God formed the man from the dust of the ground and breathed into his nostrils the breath of life, and the man became a living being" (Genesis 2:7).

If dust represented all we ever were, then the story of mankind would be a sad tale indeed. But elsewhere it says, "You made him a little lower than the heavenly beings and crowned him with glory and honor" (Psalm 8:5).

This dust, this clay, has a divine shape to it, as the first creation story confirms: "So God created man in his own image, in the image of God he created him: male and female he created them" (Genesis 1:27). The composition may be made up of the elements of the earth, but the heart is the heart crafted by the eternal love of God. Our dust nature may sully the image, but our heart continues to yearn for the holiness of God.

But as for me, I will always have hope;
I will praise you more and more.
My mouth will tell of your righteousness,
of your salvation all day long,
though I know not its measure.

—PSALM 71:14–15

HE WILL ANSWER OUR PRAYER

FAITH OFTEN IS born out of the darkness of a crisis, for a time of crisis can shake us loose from firmness of the assumptions we have lived by. When serious trouble comes our way, those assumptions easily shatter as we try to come to grips with the threat of "terror on every side" (Psalm 31:13). This is when we may awaken to the reality of our need for God, "for I am in distress; my eyes grow weak with sorrow, my soul and my body with grief" (Psalm 31:9).

When God answers us, *and he does*, it is not always in the way we might desire. And when we respond, hope will begin to open before us like a landscape of great beauty, and we say in gratitude and joy, "I will praise you more and more. My mouth will tell of your righteousness, of your salvation all day long, though I know not its measure."

It is better to take refuge in the LORD than to trust in man.

It is better to take refuge in the LORD than to trust in princes.

—PSALM 118:8–9

———⌘———

ACCEPT NO SUBSTITUTES

THE TEMPTATION TO create our own gods is almost irresistible. And once we have landed on the god of our choice, we move immediately to worship, casting aside reason and experience in our rush to laud the object of our desire. The object could be anything: a baseball team or a woman. It could be a Hollywood star or a politician. We seem to need to manufacture something or someone who is greater than we are, and so we put our trust in man and in princes even though the evidence would suggest that neither men nor princes are very trustworthy.

The tendency to worship mortals is like accepting the counterfeit for the original. The author of Hebrews addresses this human foible when he says that what we have here is "a copy and shadow of what is in heaven" (Hebrews 8:5). Jesus' claim is that He is the original and not a mere copy. While the world is always attempting to discredit and downgrade Him, Jesus keeps reminding us that He is the authentic one who can always be counted on.

Jesus said that others would come in His name (Matthew 24:5) and "many false prophets will appear and deceive many people" (Matthew 24:11), and all this has come true, especially in our own time; but Jesus continues to shine through all the darkness and confusion as the One, the only one we can trust.

I am the most ignorant of men; I do not have a man's
understanding. I have not learned wisdom, nor have I knowledge
of the Holy One. Who has gone up to heaven and come down?
Who has gathered up the wind in the hollow of his hands?

—PROVERBS 30:2–4

THE FACE OF GOD

JOB ASKS, "WHO then can understand the thunder of his power?" (Job 26:14). Solomon asks, "Who has gathered up the wind in the hollow of his hands?" (Proverbs 30:4) And Jesus, speaking to Nicodemus, says, "I tell you the truth, no one can see the kingdom of God, unless he is born again. . . . I have spoken to you of earthly things and you do not believe; how then will you believe if I speak of heavenly things?" (John 3:3, 12).

Nicodemus represents the state of the darkened human mind before the advent of the Son. Men could marvel at the vast dimensions of the universe and praise the splendor and beauty of the seas and mountains and the earth itself, but the face of God remained remote. Even the wisest and holiest of men could confess to being ignorant when standing before God.

Then God sent His Son into the world to bring the truth of His light to all men who wished to see. Jesus was not just a healer and teacher and prophet; He was and is the Son of the Living God and He made it known to all who would hear and who could see: "Don't you know me, Philip, even after I have been among you such a long time? Anyone who has seen me has seen the Father. How can you say, 'Show us the Father?' Don't you believe that I am in the Father, and that the Father is in me? The words I say to you are not just my own. Rather, it is the Father, living in me, who is doing his work" (John 14:9–10).

As Jesus speaks to Philip, He is also speaking to each one of us: "Don't you know me? Don't you believe I am who I say I am? Don't you know that the Father has sent me to you out of divine love? If you don't believe me, then who do you say that I am?"

I will declare that your love stands firm forever,

that you established your faithfulness in heaven itself.

You said, "I have made a covenant with my chosen one,

I have sworn to David my servant, 'I will establish your line

forever and make your throne firm through all generations.'"

—PSALM 89:2–4

A LIGHT FOR REVELATION

NATHAN, THE PROPHET of God, tells King David of the Word he has heard from God: "The LORD declares to you that the LORD himself will establish a house for you. . . . I will raise up your offspring to succeed you. . . . I will establish his kingdom. He is the one who will build a house for my Name, and I will establish the throne of his kingdom forever. I will be his father and he will be my son. . . . Your house [referring to David] and your kingdom will endure forever before me, your throne will be established forever" (2 Samuel 7:11–14, 16).

The Gospel of Matthew records many of the prophecies fulfilled with the birth of Christ, but many people miss the prophecy of the Davidic branch because it is recorded in a long genealogy at the very beginning of the gospel story. But Matthew knew the significance of identifying who Jesus was through the prophecies of Isaiah, Micah, Nathan, and others.

The advent of the birth of Christ was an expected event; it was the fulfillment of the promise of God to the prophets and passed down through the Hebrew Scriptures. Simeon, a righteous and devout man, says, on seeing the Christ child, "For my eyes have seen your salvation, which you have prepared in the sight of all people, a light for revelation to the Gentiles and for glory to your people Israel" (Luke 2:30–32).

A wise king winnows out the wicked;

he drives the threshing wheel over them.

The lamp of the LORD searches the spirit of a man;

it searches out his inmost being.

Love and faithfulness keep a king safe;

through love his throne is made secure.

The glory of young men is their strength,

gray hair the splendor of the old.

—PROVERBS 20:26–29

EVERYTHING IS PERMITTED

IN THE NINETEENTH century, many members of the intelligentsia decided that the God of the Bible was false and irrelevant. Whether it was through the work of Darwin, Marx, or Nietzsche, God, for the most part, was ushered off the stage. This created a new problem: Who would lead the way in establishing the new world order? If mankind were to continue to climb to ever-higher levels of technological and scientific achievement, then a substitute standard and standard bearer would be required. It was Nietzsche who proposed the idea of the Overlord or Ubermensch.

Another nineteenth-century writer, Fyodor Dostoyevsky, saw a darker side to the "God Is Dead" movement. He wrote in *The Brothers Karamazov*, "If God does not exist, then everything is permitted." It would not be until the twentieth century that the world would be able to test the practical applications underpinning the godless Overlord. And by then it was too late. The hope of the nineteenth century devolved into the horrific political and scientific perversions of the twentieth. It turns out that, when everything is permitted, "everything" inevitably includes Nazi death camps and Soviet Gulags. In the hands of the dictatorial Ubermensch, whether Hitler or Stalin or Mao, the people would be liberated into a demonic level of suffering.

David Berlinski in his book, *The Devil's Delusion*, describes how German extermination squads swept into Eastern European villages, rounded up people, had them dig their own graves, and then shot them. One man, an elderly Hasidic Jew, turned to his executioner and said, "God is watching what you are doing." He was then shot dead. Berlinski then goes on to say this: "What Hitler did not believe and what Stalin did not believe and what Mao did not believe and what the SS did not believe and what the Gestapo did not believe and what the NKVD did not believe and what the commissars, functionaries, swaggering executioners, Nazi doctors, Communist Party theoreticians, intellectuals, Brown Shirts, Black Shirts, gauleiters, and a thousand party hacks did not believe was that God was watching what they were doing. And as far as we can tell, very few of those carrying out the horrors of the twentieth century worried overmuch that God was watching what they were doing either."

Have we learned anything from the nightmares of the last century? Do we continue to look to mortals for a pathway to a better life? Or do we adhere to the words of the Psalmist: "It is better to take refuge in the LORD than to trust in man. It is better to take refuge in the LORD than to trust in princes" (Psalm 118:8–9).

Help, Lord, for the godly are no more;
the faithful have vanished from among men.
Everyone lies to his neighbor;
their flattering lips speak with deception.

—PSALM 12:1–2

ENGINES OF WAR

IN *The Lord of the Rings*, Lord Sauron seeks the ring that will give him complete power over Middle Earth. He is a dark presence who would control everything even if that means creating a wasteland using his vast forces of destruction and evil.

Sauron is a character in a novel, but we don't need to look too deeply into our own time to find the same lust for mayhem spreading its shadow of death over a credulous world. Thunderous cannons shake the land because determined rulers have banished God from the earth. When men attempt to live without God, "there is no one who does good, not even one" (Psalm 14:3).

According to Paul, a godless world looks very much like the world Sauron envisions: "Their throats are open graves; their tongues practice deceit. The poison of vipers is on their lips. Their mouths are full of cursing and bitterness. Their feet are swift to shed blood: ruin and misery mark their ways, and the way of peace they do not know" (Romans 3:13–17).

Do not revile the king even in your thoughts, or curse the
rich in your bedroom, because a bird of the air may carry your
words, and a bird on the wing may report what you say.

—ECCLESIASTES 10:20

<hr>

CAN ANYONE HIDE FROM THE LORD?

THE IDEA OF a bird, any bird, carrying an unflattering thought straight to the king may seem ridiculous. To read this literally, though, would be to miss the point because there is a spiritual truth being offered here. If the king is more than a king, if, in fact, he is God, then the truth is that nothing near or far, high or low, escapes His searching eye: "For the eyes of the LORD range throughout the earth to strengthen those whose hearts are fully committed to him" (2 Chronicles 16:9). No word uttered in the most desolate place will go unheard. No thought, however fleeting, will go unnoticed. "'Am I only a God nearby,' declares the LORD, 'and not a God far away? Can anyone hide in secret places so that I cannot see him?' declares the LORD. 'Do not I fill heaven and earth?' declares the Lord" (Jeremiah 23:23–24).

For some of us, it is uncomfortable to think that God can see everything we do and can know every thought we have. There are times when we would rather hide from the probing eyes of God. There are times when we would prefer to slink away under the cover of darkness.

King David knew the truth when he wrote: "O LORD, you have searched me and you know me. You know when I sit and when I rise; you perceive my thoughts from afar. You discern my going out and my lying down; you are familiar with all my ways" (Psalm 139:1–3).

Love and faithfulness meet together; righteousness and
peace kiss each other. . . . Righteousness goes before him
and prepares the way for his steps.

—PSALM 85:10, 13

GOD IS LOVE

HERE IS A startling thought: all righteousness comes from God.
We are surprised by this because we often assume people are
naturally good. When we hear of a neighbor who has done a
terrible thing, our first reaction is one of complete surprise. Or
when a mother hears that her son has been arrested for some
crime, we usually hear her say that her boy is really a good kid. Not
so. Jesus tells us that "there is only One who is good" (Matthew
19:17).

Despite what men and women may claim for themselves or
what others might claim for them, there is no goodness, no
righteousness, and no holiness that can be obtained without
redemption. We need to drink from the nurturing spring of the
source of all life.

Without Christ, the spring will dry up, and we will begin to die
through sin because we do not have the Holy Spirit as the source
that sustains us. "If anyone is in Christ, he is a new creation; the old
has gone, the new has come! All this is from God, who reconciled
us to himself through Christ and gave us the ministry of
reconciliation. . . . And he has committed to us the message of
reconciliation. . . . Be reconciled to God. God made him who had
no sin to be sin for us, so that in him we might become the
righteousness of God" (2 Corinthians 5:17–21).

Your statutes are wonderful; therefore I obey them. The unfolding
of your words gives light; it gives understanding to the simple.

—PSALM 119:129–130

THE WORK OF THE DISCIPLE

THE PROLOGUE TO John's gospel (John 1:1–18) serves as an overture to the revelation that Jesus Christ is the Son of God and, as the Son, he is the light that God has sent into a wayward world.

John, like all of the disciples, was an unlikely witness to the ministry of Jesus. The way had been prepared for the coming of the Christ through the word of the prophets, but then, hundreds of years of silence passed until a new prophet emerged to announce the coming of the Holy One of God. And just as John the Baptist said, "He who comes after me has surpassed me because he was before me," (John 1:15) so, too, the witnesses who would come after would be called to come forward to share the revelation that Jesus is the Christ.

The Gospel of John reveals the truth of Jesus told to a generation that did not walk with Him. The words of John are filled with light, love, and life because they are saturated by the power of the Holy Spirit. To be filled with the Holy Spirit is to know what the Psalmist means when he says, "The unfolding of your words gives light; it gives understanding to the simple."

Giving understanding of God's revelation to a new generation is the work of all disciples. Proclaiming the truth of the word through the power of the Holy Spirit is a work always in progress. "Because you have seen me, you have believed; blessed are those who have not seen and yet have believed" (John 20:29).

The angel of the LORD encamps around those who fear him,

and he delivers them. Taste and see that the LORD is good;

blessed is the man who takes refuge in him. Fear the LORD,

you his saints, for those who fear him lack nothing.

—PSALM 34:7–9

REAL FOOD

WHEN WE TAKE refuge in the Lord, our appetite for the food of this world will diminish. Speaking in the language of the Holy Spirit, Jesus tells His disciples, "I have food to eat that you know nothing about" (John 4:32). Later He says, "I am the bread of life. He who comes to me will never go hungry, and he who believes in me will never be thirsty" (John 6:35).

At the last supper, Jesus established the sacrament of the Eucharist, identifying his body and blood as the real food that opens the way to eternal life: "Jesus took bread, gave thanks and broke it, and gave it to his disciples, saying, 'Take and eat; this is my body.' Then he took the cup, gave thanks and offered it to them, saying, 'Drink from it, all of you. This is my blood of the covenant, which is poured out for many for the forgiveness of sins" (Matthew 26:26–28).

Jesus is saying, "Taste and know the Lord; taste and believe He is the Son of God; taste and receive the gift of eternal life freely given, through his death on the cross, to all who believe."

Relent, O Lord! How long will it be?
Have compassion on your servants . . .
May the favor of the Lord our God rest upon us;
establish the work of our hands for us—
yes, establish the work of our hands.

—PSALM 90:13, 17

THE ANSWER

THE ANSWER TO David's question, "How long will it be?" came one thousand years later with the collision of the supernatural and natural worlds. The answer came to a young woman in Nazareth who was engaged to be married to a man who was a descendant of David. She was visited by an angel who told her that she was highly favored by the Lord, that though she was a virgin, she would give birth to a child through the power of the Holy Spirit, and that she would give her baby child the name Jesus.

The angel Gabriel tells her, "He will be great and will be called the Son of the Most High. The Lord God will give him the throne of his father David, and he will reign over the house of Jacob forever; his kingdom will never end" (Luke 1:32–33). When Mary asks, "How will this be . . . since I am a virgin?" the angel answers: "Nothing is impossible with God" (Luke 1:37).

Just as Mary submitted to the impossible, so we are called to believe, saying with her, "My soul glorifies the Lord and my spirit rejoices in God my savior, for he has been mindful of the humble state of his servant" (Luke 1:46–48).

"Because he loves me," says the Lord, "I will rescue him;
I will protect him, for he acknowledges my name.
He will call upon me, and I will answer him;
I will be with him in trouble, I will deliver him and honor him.
With long life will I satisfy him and show him my salvation."

—PSALM 91:14–16

THE GOD OF LIGHT, LIFE, AND LOVE

WE HAVE HEARD it said that the God of the Old Testament is an angry and distant God. People who say this might point to the destruction of Sodom and Gomorrah or the Great Flood that nearly destroyed everything living on the earth.

But all of this is a point of view seeking a justification. God is never cruel, but humans are; God hates sin, but we are steeped in it. He loves righteousness, yet we flee from it.

God's purpose for us began to be worked out when He chose Abram to become the father of many nations. Even so, God's purpose would not be fully revealed for two thousand years. And that purpose was built on love. "'Because he loves me,' says the Lord, 'I will rescue him; I will protect him, for he acknowledges my name.'"

This clearly is the God of Abraham, Isaac, and Jacob, and it is the God who sent his only Son into the world to "save us from our sins." (Matthew 1:21). This is the God who will answer prayers, who will protect us from trouble, and who will point the way to eternal life. This is the God who troubled to reopen the door to a relationship with each one of His children through His Son, Jesus Christ. This is the same God who will pluck me out of disaster and place me on firm ground. This is the God of life, the God of light, and, most of all, the God of love. "God is love and whoever abides in love abides in God and God abides in him." (1 John 4:16)

Sons are a heritage from the LORD, children a reward from him.

Like arrows in the hands of a warrior are sons born in one's youth.

Blessed is the man whose quiver is full of them. They will not be

put to shame when they contend with their enemies in the gate.

—PSALM 127:3–5

PARENTING

EVERY CHILD IS a miracle. How else should we view it? So small, so beautiful, so dependent! If we see the child as a blessed gift from God, then we are going to take our parenting seriously and will instruct our children in the way of the Lord. But here is where we often go wrong. When we fail in this vital role, we either spoil or discourage the child, and everyone suffers as a result.

Eli was a great priest of Israel, and he had two sons, Hophni and Phinehas; but they were wicked men in the eyes of the Lord, for their father would not control them. They stole from the offerings of sacrifice, and by their foolish behavior showed contempt for the God of Israel. Finally, Eli confronted his sons, but it was too late. The Lord declared, "Those who honor me I will honor, but those who despise me will be disdained. The time is coming when I will cut short your strength and the strength of your father's house, so that there will not be an old man in your family line and you will see distress in my dwelling" (1 Samuel 2:30–32).

And it happened as God said. As parents, we are called to be wise parents so that the wonderful blessing of having children does not grow into something other than what we would want.

Those who are far from you will perish;
you destroy all who are unfaithful to you.
But as for me, it is good to be near God.
I have made the Sovereign LORD my refuge;
I will tell of all your deeds.

—PSALM 73:27–28

THE GIFT

THE WORLD ON the eve of the birth of Jesus Christ was a world soaked in sin. Violence flashed in the cold air as Jerusalem cringed under the iron yoke of Rome. The world was threatening and heartless, but there was also an air of expectation that something momentous was taking place. Wise men from the east had traveled long distances to come to Jerusalem to find the child destined to be king. They asked, "Where is the one who has been born king of the Jews? We saw his star in the east and have come to worship him" (Matthew 2:2).

Herod, who ruled in Jerusalem as a Roman puppet, was the perfect embodiment of all the corruption and darkness that permeated David's holy city. When Herod heard of the Magi's sacred mission, he sent his soldiers to search out and destroy the defenseless child. The rich and powerful, steeped in sin and corruption, choose, from the outset, to destroy this Savior rather than embrace Him.

Now as we prepare to celebrate the feast of the miracle of the birth of the Christ child, we should remember that he entered a dangerous and unwelcoming world. Still he came into this world at a particular time to a particular place so that he could seek out sinners for all time and from any place.

When we think of Christmas, we think of gifts, not fully realizing that the gifts we give are merely symbols of the greatest gift of all. Jesus was born into a troubled world as a way to reveal the true heart of God. Jesus came into our world on that cold night not as a conqueror, but as a Savior. He came to set the prisoners free once and for all.

The LORD swore an oath to David, a sure oath that he will not
revoke: "One of your own descendants I will place on your
throne—
if your sons keep my covenant and the statutes I teach them,
then their sons will sit on your throne for ever and ever."

—PSALM 132:11–12

THE PROMISE FULFILLED

GOD'S PROMISE TO King David would find its fulfillment a thousand years later in a small town on the outskirts of Jerusalem. Prophets who lived after David's time told of signs that would confirm the coming of the Messiah. One sign was told by Isaiah: "The virgin will be with child and will give birth to a son, and will call him Immanuel" (Isaiah 7:14).

Another prophet, Micah, said that the Messiah would be born in the city of David: "But you, Bethlehem, in the land of Judah, are by no means least among the rulers of Judah, for out of you will come a ruler who will be a shepherd of my people Israel" (Micah 5:2). Other prophecies include the flight into Egypt (Hosea 11:1) and the slaughter of the innocents (Jeremiah 31:15).

Christmas Day has been celebrated for nearly two thousand years, but the advent of the child named Jesus was anticipated for a full thousand years before it actually occurred. All the Scriptures point to this child as the one Israel had been waiting for. Later, during Christ's three-year public ministry, John the Baptist asked, "Are you the one who was to come, or should we expect someone else?" (Luke 7:20).

Jesus answered John, but the question still stands for each one of us: Do we believe the weight of all the evidence—the prophets, the Scriptures, the apostles, the words of Christ Himself, or do we believe something else?

Your love, O LORD, reaches to the heavens, your faithfulness
to the skies. Your righteousness is like the mighty mountains,
your justice like the great deep. O LORD, you preserve both
man and beast. How priceless is your unfailing love!

—PSALM 36:5–7

WALKING IN THE LIGHT

"IF WE CLAIM to have fellowship with him yet walk in the darkness, we lie and do not live by the truth" (1 John 1:6). By walking in the light, we turn away the works of darkness that, among other things, serve as a barrier to a life-giving relationship to God the Father through the work of his Son. When we claim to walk in the light of fellowship with God, we put the very honor of God on the line with our actions and our lives. Thus, when we claim the gift of God's love, we are also proclaiming, not just in words but in action, that we are children of God, staking everything on that fact.

So how are we to live if we claim to be children of God? If we live by the first great commandment (Mark 12:28–31) to give our all to God, then we are also called to live by the second commandment to love our neighbors as ourselves as well. The two commandments cannot be separated from one another; otherwise, we will proclaim our love of God with our lips but deny it in our lives.

The God-given purpose of our time here is to be beacons of light in a darkened and dangerous world by spreading the truth of God's love and faithfulness for anyone to see as God has gifted us to see.

*"Because of the oppression of the weak and the
groaning of the needy, I will now arise," says the LORD.
"I will protect them from those who malign them."
And the words of the LORD are flawless, like silver
refined in a furnace of clay, purified seven times.*

—PSALM 12:5–6

BLESSED ARE THE POOR

GOD LOOKS AFTER the most insignificant among us. It does not matter to Him that we may be poor or powerless in worldly terms; He only asks that we trust in Him and His Word. This is exactly what Christ taught in His Sermon on the Mount: "Blessed are the poor in spirit for theirs is the kingdom of heaven. Blessed are those who mourn, for they will be comforted. Blessed are the meek, for they will inherit the earth" (Matthew 5:3–5).

God's Word is flawless for He never shows the kind of favoritism that men habitually show to those who have political power or great wealth. He demonstrated this in the very life and circumstances of His own son, Jesus, who was not born in a palace built for kings. And when it came time for the Son to die, He was sentenced along with common criminals and was mocked by His tormentors who put a crown of thorns on His head. "He was despised and rejected by men, a man of sorrows, and familiar with suffering" (Isaiah 53:3).

Yet this is the one who is called "KING OF KINGS AND LORD OF LORDS" (Revelation 19:16). God's ways are surely wondrous, and His Word is surely flawless. For His love caused Him to become one of us so that we could become more like Him.

Call upon me in the day of trouble;
I will deliver you, and you will honor me.

—PSALM 50:15

CALL UPON ME

WHO HASN'T EXPERIENCED trouble? Who hasn't been at the end of their rope? Job tells us "man is born to trouble" (Job 5:7), which runs contrary to the fantasy that life is a pathway to a series of peak experiences on the stairway to the executive suite. The truth is that "in this world you will have trouble" (John 16:33).

When trouble came my way, I was only vaguely aware of the severity of the coming storm. I assured myself that I could navigate to a safe harbor. Yet the storm only intensified, and I found myself overcome by the waves of the sea and blown and tossed by the wind (James 1:6). Like Jonah, "The engulfing waters threatened me, the deep surrounded me . . . to the roots of the mountains I sank down; the earth barred me in forever" (Jonah 2:5–6). But before the storm could destroy him, Jonah says that "in my distress I called to the LORD, and he answered me. From the depths of the grave I called for help, and you listened to my cry" (Jonah 2:2).

In my own time of impending trouble, all the usual answers proved to be empty. And so when all options seemed to be exhausted and all doors closed, I turned to the Lord in my desperation, and He delivered me to a safe shore. As undeserving as I am, God graciously reached down and took my hand and saved me.

Twelve years later, I was attending a Christmas Eve service with my family. During the service, the young children of the church handed out little candy canes with an attached handwritten note. When one of the children with the basket came to my row, I at first thought to let the basket pass, but at the last moment, I reached out and took one of the candy canes. The note said this: "'Call upon me in the day of trouble; I will deliver you, and you will honor me.'" I have kept that little Christmas message in my possession from that day to this. I read it as an affirmation of God's grace and my gratitude.

The LORD blessed the latter part of Job's life more than the
first . . . After this, Job lived a hundred and forty years;
he saw his children and their children to the fourth generation.

—JOB 42:12, 16

———— ∞ ————

TO KNOW GOD

THE STORY OF Job ends as it began. We first meet him as a man who is rich in every way—rich in family, rich in property, and rich in God's love. This is a man we would certainly count as blessed. But between the beginning and end, Job experiences what it is like to live without God's full protection. Job's afflictions were terrible, and it seemed to him that God had completely abandoned him to Satan.

Through it all, Job remains faithful, refusing to compromise his integrity just to relieve his suffering. While Job understands that God is not punishing him for a particular transgression, reconciliation can only come when he completely submits himself to God's will. Job comes to understand that every blessing comes from God: "Surely I spoke of things I did not understand, things too wonderful for me to know" (Job 42:3). Then he acknowledges what it means to actually experience God: "My ears had heard of you but now my eyes have seen you. Therefore I despise myself and repent in dust and ashes" (Job 42:5–6).

To know *about* God is not to *know* God. Knowing God takes our whole being: our heart, soul, strength, and mind. For to know God is to love God, and to love God is the source of all joy, all abundance, and all goodness.

Sing to the LORD, you saints of his; praise his holy name.

For his anger lasts only a moment, but his favor lasts a lifetime;

weeping may remain for a night, but rejoicing comes in the morning.

—PSALM 30:4–5

THE COLOR OF LOVE

REVELERS OF THE night seek to escape the light of the emerging dawn. They need to find shelter in the shadows, for they are naturally creatures who prefer darkness.

For the man of God, the new light of day represents all the spiritual blessings of God in all their natural glory. The rising sun extinguishes the gloom of the fading darkness and paints the world with the same brush that God used to create it in the first place. The primary color is the color of love, for "the heavens declare the glory of God, the skies proclaim the work of his hands" (Psalm 19:1). And that color reveals the splendor and the majesty of creation everywhere: "The streams of God are filled with water to provide the people with grain, for so you have ordained it. You drench its furrows and level its ridges; you soften it with showers and bless its crops. You crown the year with your bounty, and your carts overflow with abundance" (Psalm 65:9–11). It is as if we get to see God at work creating the earth and everything in it every morning of every day of the year when "the morning stars sang together and all the angels shouted for joy" (Job 38:7). Truly, "where morning dawns and evening fades you call forth songs of joy" (Psalm 65:8).

Now all has been heard; here is the conclusion of the matter:
Fear God and keep his commandments, for this is the whole
duty of man. For God will bring every deed into judgment,
including every hidden thing, whether it is good or evil.

—ECCLESIASTES 12:13–14

A NEW YOU?

IF YOU HAVE stayed with me on this daily journey through *Signposts,*
you might recall that on January 1, I wrote about being on the
precipice of a new year. Now we have arrived at the last day of that
year, and we find it to be bittersweet. We look forward with hope,
but we look back with perhaps a hint of regret.

Before the calendar flips to a new year (and all the advertisements
that will pave the way to a "new you"), we might take some time to
reflect on the desire for change in the first place. For example,
physical well-being is important, but is it the key to our spiritual
well-being?

I also wrote on January 1 that our desire to change might have
something to do with a deep desire to reconnect with the holiness
of God. If that is the case, and I believe it is, perhaps a better way
to look back over this past year is to ask yourself if you have taken
steps to bring God back into your daily life. And as you look forward
to the next year, what will you do to keep renewing that relationship?

For me, I plan to continue to begin each day in the Word of
God. I am constantly amazed at how new my everyday encounters
with Scripture turn out to be. And I plan to reinvigorate my prayer
life because prayer brings intimacy and intimacy opens the door to
insight and wisdom. I am sure all of us could use a little more of
the wisdom of God as we continue to engage the world day by day.

TOPICAL INDEX

HOPE January 4, 18, 20, 31, February 16, 21, 25, March 18, 23, 28, April 22, 29, May 1, 19, 24, June 9, 15, 16, 25, July 30, August 9, 15, 20, 24, 29, September 1, 4, October 6, December 6, 11, 31

IDOLATRY January 9, March 4, September 25, November 26

KNOWLEDGE January 21, 28, 29, February 4, 27, March 11, 19, April 29, May 28, 29, June 18, 19, August 15, September 3, 21, 27, October 12, 19, November 12, December 4

LONELINESS January 18, March 17, February 10, March 8, May 19, June 21, August 5, September 8, 16

LOVE January 1, 2, 13, 25, February 4, 7, 14, 16, 22, March 28, 31, April 1, 4, 5, 12, 13, 21, May 6, 7, 12, 13, 22, 30, 31, June 2, 8, 14, 16, 17, 21, 27, 28, July 7, 10, 11, 19, 20, 24, 25, 29, 30,31, August 1, 12, 14, 26, September 1, 4, 6, 8, 13, 14, 15, 18, 23, October 3, 11, 22, 27, November 4, 5, 7, 18, 20, 27, December 6, 10, 11, 13, 18, 19, 22, 26, 27, 29, 30

MARRIAGE AND FAMILY February 9, 18, 25, March 13, 24, April 4, 15, May 7, 12, 23, 28, 29 June 16, 21, July 5, 8, 16, 23, 29, 30, August 11, September 15, 23, 30, October 20, November 5, 8, 11, 20

MERCY January 13, May 8, 18, 25, June 20, 28, July 11, August 9, 10, September 13, 22, November 3, 9, 18, 20, 29, December 11

MONEY January 17, February 29, March 2, 6, 15, April 17, 25, May 31, June 1, July 24, 26, August 20, August 31, September 10, 11, 14, October 5, 10, November 6, 10, 12, 26, December 27

MORTALITY February 23, May 20, July 26, August 31, September 7

OLD AGE January 31, May 5

PRAISE February 14, 16, March 8, 23, April 1, 6, 8, 11, May 4, June 19, July 18, November 27, 29, December 1, 11

PRAYER January 12, 19, 29, February 26, April 3, 8, May 3, 4, June 11, July 22, August 9, 28, September 11, 13, 26, October 23, November 29, December 11, 31

REPENTANCE January 15, March 19, April 28, November 3, December 29

SALVATION January 5, March 3, 8, May 18, 29, June 25, August 6, 9, September 7, October 3, December 5, 11, 14

SINFUL NATURE January 2, 7, 9, 19, 20, 21, 22, 24, 25, 28, February 18, 25, March 8, 9, 10, 19, 28, April 4, 10, 15, 18, 20, 30, May 2, 13, 26, 28, June 4, 6, 8, 23, July 6, 7, 8, 12, 16, 19, 21, 24, 27, 28, 30, 31 August 12, 13, 14, 16, 18, 19, 22, 27, September 3, 4, 18, 22, 24, 29, October 5, 12, 19, 20, 27, November 4, 9, 14, 22, 25, December 23

SUFFERING January 12, 13, 24, February 4, 9, March 8, 26, April 4, 6, 29, May 24, June 5, July 9, August 13, September 20, October 2, 11, 27, 28, November 3, 13, December. 9, 27, 29

TEMPTATION February 28, March 3, 8, April 24, May 15, 17, 21, June 30, July 16, August 12, September 10, October 5, and December 12

THANKSGIVING January 30, April. 1, May 4, June 2, July 18, October 11

TIME January 10, 15, 26, February 2, 13, 20, March 5, 18, 27, April 9, 30, May 1, 5, 11, 14, 16, 20, 27, June 27, July 10, 11, 15, 26, August 2, 31, September 14, 24, October 6, 21, 24, November 3, 30, December 24, 26

TRUST February 28, June 7, 26, July 4, 30, August 18, September 4, 16, 23, October 6, November 13, December 3, 12, 15, 27

WISDOM January 4, 7, 20, 29, February 5, 6, 17, 23, 27, March 28, July 16, April 15, 22, 26, May 8, 23, 27, 31, June 8, 19, 27, July 8, 16, 26, 28, 31, September 3, 7, 18, 21, 24, 27, 28, October 7, 12, 15, November 12, December 2, 31

WORK April 17, 25, June 18, 26, August 25, October 12, 30, December 9, 19

YOUTH January 20, 29, 30, May 5, 21, 23, June 15, July 10, 28, August 11, 16, December 23

BIBLIOGRAPHY

Aquinas, Thomas. *Meditations for Everyday*. Ft. Collins, Colorado: Roman Catholic Books, 1945

Berlinski, David. *The Devil's Delusion*. New York, New York: Crown Publishing, 2008, pp. 26-27

Augustine, Saint. *Confessions*. Trans. by Henry Chadwick. New York and Oxford: Oxford University Press, 1991

Chambers, Oswald. *Biblical Psychology: Christ-Centered Solutions for Daily Problems*. Grand Rapids, Michigan: Discovery House, 1995, pp. 91-92

Chambers, Oswald. *Devotions for a Deeper Life*. Grand Rapids, Michigan: Zondervan, 1970

Chambers, Oswald. *My Utmost for His Highest: An Updated Edition in Today's Language*. Edited by James Reimann. Grand Rapids, Michigan: Discovery House, 1992

Chambers, Oswald. *Still Higher for His Highest*. Grand Rapids, Michigan: Zondervan, 1970

Chesterton, G.K. *Orthodoxy*. Colorado Springs, CO: WaterBrook Press, 2001

Cranmer, Thomas. *The First English Prayer Book*. Edited by Robert Van De Meyer. Harrisburg, Pennsylvania: Morehouse Publishing, 1999

Dostoyevsky, Fyodor. *The Brothers Karamazov*. Translated by Constance Garnett. Mineola, NY: Dover Publications, 2005

Eldredge, John. *Epic: The Story God Is Telling and the Role That Is Yours to Play*. Nashville, Tennessee: Nelson Books, 2004

Gardner, Helen, editor. *The New Oxford Book of English Verse, 1250-1950*. Oxford University Press, 1972, p. 703

Gilder, George. *Men and Marriage*. Gretna, Louisiana: Pelican Publishing Co., 1986

Kampmann, Eric. *Tree of Life: A Book of Wisdom for Men: Biblical Wisdom For Everyday Living*. New York, New York: Beaufort Books, 2003

Kempis, Thomas à. *The Imitation of Christ*. Trans. by Joseph N. Tylenda. New York, New York: Vintage Books, a division of Random House, 1998

Kempis, Thomas à. *On the Passion of Christ: According to the Four Evangelists: Prayers and Meditations*. Translated by Joseph N. Tylenda. San Francisco, California: Ignatius Press, 2004

Lewis, C.S. *Mere Christianity*. New York, New York: Harper San Francisco, a division of HarperCollins, 2001, p.92

Lewis, C.S. *The Weight of Glory*. New York, New York: Harper San Francisco, a division of HarperCollins, 2001, p.136

Lewis, C.S. *A Year with C.S. Lewis: Daily Readings from His Classic Works*. New York, New York: Harper San Francisco, a division of HarperCollins, 2003

New International Version Holy Bible, Scofield Study System, New York, New York: Oxford University Press, 2004

Shakespeare, William. *Merchant of Venice*. New York, New York: Everyman Library, Knopf, a division of Random House, 1996

St. Augustine. *Traditional St. Augustine Prayer Book*. Compiled and Edited by: Rev. Loren Gavitt and Rev. Archie Drake. Athens, GA: Anglican Parishes Association, 2005

Storm, Howard. *My Descent Into Death: A Second Chance at Life*. New York, New York: Doubleday Publishers, a division of Random House, 2005

Stott, John. *Basic Christianity*. Downers Grove, Illinois: InterVarsity Press, 1971

Warren, Rick. *The Purpose Driven Life: What On Earth Am I Here For?* Grand Rapids, Michigan: Zondervan, 2002